CHEROKEE COUNTY, GEORGIA
A HISTORY

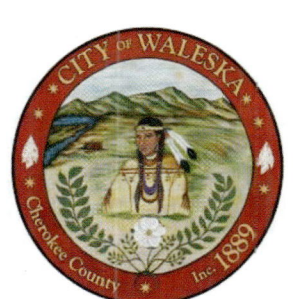

BALL GROUND 4
1832

CROSS ROADS 1000

MULLINS NO. 818

Prominent place and property names:

- J.R. BROWN PROP
- L. WILLIAMS
- J.M. ROBE...
- J.A. BYERS
- MARBLE
- T.A. SHEL...
- CHERRY GROVE ACDY.
- A.S. COCHRAN
- B. ATHINS
- L.A. In...
- LAREDO
- CONNS C.
- J.T. WOODALL
- BALL GROUND
- A.C. CONN
- FREEMANS MILL
- S.U. EDWARDS
- J.N. FARMER
- OAK GROVE ACDY.
- W.P. BOBO
- J. PRICE
- D.P. HILL
- B. PERCEL
- N. DARBY
- MARY WATKINS
- J.H. HENDRIX
- VILMERS BRG
- W. HOGAN
- SHARP MOUNTAIN
- BOLING
- J.M. HICH...
- J.B. REVIS
- J.H. GREEN
- N.E. BRANNON
- R.J. PERCELL
- H.M. BISH...
- J.W. JARVIS
- W. HOGAN
- HILLS
- RAYS MILL
- McGRAUS FORD
- J.N. DONALD
- J.N. DONALD
- J.P. SAY
- L.J. GREEN
- R. CHEEK FERRY
- MARY JARVIS
- R.A. WILSON
- S.L. COKER
- J.H. HESTER
- J.P. SAY
- J.E.S. COKER
- G.M. WHEELER
- H.C. BOLING
- S.Y.C. GOA...
- MRS. CYNTHIE PERKINS
- D. SPRINGER
- F.H. SMITHWICK
- C.J.A. BARRETT
- J.B. RICHARDS
- S.M. SANDO
- F.H. BURTS' GOLD MINE
- J.H. LATHEM
- ORANGE CH
- ORANGE
- J.D. IDWELL
- J. GALT
- CHESTER MINE
- MRS. A.C. LATHAM
- T.W. LATHAM
- S.W. SMITHWICK
- MACEDONIA CH.
- W.A. LATHA...
- FT. BUFFINGTON ACDY.
- T.N. SMITH
- HARMONY CH.
- FT. BUFFINGTON
- R. PERRY
- E.J. WHITE
- R.C.
- J. BELL
- N.N. WILSONS GN
- T.G. FOWLER
- J.M. DRUMM...
- C.C. DAVIS
- B.F. PERRY
- MRS. E. BRUCE
- JAMES DANIEL
- W.N. WILLSON

ETOWAH River, CREEK notations throughout.

CHEROKEE COUNTY, GEORGIA

A HISTORY

Rebecca Johnston

For the Cherokee County Historical Society

The Cherokee County Historical Society
PO Box 1287
Canton, GA 30169
770.345.3288   www.rockbarn.org

Stefanie Joyner, Executive Director
Meghan Griffin, Archivist

Johnston, Rebecca
Cherokee County, Georgia: A History/ Rebecca Johnston
for the Cherokee County Historical Society
ISBN 978-1-936815-28-9

Creative Design and Layout by Cherokee County Historical Society Staff
Stefanie Joyner and Meghan Griffin

Published by Yawn's Publishing
210 East Main Street
Canton, Georgia 30114
678.880.1922   www.yawnspublishing.com

Previous photograph of Gresham Mill by Jim Harris, following photographs
of Holly Springs Depot by Jim Kirk; Gibbs Gardens by Gibbs Gardens;
Shingle House by Sarah Kruger; Etowah River by Steve Lamb;
Historic Marble Courthouse by Stefanie Joyner;
J.H. Johnston House (circa 1913) by Jim Harris.
Map on endsheets is from the 1895 Cherokee County Map.

Table of Contents

Introduction

No other community in the state has the diverse history that the account of Cherokee County's past offers. Cherokee County's history parallels the story of Georgia and often claims center stage in the state's narration. From early Native American times through the Civil War to the early twentieth century and forward to the present, Cherokee County plays an important role in the recounting of the events of each time period. With such a complex and layered history, it is impossible to recount everything and mention everyone who made a contribution in just one book. For those who wish to explore more about Cherokee County there are entire volumes on topics that are included here only briefly.

When I set out on the journey to write the history of Cherokee County my main wish was to share my love and knowledge of my native county with those who live here and who are interested in our collective past. My goal was to write an interesting and factual account of the land, people, events, advancements and opportunities which shaped us into what we are today. I credit my father, the late James Walter Wheeler, Jr., with instilling in me a deep respect for Cherokee County and its history. His love for the county where he was born was always evident in all he stood for and taught me. I know he would be proud that I was able to be a part of this project for the Cherokee County Historical Society.

No project of this type can ever be completed without support from a group of people who give unselfishly of their time and talents to bring it to fruition. First and foremost is the amazing staff at the Cherokee County Historical Society, comprised of Director Stefanie Joyner and Archivist Meghan Griffin. They work tirelessly each and every day to help preserve and protect our past for us and they do it professionally and competently. They are invaluable to our community and are at the core of historical efforts such as numerous publications, the history museum, archiving of thousands of documents and photographs and historic preservation. They have both brought their substantial talents to this project and worked as equal partners in the endeavor.

The Joe E. Johnston Foundation made this important project possible financially and its support enables the proceeds from the publication of this history book to be used entirely for the work of the Cherokee County Historical Society. For that generous support all of us are eternally grateful.

Heartfelt thanks to Juanita Hughes for editing every word for content and grammar with her usual thoroughness and attention to detail. Thanks also to Reinhardt University History Professor Dr. Kenneth Wheeler for reading my early attempts and his impeccable input. Many other members of the Historical Society including Karen Smithwick, James "Skip" Spears, Lisa Tressler, Kathy Day, and Judson Roberts have taken the time to read drafts and give input into the final product. I am so glad that the Sequoyah Regional Library and its employees place such an emphasis on local history and records and appreciate the staff in assisting me in my research. Sincere thanks go to all the many residents who took time to talk with me, share family histories and photographs, and open their personal memories to me.

Most of all I thank my wonderful and patient husband of more than 35 years, Harry Buchanan Johnston III. Once more throughout this project his support and help have proven invaluable and I could never have completed this book without him.

When I think back on my life in Cherokee County, I am astounded at all the people who have influenced me, from my teachers at Canton Elementary and Cherokee High School to church leaders to friends and their parents to my own family. Over the years I have had so many wonderful opportunities to sit around the kitchen table and talk about our history and the events that have shaped our lives. I am appreciative of my years working at the *Cherokee Tribune* and the information I gleaned and the lessons I was taught while employed there.

The people of Cherokee County have always demonstrated their character, resilience, love of family and God, thirst for knowledge, vision and work ethic. Most of all they have had within them the will to survive and thrive. Along with the first crops, the earliest settlers planted those beliefs and virtues. The seeds of their characters took root and are evident throughout the narration of this county, because history is really the story of people.

- Rebecca Johnston

Dedication

The greatest men are those who quietly go about doing good deeds never seeking recognition or thanks. Such a man was Joseph Egleston Johnston of Woodstock. Joe Johnston, in fact, came from a family of great men and was carrying on the tradition begun by his father of giving back without fanfare to the community which gave so much to him. Along with his brother Smith L. Johnston, Sr. and many other members of his family, Joe Johnston made a major and lasting impact on Cherokee County. Today, the family of Joe E. Johnston continues its philanthropic endeavors which have helped numerous people in time of need and enhanced the lives of many. Whether through the church, the community, business or leisure, the Johnston family has for generations generously contributed their time, resources and commitment to make Cherokee County a better place. Because of those significant contributions throughout the history of Cherokee County, this book is dedicated to Joseph Egleston Johnston and his family.

Joe Johnston was a native of Cherokee County born on March 1, 1890, the son of J.H. Johnston and Sarah Avis Benson Johnston. Joseph E. Johnston received his formal education in the public schools of Woodstock and at Creighton Business College of Atlanta. In 1911 at the age of 21, he joined his father at the J.H. Johnston Company in Woodstock, which dealt in general merchandise, fertilizers and cotton.

Joe Johnston served in World War I in the United States Army for 18 months and achieved the rank of second lieutenant. Johnston was elected to the Georgia House of Representatives in 1929 and served until 1933. In 1935 he served one term in the Georgia Senate. Johnston was active in his community as a member of numerous civic organizations, including the Lions Club and the Masonic Lodge.

The Johnston family, including Joe Johnston, was active in the Woodstock United Methodist Church. Joe Johnston served in numerous capacities at the church. Through the church, the Johnston family contributed to the community in many ways. The Johnston family has always been supportive of the Cherokee County public libraries and Reinhardt University.

The Johnston family was instrumental in the Bank of Woodstock and J.H. Johnston was one of the founders. Joe Johnston, Smith Johnston, Sr. and Smith Johnston, Jr. each served terms as president of the bank. Joe Johnston and his brother Smith Johnston, Sr. were active in the management of the Cherokee Cotton Mills. The mill was located on Little River and was operated until 1950 when the business was discontinued due to the construction of Allatoona Dam. Joe Johnston also served on the Board of Directors of Canton Cotton Mills.

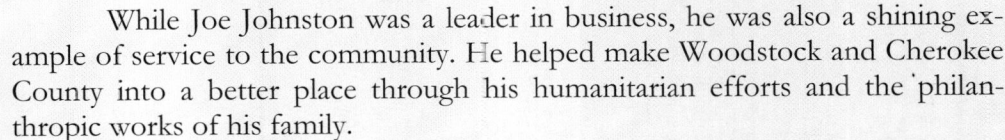

While Joe Johnston was a leader in business, he was also a shining example of service to the community. He helped make Woodstock and Cherokee County into a better place through his humanitarian efforts and the philanthropic works of his family.

The family continues to help others through the Habitat for Humanity, Cherokee Court Appointed Special Advocates, Cherokee YMCA, Boy Scouts of America, Young Life of Cherokee County, Preservation Woodstock, and numerous other organizations. The Johnston family supports historic preservation through the Cherokee County Historical Society and other efforts.

Joe Johnston's successes were many but his greatest successes were in caring for his fellow man, and in giving back to his community. His story provides an example of greatness, in great part because he went about the work of sharing with others quietly and without seeking recognition for himself. It is an honor to dedicate this history to him. Cherokee County is indeed a better place because of Joseph Egleston Johnston.

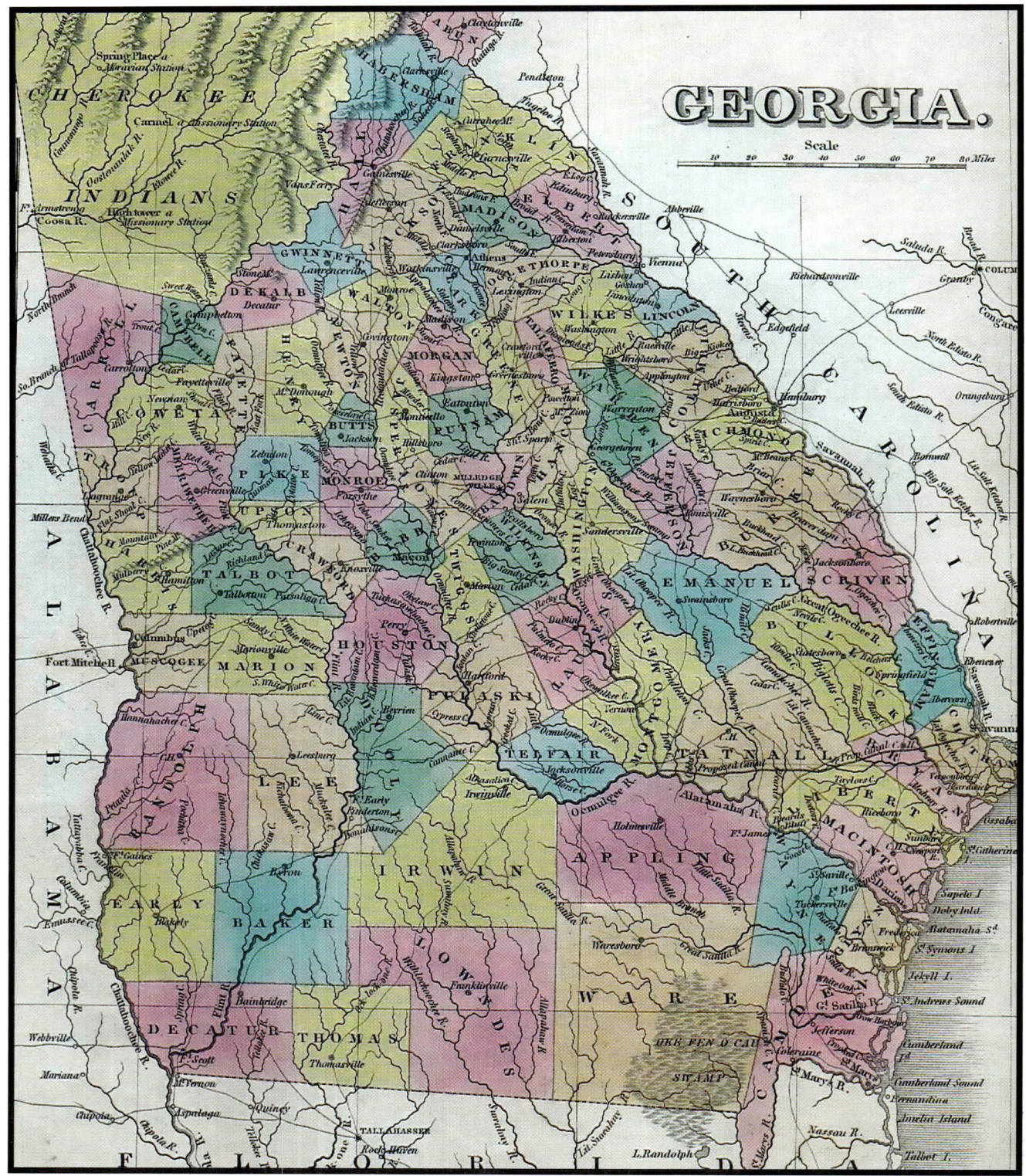

An 1831 map of Georgia shows the Cherokee Indian territory before Cherokee County was chartered in December of that year.

Chapter One

Origins of County Steeped in Conflict

The clash for control between the last native inhabitants making their home in North Georgia and the white settlers who sought to lay claim to the rich territory was fought for the most part politically and legally, but was nonetheless a brutal conflict with many vicious skirmishes. The formal creation of Cherokee County on December 26, 1831, was only one step in the continuation of the battle for the rights to what was before that date designated Cherokee Indian territory. At the time of the county's incorporation, the Cherokees had yet to relinquish their claims to the federal or state governments, and still maintained their ownership of the region. When the Georgia Legislature passed the act creating a new county in Northwest Georgia the Cherokees were still firmly entrenched in their homeland with thriving farms, businesses and towns. Despite the presence of the native people, pioneers were already beginning to push into what they viewed as a new frontier ripe for settlement. Georgia's government already maintained control of the rest of the state, with neighboring counties such as Hall and Carroll settled and incorporated years earlier. The settlers, who began arriving in the Cherokee territory in earnest around 1827, were impatient to lay claim to the right to carve a livelihood out of the rich Indian domain. The year 1828 was a turning point when gold was discovered in Dahlonega and the subsequent gold rush inundated much of North Georgia with those seeking their fortune. The stage was set for a fight that would end with the removal of the native Indians who occupied the region in the cruel episode of American history now known as the Trail of Tears. The march started in Cherokee County and surrounding regions in 1838 with roundups and imprisonment and resulted in the deaths of thousands of those who were forced to leave their homeland for the brutal march to the West.

The origins of the history of Cherokee County began thousands of years before the arrival of the Europeans and the white settlers. Archaeological studies conducted in Cherokee County revealed the first inhabitants were the Paleo-Indians, the earliest hunters and gatherers of the Western Hemisphere. These nomads moved across the land looking for food, leaving behind evidence of the weapons they used to kill their prey. From the time of those first inhabitants until the journey of European explorers into the region a long history of inhabitants left their mark on the land that would eventually be incorporated into Cherokee County.

From the beginning of civilization, Cherokee County blessed those who chose it as their home with an abundance of natural resources. First and foremost among those is the winding Etowah River, along with its tributaries, which supplied not only water, but sustenance and a means of transportation as well. It was along the banks of the waters that the Native Americans began to settle. Numerous archaeological studies have unearthed evidence of those early civilizations in Cherokee County.

While the Native Americans occupied Cherokee County for thousands of years, it was the pioneers whose presence charted a new direction that led to the future. The early settlers were a determined and dedicated people looking for the opportunity to carve a home for their families out of the areas of wilderness and to take advantage of the opportunities they encountered when they arrived in Cherokee County. Many of those who settled in Cherokee County were of English, Irish, Scotch, Dutch and German descent. They brought with them their heritage, religions, and desire for a better life for their families. The new settlements grew up around transportation routes, such as established trails which were used by the Native Americans. Soon after settling into the region they began to establish schools, churches and businesses. They also began to set up local governments. Through the foresight of those first early residents of Cherokee County the foundation was laid for a strong and vibrant community.

Early People Leave Their Mark

Thousands of years ago, millennia before the birth of Christ and the discovery of the New World by European explorers, the Paleo-Indians inhabited Cherokee County along the Etowah River, drawing life from its waters. Modern day construction projects and archaeological studies have unearthed some degree of evidence that inhabited villages were located along the Etowah River as early as the Paleo Period 13,000 to 10,000 years ago. Those first people of the New World made their way out of Siberia around 13,000 B.C. across a land bridge which at the time connected it to Alaska. They then migrated over the next several generations across the United States, eventually reaching the Southeast of the landmass of North America.

Prehistoric and Historic Periods in Georgia

- Paleo Period - 11,000 B.C. to 8,000 B.C.
- Archaic Period - 8,000 B.C. to 1,000 B.C.
- Woodland Period - 1,000 B.C. to 800 A.D.
- Mississippian Period - 1000 A.D. to 1600 A.D.
- Historic Period 1600 A.D. to 1838 A.D.

Surface finds of artifacts, many in private collections, still constitute the bulk of the evidence for Paleo-Indian occupation in the state of Georgia. Those early Native Americans traveled in small bands of 25 to 50 and originally hunted large game, but in some regions could have begun to depend on small game and vegetables for livelihood. In Georgia, the Paleo-Indian period is divided into Early, Middle and Late subperiods. The majority of the finds in today's Cherokee County and surrounding region suggest the Paleo-Indians occupied it during the Early and Late time frames. Artifacts have been discovered here in plowed fields, shorelines, stream beds and cleared areas or those devoid of vegetation for other reasons. Archaeologists for the Smithsonian Institution in 1946 conducted a survey of the area that would eventually become Allatoona Lake, but recovered no Paleo-Indian artifacts, although they did recover artifacts from later periods. In the 1980s the Southeastern Archeological Services, Inc. revisited some of the sites from the earlier survey, focusing on land uncovered by the lake during a drawdown of the waters. They found artifacts from the Paleo-Indian period at nine sites out of more than 1,000 they visited.

The archaeologists also studied another site known as the Laffingal site, 400 acres on an upland ridge, which produced an even higher number of Paleo-Indian artifacts. While it is clear from the information gathered that Paleo-Indians did occupy the region, many questions about the period are unanswered.

Following the Paleo Period, the Archaic Period began to take shape around 8,000 to 7,000 B.C. in the eastern United States. In Georgia the beginning of the Archaic Period is placed around 8,000 B.C. The people of the Archaic Period depended on vegetable foods such as nuts, seeds and berries, as well as fish and small game. The Archaic people were also more sedentary than the Paleo-Indians, who had followed the herds of game off which they lived. The Archaic may have developed out of the Paleo Period as it evolved away from hunting and the large game died off. Those of the Archaic Period in north Georgia moved with the season, although they sometimes would set up a resident camp which might contain homes, some with hearths, but they did not occupy them for long periods. The Cagle site in Cherokee County offers an example of this type of residential camp. The site is located just west of Hickory Log Creek and was discovered during the work in preparation for Interstate 575 in the early 1980s. Archaeological work for the Cagle site was conducted for the state Department of Transportation by Dr. Morgan Crook, Jr. Plant remains such as hickory nut shells and persimmon seeds, as well as projectile points made from quartz and other minerals indigenous to the region gave indication of the Late Archaic or the early Woodland Period which followed it.

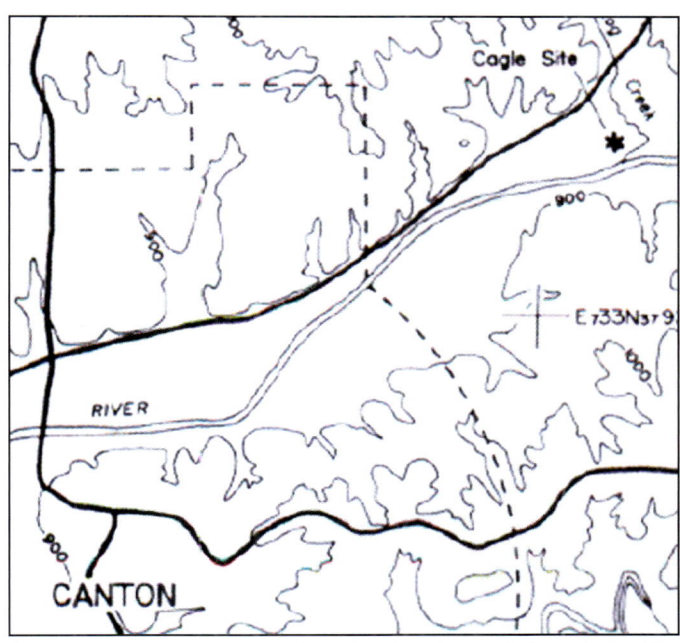

A topographic map provides the location of the Cagle Site (Ck9). *Cagle Site Report, Georgia Department of Transportation, March 1985.*

As those of the Archaic Period began to be more efficient at finding enough food on which to live they began other pursuits such as making jewelry and stone pipes. They also began to bury their dead, often with weapons and tools. However, concern with proper burial would be a key characteristic of the next age, the Woodland Period, which is dated from around 1,000 years B.C. to 800 years A.D.

The Native Americans of the Woodland Period began to build more permanent abodes than those of the Archaic Period. The population in the area increased and residential groups were larger than in early times. Evidence shows they relied more heavily on vegetation and that agriculture began to replace some of the gathering and hunting that marked earlier periods. The people of the Woodland Period also made pottery and were known for building large ceremonial mounds. Burials of some of the Indians took place in the large earthworks. Large mounds of varying sizes were constructed, some of them massive in dimension, containing one or more corpses.

The Mississippian tradition of the native inhabitants dating from about 1000 A.D. to 1600 A.D. reached a pinnacle around 1200 A.D. During the Mississippian Period in the Southeast some of the most complex civilizations to exist in North America were formed. The people of the Mississippian culture lived in Chieftain Societies, which were ranked socially into the elite and commoners. The Etowah Indian Mounds Historic Site in present day Cartersville in Bartow County from this period offers some of the best examples of Southeastern Indian art, including statues, monolithic axes, an elaborate headdress of copper, and large copper plaques depicting scenes. Designated by archaeologists as the Etowah Site, it was one of the most impressive chieftain capitals to be discovered. The site was home to several thousand Native Americans from 1000 to 1550 A.D. It is 54 acres in size and contains six earthen mounds. The site also has a plaza, defensive ditch and village area. The historic site is the most intact example of Mississippian Culture in the Southeastern United States.

An example of a palisade, or fortified village, was uncovered in Cherokee County in 1995 when excavation work was done in preparation for a Walmart shopping center on Old Highway 5 in Canton. The discovery is designated the Hickory Log site by archaeologists. Palisades were barricades of vertical walls usually constructed from logs for protection from hostile tribes. The site on the Etowah River shows evidence of occupation from at least 200 B.C. up until the Cherokee removal in the 1830s. Evidence of occupation during the late Woodland Period included the palisade, which was well-situated with a strong defensive position and large enough that it is believed to have sheltered a substantial population. The palisade would have been used not just for protection of those who lived inside it, but also for those who lived in the surrounding area to seek shelter in time of battle or danger. Human burials

A sampling of artifacts from the Cherokee County Historical Society archives, including a ceramic jar, projectile points, pottery shards, platform pipe, and banner stones. The items were donated by Harold Johnston and were found in Cherokee County. They are on display in the *Cherokee County History Museum and Visitors Center.*

were located at the site with a total of 22 positive human remains and 12 possible remains found. The site also yielded three structures from the Mississippian period which followed, as well as evidence of the Creek and Cherokee inhabitants who lived there in the late 1700s and early 1800s.

Two archaeological locations, the Wilbanks site and the Long Swamp site, provide evidence of occupation from 1000 to 1100 A.D in Cherokee County during the early Etowah phase of the Mississippian Period. The Long Swamp site near where Long Swamp Creek runs into the Etowah River was initially excavated by Robert Wauchope in the late 1930s. There he located a prehistoric mound, a possible village and other archaeological findings that indicated evidence of Early and Middle Woodland, Early to Late Mississippian and Cherokee components. In 2008 further work was done at the site by Edwards-Pitman Environmental, Inc. of Smyrna. In addition to a large residence and possible outbuildings such as a corn crib and summer sleeping cabins, the site revealed an extensive palisade that could have enclosed the entire village situated there. Artifacts from the Woodstock phase of the Late Woodland Period and the Etowah phase of the Mississippi Period were also found there. One possible structure and one definite structure were found on the upper terrace of the site. The well-preserved structure was fully excavated and was dated using radiocarbon science to about 1600 A.D. It appears to be a winter house, or hot house, which was used during the colder months by the inhabitants.

Carl Etheridge, a senior field archaeologist, at work in 2008 at the Long Swamp Creek archaeological site.

Several major artifacts have been located in Cherokee County in addition to discoveries by archaeologists and to numerous smaller artifacts found by residents along rivers, streams, and in cleared fields. One of those is the Reinhardt Rock which is now on display at the Funk Heritage Center at Reinhardt University in Waleska. The artifact is a boulder known as a petroglyph for its rock carvings and was found near Keithburg on a hilltop in the Hickory Log area of Cherokee County. The Reinhardt Rock was donated to the school by the Cline family and is on display in the "Hall of Ancients" at the center. Petroglyphs

have been located throughout the world. While many date back thousands of years, those in north Georgia are believed to date from 600 to 1400 A.D. Theories abound to explain the meanings of the carvings depending on their location and age. Those in north Georgia were often placed along trails or geographically significant locations such as creeks and crossroads. They might have given useful information about the area to passers-by. Often they were decorated with crosses, bird tracks, human feet and anthropomorphic symbols.

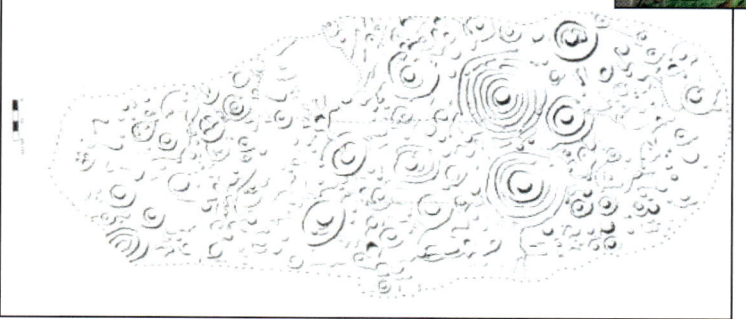

A diagram, above, of the markings on the Reinhardt Rock. *Recent Recording of Petroglyphs in Georgia, The Profile, Winter 2002 - 2003.*

The Reinhardt Rock, above, is a major artifact found in the Keithburg community region of Cherokee County and on display at the Funk Heritage Center of Reinhardt University in Waleska.

The Historic Period of Georgia history is often dated to Hernando de Soto's 1540 expedition into Georgia. De Soto was a Spanish explorer who came to the New World as part of the effort to conquer the Inca Empire in Peru. He then served as governor of Cuba before embarking on an expedition into North America which would eventually lead him through North Georgia. When de Soto undertook his brutal exploration of the New World, the Mississippian culture was already in decline. He and his men are believed to have entered the southwestern corner of Georgia and embarked on a route that led them northeast to where the border of South Carolina and Georgia are today. They then traveled

west to what is now the border of Georgia and Tennessee. Their journey had far-reaching effects on the area and its people, including the spread of disease which threatened the population and caused considerable sickness and death. The explorers plundered temples and robbed the native inhabitants of their riches, according to Charles Hudson in his book *The Southeast Indians.* Hudson writes that the Southeastern Indians were "biologically unprepared for the diseases that arrived with the European invaders: they were unprepared to deal with a people who knew no limit, and who recklessly exploited the earth and its creatures, and they were unequal to a people whose use of writing enabled them to plan and coordinate aggressive political strategies for decades and even centuries until they had conquered the people who stood in their way."

This engraved monolithic axe was found on the banks of the Etowah River near Ball Ground in 1917. It is on exhibit at the U.S. National Museum in Washington, D.C.

In May 1540, de Soto crossed the Blue Ridge Mountains into Cherokee territory, according to Hudson. The explorers rapidly passed through the Cherokee region along a route that followed the Hiawassee River then southward to the Coosa River and into what is today Alabama. Hudson writes that the Cherokee could have already been weakened by smallpox, which would have made it easier for the expedition to move through rapidly and unchallenged. De Soto also discovered evidence of the gold in north Georgia, according to Hudson, but noted that it would have to be mined. Evidence to prove whether de Soto actually was in present-day Cherokee County is inconclusive, as no signs of attempts to colonize have been uncovered. Some European artifacts were identified at the Etowah site in today's Bartow County. After de Soto and his men passed through it would be another 150 years before Europeans visited North Georgia again.

An 1815 map shows the division of lands in Georgia between the Cherokee and Upper Creek people, the Native Americans who occupied most of the area when the Europeans first came into the region.

Cherokees Gain Control of Region

Prevalent accounts of how the Cherokees came to control the area that is today Cherokee County, Georgia, are often based on legend and myth since few written records before the late 1700s are available. When the Europeans began to settle Georgia, two Native American populations made their home there, the Creek people who occupied the southern portions of the state and the Cherokee who lived in the northern region. At one time, the Creek Indians inhabited the lands which now make up North Georgia, but possibly sometime in the late 1500s the Cherokee Indians began pushing down into the region. In the late 1600s the Cherokee defeated the Creeks in the northern parts of the region in a battle in today's Lumpkin County, and the Creeks were pushed south to the banks of the Etowah River. By the 1740s the Cherokee and Creek were in a continuous fight for control of the north Georgia region. During the French and Indian War, the Creeks sided with the French and the Cherokees with the British. In 1755 the first of two major historical events at the Cherokee Village at Long Swamp Creek took place, according to Charles O. Walker in *Cherokee Footprints*. The battle of Taliwa, which was fought in the vicinity of where Long Swamp Creek runs into the Etowah River, finally settled the issue with the Cherokee achieving victory. The Creek were forced further south along the Chattahoochee and Flint

Rivers and west to the Coosa River and eventually ceded all lands in the state of Georgia, withdrawing further west into Alabama.

James Mooney was an ethnologist who worked with the federal government and became fascinated with the Native Americans he tracked. In his 1888 work, *Myths of the Cherokee*, Mooney wrote that the Cherokees won their land from the Creeks during the French and Indian War in a battle at the site of the present day Ball Ground.

"The battle of Taliwa," wrote Mooney, "which decided in favor of the Cherokee the long war between themselves and the Creeks, was fought about 1755 or a few years later at a spot on Mountain Creek or Long Swamp Creek which enters Etowah River above Canton, Georgia, near where the old trail crossed the river about Long Swamp town. All our information is traditional, obtained from James Wafford, who heard the story as a boy, about the year 1815, from an old trader named Brian Ward who witnessed the battle sixty years before. According to his account, it was the hardest battle ever fought between the two tribes, with about 500 Cherokee and twice that number of Creek warriors engaged in the conflict. The Cherokee were at first overmatched and fell back, but rallied again and returned to the attack, driving the Creeks to cover so that they broke and ran. The victory was complete and decisive and the defeated tribe immediately afterward abandoning the whole upper portion of Georgia…"

An historical marker erected in 1953 states in downtown Ball Ground, "Two and one-half miles to the east, near the confluence of Long-Swamp Creek and the Etowah River, is the traditional site of Taliwa, scene of the fiercest and most decisive battle in the long war of the 1740's and 50's between the Cherokee and Creek Indians. There, about 1755, the great Cherokee war-chief Oconostota, led 500 of his warriors to victory over a larger band of Creeks. So complete was the defeat that the Creeks retreated south of the Chattahoochee River, leaving to their opponents the region later to become the heart of the ill-fated Cherokee Nation."

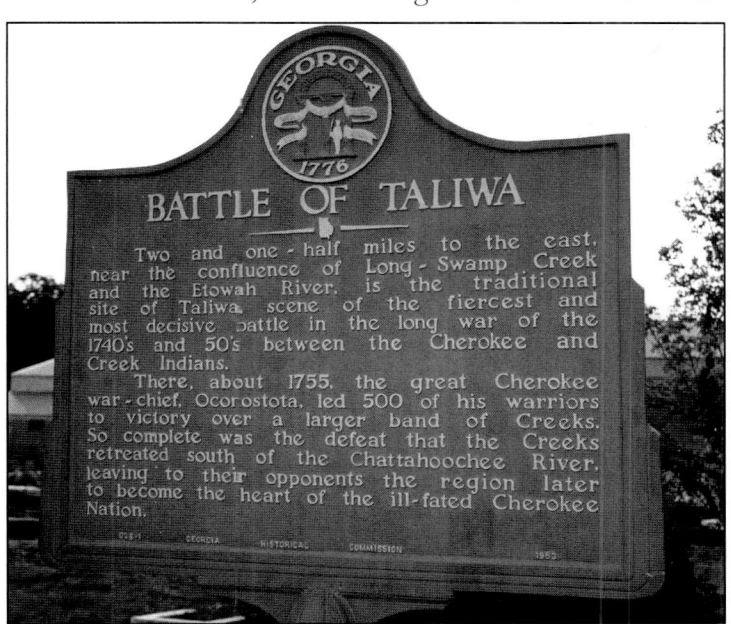

The historical marker for the Battle of Taliwa erected in downtown Ball Ground in 1953.

Traditional accounts of the battle vary, including a part of the story surrounding Nancy Ward, a Cherokee woman who is thought to have fought in the battle of Taliwa. According to Charles Hudson, Cherokee women sometimes played a man's role, and Nancy Ward was one such woman. She fought like a man and was given the name Ghigia which meant "war woman" or "beloved woman." At the time of the battle of Taliwa she was married to the Cherokee chieftain Kingfisher. Kingfisher was killed during the battle and it is said that Nancy picked up his rifle and helped rally the Cherokee to their victory. She later married Ward. Throughout her life she continued to be a major influence in the Cherokee nation. She spoke in Cherokee Councils and in 1781 engaged in negotiations with the invading American army, according to Hudson.

Some accounts of how it was decided whether the Creeks or the Cherokees controlled the lands of northwest Georgia state the issue was decided by an actual ball game. Whether these tales mean it was literally a ball game of the type the Indians typically played or whether the word used for ball game was a double entendre meaning fighting a battle is a matter of speculation. The Cherokee, along with other Native American tribes, played a type of lacrosse that was both rough and aggressive, sometimes even ending in death for some players. Weeks of negotiation led up to a game and a loss was a serious matter. These ball games, some played only once a year, were so rigorously fought that they were something of a cross between peace and war. Mooney, who lived among the Cherokee in North Carolina as part of his research, interviewing and chronicling his findings, said, "As originally told it may have a veiled meaning, as among the Cherokee 'to play a ballgame' is frequently used to denote fighting a battle." Some old maps do designate the early name of Ball Ground as Battle Ground.

According to Lloyd Marlin and other local historians, the game played between the Creeks and the Cherokee near today's Ball Ground was to decide the ownership of a large tract of land that included as much as one thousand acres. Whether it was an actual battle or a game, the results were the same.

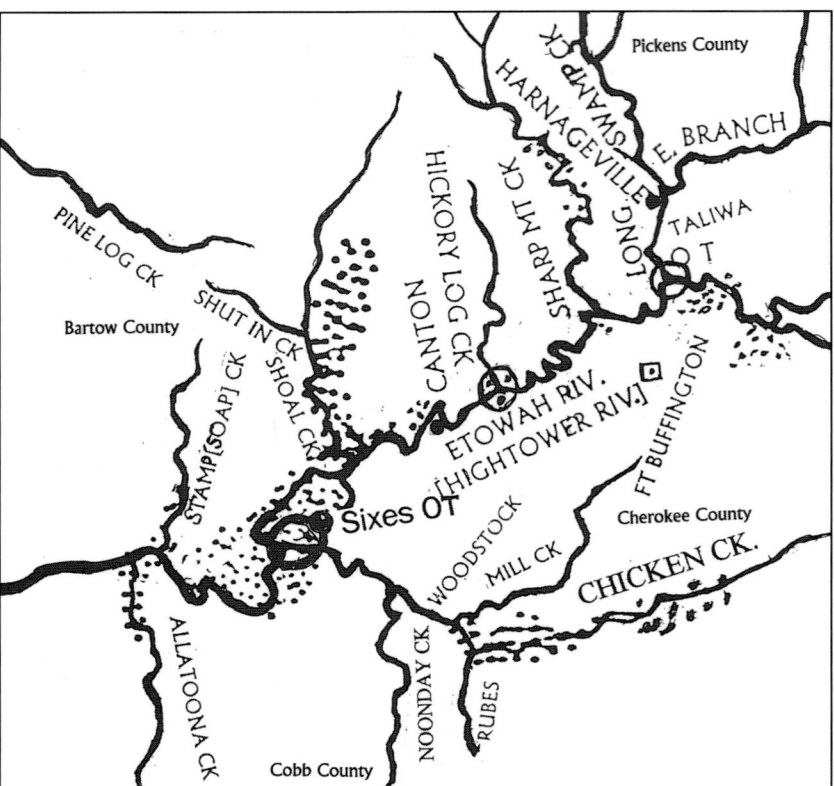

The Cherokees lived along the Etowah River and its tributaries circa 1835. This map shows the major areas they inhabited before the Indian Removal and includes the site of Taliwa/Long Swamp Creek. *Courtesy of collection of the Reverend Charles O. Walker, Cherokee Footprints Volume III.*

A 1900 image of a Cherokee playing ball taken by James Mooney. *Smithsonian Institute.*

The Cherokee were victorious. The Creeks retreated and the Cherokee were left in control of the region that would eventually become Cherokee County and its surrounding area.

The other major event that took place at Long Swamp Creek was what is sometimes designated the last battle of the American Revolution in Georgia. According to various accounts, in the late 1770s, the British were using the Cherokee villages in Northwest Georgia as bases of support against the American colonists. Their agents were hiding in the villages and enlisting the Cherokee to help them in their fight against the American troops. British Deputy Indian Superintendent Colonel Thomas Waters had moved to the Long Swamp village in early 1782. His charge was to organize the Cherokee for raids against the southern frontier and to draw away the British from the coastal towns they held.

Brigadier General Andrew Pickens, a militia leader from South Carolina who had played a major part in the Battle of Kettle Creek in North Georgia earlier in the war and was later captured in Charleston during fighting there, decided he must stop the Cherokee in the fall of 1782. He was joined by Lieutenant Colonel Elijah Clarke and they with about 400 men marched north to cross the Etowah River and engage the Cherokee settlement at Long Swamp, according to *Cherokee Footprints* by Charles O. Walker.

Historian and author Don L. Shadburn also writes of the battle, "About 12 miles east of Hickory Log was the village of Long Swamp, situated at the mouth of that stream on the north side of the Etowah, in Gold District 3. Historically, this site was occupied at an early date, at least in the years of the colonial rebellion, for it served as a stronghold in the last days of the war for a small army of raiders commanded by Thomas Waters, a British colonel, before they were finally put to flight in the autumn of 1782 by militiamen under Andrew Pickens and Elijah Clarke."

Most of the Cherokee's warriors escaped, according to Walker's account, but Pickens did capture about 50 women, children and older men of the village. After he gained control of the village, on October 12, 1782, he summoned 12 chiefs and about 200 warriors to meet him there. Following negotiations that included the mandate that all Loyalists and all African slaves owned by the Cherokee be turned over to the Americans, Pickens pre-

Brigadier General Andrew Pickens was called Skyagusta or Wizard Owl by the Cherokee.

pared to leave north Georgia. Waters was not captured and subsequently made his way to Florida. Pickens then helped the Cherokee define the border with the whites in the Long Swamp Treaty, which signed over portions of land between the Savannah and Chattahoochee River to the colonists. Pickens was well regarded by Native Americans with whom he dealt, and was given the name Skyagusta, or "The Wizard Owl," by the Cherokee. Following the signing of the treaty, he and his men went home to South Carolina.

In 1792 during the shaky peace between the Cherokee and whites that followed, a group of militiamen from Tennessee under the command of John Sevier attacked the Cherokee and it is believed the Long Swamp village was burned, but the Cherokee continued to live in the area and the community was revived in the early 1800s when the Federal Road was opened into the region.

Several Native American towns were settled in today's Cherokee County, including Sixes Old Town, which was at the junction of Little River and the Etowah River and was headed by Chief Stop. The town was about seven miles southwest of today's Canton. By 1833 as many as 400 Indians were living there. The name may have denoted the number of outstanding fighters or warriors the town boasted and is

Early maps, including this one in 1855, show present day Ball Ground as "Battle Ground."

the origin of today's Sixes community's name. Sixes had been first settled by the Cherokee around 1799 on the north and south banks of the river and was in the Hickory Log District of the Cherokee Nation. The Cherokee Nation was comprised at the time of eight districts and other districts were Chicamaugee, Chattoogee, Amoah, Etowah, Aquohee, Tahquohee and Coosewatee.

In addition to Hickory Log District, the name Hickory Log was also given to another Cherokee settlement along the Etowah River near Ball Ground. Other known settlements included Red Bank and an unnamed settlement that was about 14 miles east of Hickory Log on the north side of the Etowah. Lost Town was in north Cherokee County in a valley of Pine Log Mountain. There was also a mission outpost at Hickory Log Town that was supervised by the Reverend Duncan O'Briant until he moved west in 1832. Hudson writes, "In 1834 the Cherokee towns of Hickory Log and Coosawattee played a game near the present day Jasper, Georgia, in which the chiefs of the towns bet $1,000 on the outcome of the game, an enormous sum for that time."

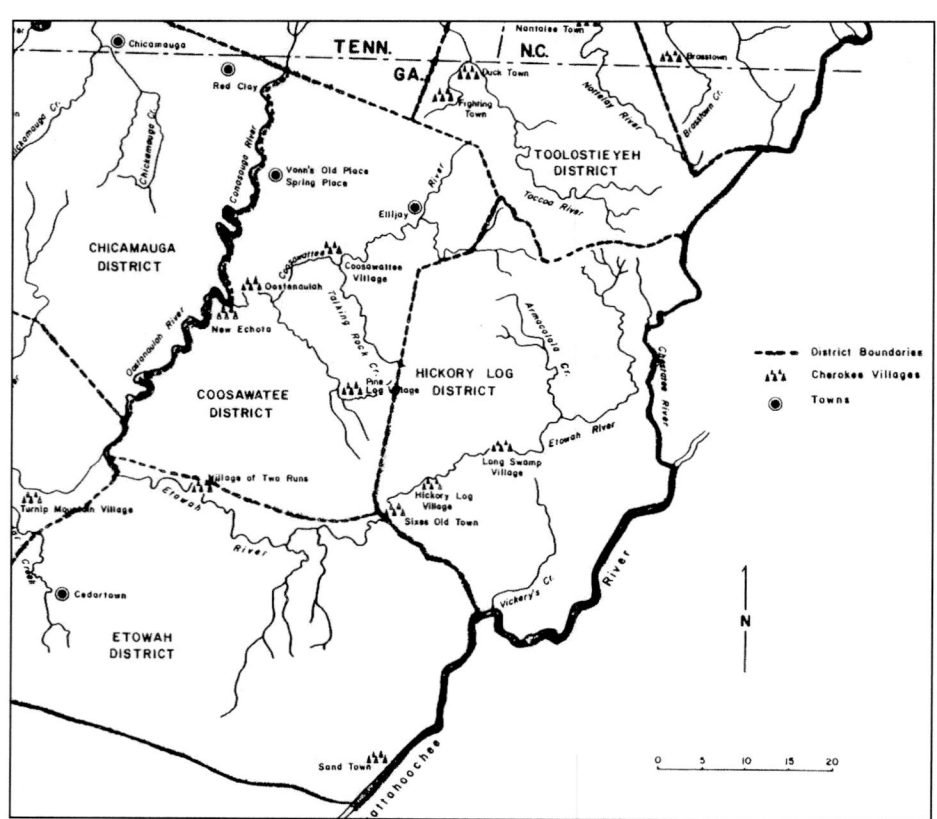

District Boundaries of the Cherokee Nation 1802. *Compiled by Douglas Wilmer and Marian Hemperly.*

In the early 1800s the Cherokee began adopting Euro-American farming methods. Before the arrival of the Europeans, the Cherokee had a communal system of land ownership, according to Hudson. "Only after the arrival of the Europeans did the Indians have a need to codify their notions of communal ownership," Hudson writes. Following the War of 1812, many of the Cherokee Indians began building gristmills and accumulating large tracts of property. The Cherokee were moving toward cotton production and the use of cotton gins, agricultural tools and machines familiar to the settlers who were moving into the region.

The Cherokee Indians set up a centralized government and in 1817 they formed a two-house Legislature patterned after the United States government. In 1821 the Cherokee Sequoyah, who at that time was living in the region that is today Alabama, devised a Cherokee alphabet. He was the first person who was illiterate to invent an alphabet. In just a few years following his work, thousands of Cherokees were able to read and write in greater percentages than their white neighbors. In 1827 the Cherokee adopted a formal constitution chartering a government with separate legislative, executive and judiciary branches. In 1828, they began publishing their own newspaper, *The Cherokee Phoenix* at their capital, New Echota, in northwest Georgia. The newspaper drew much attention from around the world. But six years later the state of Georgia confiscated the printing press and shut down the publication.

Even as these advances in government and communication were taking place among the Cherokee, Hudson writes that wealthy Cherokee had begun buying slaves. The Cherokee also passed a law making it illegal for blacks to marry Cherokees. In the 1835 census, James Daniel, of mixed European and Native American heritage, was one of the wealthiest men in Cherokee County, a rich planter and a slave owner. Records show that he owned 37 slaves, 30 houses and 300 acres at his Long Swamp plantation. Mose Downing, another Cherokee with mixed ancestry, had five slaves, 11 houses and 157 acres of land in the census. George Still lived at Red Bank Town on the Etowah and owned 10 slaves, 10 houses, three farms and 100 acres of land in cultivation.

James Daniel, of Euro-Native American ancestry, was one of the wealthiest men in Cherokee County and settled his homeplace on Long Swamp Creek well before 1820. His property at Long Swamp Creek totaled 300 acres. *Courtesy of the collection of the Reverend Charles Walker, Cherokee Images.*

Most of the Cherokee lived in log cabins or wooden structures. The largest building in the settlement was usually the council house. Writers of the day called the Cherokee people at times grave, dignified and reserved in manner. As a nation they were described as cheerful and humane, honest and territorial. Women occupied a high status in the villages, and for centuries were allowed to own land. But as the Cherokee worked to hold onto their lands and to prosper in the early 19th century, events and opinions among the governments in Washington and the state of Georgia that would eventually lead to their removal were growing on the horizon.

Settlers Begin Their Push into the Territory

White settlers had already staked their claim to the lands in Georgia bordering Indian Territory as well as South and North Carolina, and the ever-increasing surge of families looking for a home on what was then the frontier of a young nation was increasing the demand for more land. The facts only hint at the drama that surrounded the creation of Cherokee County. After years of treaties and broken promises, and with the lure of gold dazzling white pioneers pouring into the area, events were in motion to make the rich Indian Territory a property of the state of Georgia in the form of a new county.

Many factors combined to lead to the removal of the Cherokee from Georgia and Cherokee County, including the discovery of gold around 1828 and the election to the office of United States president by Andrew Jackson, who was long an advocate of removing the native population to the West. It would be 10 years before all Native American lands were seized, and a few historians argue that the discovery of the precious mineral did not hasten the process. But it is accepted by most historians and researchers as a significant reason for accelerating the removal of the Cherokee from their lands. Some say that the first gold found in Cherokee County was in the area of the Cherokee settlement of Sixes Old Town. But when news in 1828 that a large nugget of gold was found near today's Dahlonega spread across the nation through newspaper reports, opportunists looking for wealth began descending into the north parts of Georgia where the precious metal was discovered.

Standing in the shallows of the Etowah River, in the creeks and streams that made up its tributaries, those lured by the prospect of gold searched for the precious metal. At night they would gather around campfires and outposts to drink and fight, and get a little sleep. Gold rush fever was at a high pitch, with nuggets worth as much as $200 being found, fueling the promise of riches for those who had little. Those men were looking for placer gold, or gold that is free for the taking from creeks and streams. It would be several years before mines were established in Cherokee County to look below the surface for further mineral riches.

Today's Cherokee County was located in the center of the gold belt and was one of the top gold-producing regions in the state. Thousands of prospectors came into the Indian Territory between 1828 and 1830, onto the lands still held at the time, at least officially, by the Cherokee. While the Georgia Gold Rush was certainly not the only factor in the government's push toward taking over the lands of North Georgia, it appears to have played a significant part. The state of Georgia passed a series of anti-Indian Acts in the wake of the discovery of gold, including a law that the Cherokees were forbidden to mine gold on their lands. They could not assemble in groups of three or more persons, including for religious purposes, and they were not allowed to testify against a white person in a court of law, a restriction that placed them in an impossible situation.

The main justifications used, however, for the removal of the Native Americans was that the white man could make better use of the land and that it was for the Indians' own good, Charles Hudson tells in his book about the Southeastern Indians. Hudson states that the argument of the day contended the Cherokee were mere heathen hunters, and that the settlers were Christian farmers who could use the land more effectively. That ignored the facts that the Indians had been agriculturists for hundreds of years, he wrote, and that they were even then adopting modern-day "agricultural techniques from the whites." Government leaders also argued that the Cherokee needed protection from the unruly whites moving into the area and that they did not pay taxes.

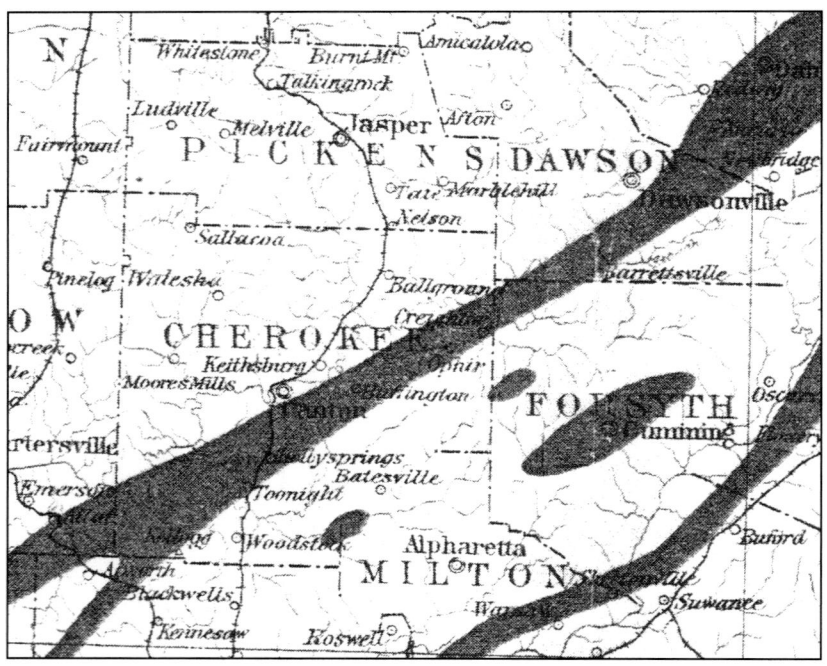

Cherokee County was in the gold belt as shown by this geological survey map of the gold deposits of Georgia dated 1909.

In 1829 in his inaugural address, President Jackson said that he had advised the Cherokee people to emigrate beyond the Mississippi or submit to the laws of the state. He said that no independent government could be formed in the jurisdiction of an existing state, effectively countering the claim by the Cherokees that the state of Georgia was infringing on their rights.

In May 1830 the United States Congress with Jackson's influence passed the Indian Removal Act, which ultimately led to the forced removal of the Cherokees in 1838 and set the stage for the tragedy later named the Trail of Tears. Only three days after the bill was signed into law by President Jackson on May 28, 1830, the state of Georgia moved to confiscate the Cherokee lands of approximately 4,600,000 acres, as well as all the Creek lands in the state.

The United States Supreme Court heard cases involving the Cherokee in the early 1830s. The first, *Cherokee Nation v. Georgia*, put forth the case that the state of Georgia did not have the right to extend its laws over the Cherokee, as they were an independent foreign state and owned their lands. The court, however, concluded that the Cherokees comprised a dependent sovereign nation. In the second case, the Supreme Court agreed to hear an appeal of the conviction by a judge in Hall County of a Cherokee named Corn Tassel who was sentenced to hang for the murder of another Cherokee. The court requested Georgia Governor George Gilmer to appear before the bench, but he refused and Corn Tassel was ultimately hanged despite the appeal.

In another instance, two missionaries, Samuel Worcester and Elizur Butler, were arrested and sentenced to four years of hard labor for refusing to take an oath of allegiance to the state of Georgia required of all white men living among the Cherokee Nation. The Supreme Court and Chief Justice John Marshall handed down a decision that the missionaries should be released. The state of Georgia refused and the missionaries were forced to accept the authority of the state, taking the oath before their release in 1833 from the state penitentiary.

Land lotteries were a means of distributing property in the state of Georgia starting in the early 1800s. Georgia is possibly the only state to have used a lottery system, and it was utilized only in part of the state, mainly for the properties taken from the Creeks and the Cherokee. Over the next two decades several such lotteries were held in portions of the state once belonging to the Creeks, but the Cherokee held much of the northern region of Georgia, and it was not until the sixth land lottery in 1832 that their lands were awarded to settlers.

The Act of December 21, 1830, and the Act of December 24, 1831, passed by the state's Legislature set the stage for the Cherokee Indian Territory in Georgia to be divided up among those eligible for the lotteries. Those settlers already living in Georgia for three years were eligible if they were bachelors over 18 years of age, married or widowed, and United States citizens. Veterans of the Revolutionary War were eligible for two draws, while wounded or disabled veterans of the War of 1812 and the Indian War also could take two draws. There were a number of other eligible categories under the acts. Those who had mined in the Cherokee Indian territory since June 1, 1830, or lived in the territories could not draw for land under the state laws.

Since the area was so large, it was divided into four sections, with each section divided to create a total of 60 land districts. Each of those was then divided by survey into land lots of 160 acres for the Sixth Land Lottery. To be granted a land lot, those lucky enough to draw one also had to pay a total of eighteen dollars. The Act of December 24, 1831, created the seventh and last land lottery which was called the Gold Lottery. It took about a third of the land lots from the 1830 act and designated them as gold districts of 40 acres each, with a

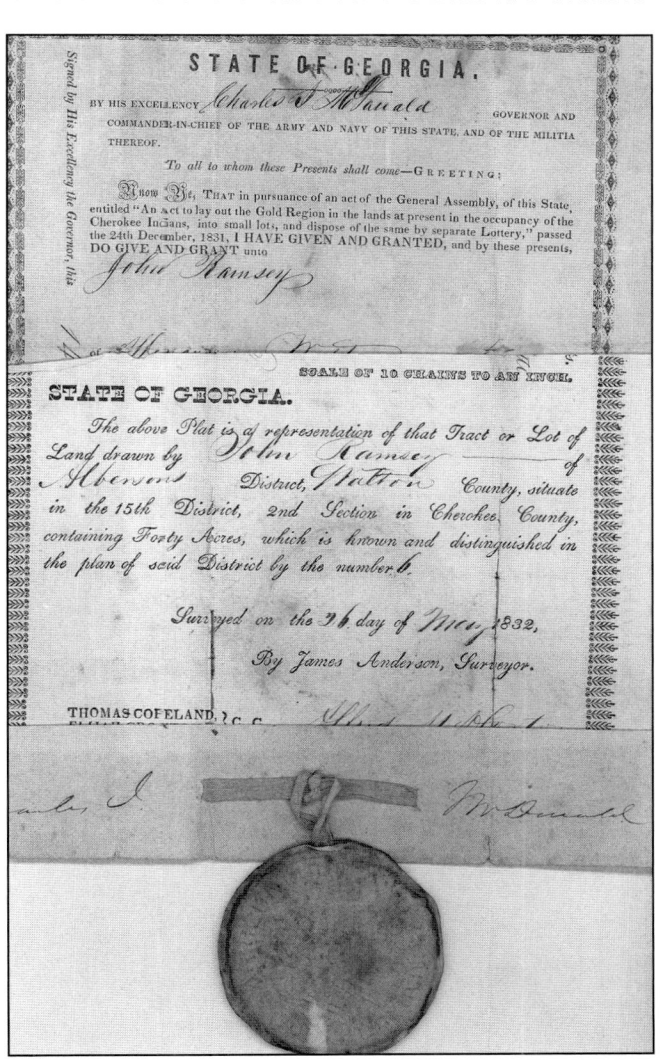

A Gold Lottery Deed signed in 1832 awarded forty acres to John Ramsey in Land Lot No. 6, District 15 of Cherokee County.

grant fee of ten dollars per lot. These lots were located in what was known by geologists as the Gold Belt of the state. The new owners of the land lots received them with whatever improvements the Cherokee had made on them, a practice that was considered particularly unjust to the Native Americans. Chief John Ross returned home from a trip to Washington to plead the Cherokees' case to find his wife paying rent to the new "owners" for the privilege to stay at the chief's own home.

There were very few white settlers permanently living in Cherokee County at the time of the land lotteries. But that quickly changed as the winners of the drawings began to claim their stakes and move into the region. Those early settlers migrated from South Carolina and North Carolina and even from as far away as Virginia. Many came from already established counties in Georgia, such as Hall County.

Only two days after passing the Act of December 24, 1831, the Georgia Legislature created the original Cherokee County, Georgia. The original Cherokee County was drawn

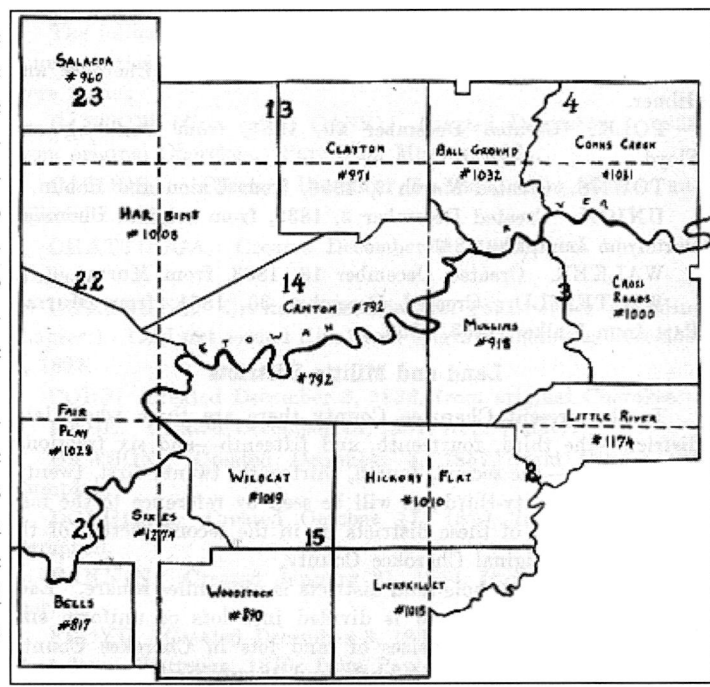

This map shows Militia and Land Districts of Cherokee County. The area was divided into Sections, then Districts, then land lots of 40 or 160 acres. This method of land division is still used today. Militia districts of Georgia were used to organize military companies from a time soon after the War of 1812 until the Civil War period.

An 1832 survey map of Section 2, District 14 of Cherokee County locating trees and their species to show the delineation of the land lots.

from all the territory held at that time by the Cherokee Indians. The official birthday of Cherokee County is December 26, 1831, when the Act creating Cherokee County was signed into law. The boundaries of the county were "All the territory, lying west of the Chattahoochee River and north of Carroll County, within the limits of Georgia," according to the Acts, Georgia, 1831.

The new law dictated that on the first Monday of February 1832, those settlers who were entitled to vote for members of the General Assembly could meet at the home of "one Ambrose Harnage," and there elect officials for the new county, including five justices of the Inferior Court, a Clerk of the Superior Court, a Clerk of the Inferior Court, a sheriff, coroner, receiver of tax returns, tax collector and county surveyor. Court was also to be held at the home of Harnage and the county was made a part of the Western Judicial Circuit by the new law. There is some debate about where the home of Harnage actually was located. Some accounts place it in Tate in Pickens County, while others put it on the old Harnage Road in north Cherokee County between Waleska and Ball Ground. According to an excerpt of an article published in the *Atlanta Constitution* in 1889 and reprinted in *Cherokee Footprints* by Charles O. Walker, "Harnage was so-called from the man who settled this place, and his house was for a long time a sort of public inn, where the mountain wayfarers, stock drovers from Kentucky and Tennessee, sought and found shelter. The old Harnage house fronted North and South, and was a story and a half high…. This house, which has long been pulled down, once occupied the present site of Col. Steven C. Tate's beautiful mountain home, and was within 400 yards of the great quarries of the Georgia Marble works. The first court was held in this house, in

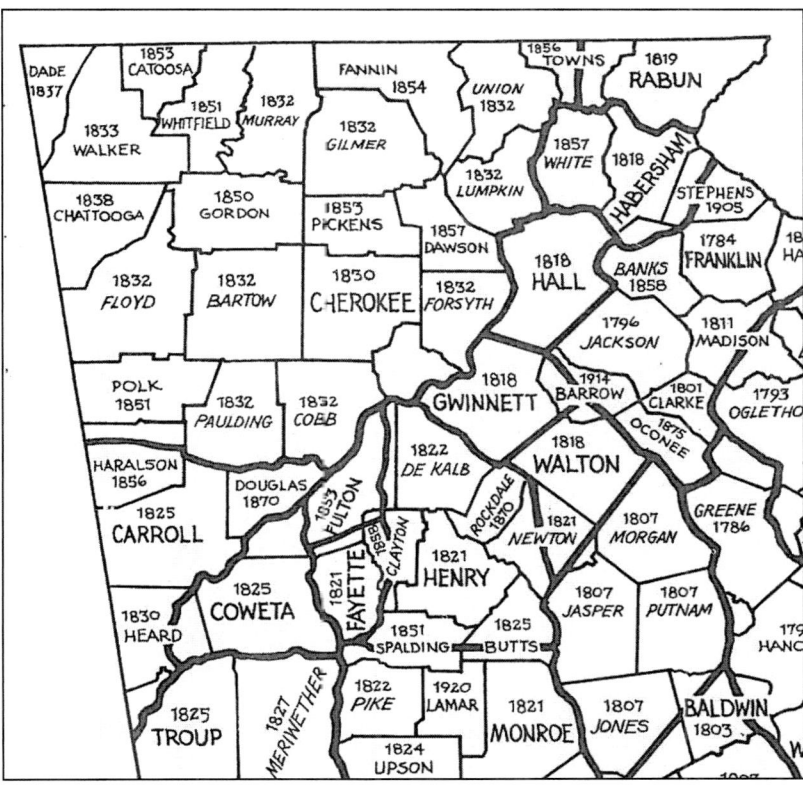

The original Cherokee County was divided into 10 counties on December 3, 1832. Later divisions eventually brought the total number of counties carved out of Cherokee County to twenty-one as well as portions of several other counties.

February, 1832, the Hon. Charles Dougherty presiding, and Mr. Turner T. Tripp solicitor general. The jurors were drawn from all sections of this immense County. The second Superior Court was held at Etowah, now Canton."

In December 1832, the first state senator elected from Cherokee County, Jacob M. Scudder (b.1788-d.1870), introduced a bill in the General Assembly to subdivide Cherokee County into 10 units, realizing that the original county was too large. Those new counties formed were Cherokee, Cass, Cobb, Floyd, Gilmer, Lumpkin, Murray, Paulding and Union. Campbell County was added later that month. Governor Wilson Lumpkin signed the bill into law on December 3, 1832. That bill set the new election for county officials and for the first court session to be held at the home of John Lay, a merchant on the Alabama Road, which is today Georgia State Highway 20.

The Cherokee County seat was incorporated by the state Legislature on December 24, 1833, and at that time given the name Etowah, believed to come from the Native American word Itawa or Etalwa, which meant trail crossing or town. The first settlers thought the Indians were saying Hightower, and the name Etowah might also be a corruption of Hightower, which was also the name given the Indian village located where the Etowah mounds are in today's Bartow County. The name also designated the river that flowed through the region. The new town was originally known as Cherokee Courthouse, according to early federal post office records. The first official name given by the state was Etowah.

Among the first to settle in the town in 1832 was an enterprising businessman from South Carolina named William Grisham, a founder of the county seat whose descendants continue to live in the home he eventually established there. Grisham was born on March 6, 1803, in the Pendleton District of South Carolina. In 1825 he married Susan Bradford and the couple moved to Decatur, Georgia, that same year. Grisham set up business in Decatur and when the gold lottery took place in 1832 he drew for land in Cherokee County. According to his descendant, Nell Galt Magruder, Grisham chose carefully where he planned to settle, perusing the land lot booklet, and deciding on Cherokee County because of its rich natural resources and location. After receiving his lot in 1832, he moved to Cherokee County. Letters received by Grisham in those early days show they were posted to the town designated Cherokee Courthouse and that he was the first postmaster. Grisham partnered in early enterprises with Dr. John W. Lewis, whom he had known in South Carolina. Grisham subsequently purchased other land lots and had control of about a dozen gold parcels. He had ownership of thousands of acres in Cherokee County and surrounding counties during his lifetime.

The county seat's name was changed to Canton a year later. It has long been an accepted fact that the name was selected because the early settlers were trying to establish a silk-growing industry in the county. However, there is some disagreement from descendants of the early settlers that the name Canton was chosen for that reason or even whether the silk industry was begun in the town at the time. The history of the state is threaded with references to the silk industry. The original settlers of Georgia who arrived with James Oglethorpe in 1732 hoped to find wealth from producing silk. In Cherokee County there is evidence that several of the early settlers of Cherokee County planted mulberry trees with which to feed silk worms. The 1841 home of William Grisham had a "silk room" where mulberry leaves could be used to feed the worms, and mulberry trees still exist on the grounds of his home. The house was not built until 1841, which disputes that the town name in 1833 came from that endeavor. One theory could be that the settlers were already considering a try at the silk industry several years before the attempt or that silk was being produced elsewhere in the community. The known attempt did fail, and no silk was ever produced in Cherokee County.

The location of the county seat was chosen because it was the center of the most heavily populated area, court and elections were already taking place there, and some of the early settlers were enthusiastically lobbying for the location. Two other early pioneer settlers along with Grisham, Judge Joseph Donaldson and John P. Brooke, donated the land for the city to be established as a way to guarantee the county seat was located where it was most advantageous to the fledgling attempts at local industry and commerce.

Brooke, another of the earliest settlers of Cherokee County, owned a ferry on the Etowah River near Canton. That early site was one of the first three known ferries on the Etowah River in the region. The first ferry was owned by a Cherokee known as Dickeski or Dick Estay, and could have been at the site of the later Gilmer Ferry west of Long Swamp Creek. The second known ferry was owned by a man of mixed Euro-Indian ancestry named Mose Downing and was where the Alabama Road crossed the Etowah River. Once the city was chartered, town lots were surveyed and sold. William K. McCanless, an early pioneer who was a wheelwright and builder, is said to have purchased the first lot in the new city of Canton.

Final Indian Removal and the Trail of Tears

Even as the white settlers were forging ahead to establish their claims in North Georgia, matters with the Cherokees were moving rapidly to a head. In what has become the most recognized and studied incident of harsh treatment of the Native Americans at the hands of the whites, the forced Cherokee Indian Removal of 1838 and 1839 was about to begin. On December 29, 1835, in events leading up to the removal, a minority faction of Cherokee chiefs signed the Treaty of New Echota with the United States Government. Under the provisions of the treaty the Cherokee were given two years to voluntarily remove from their lands and in return they would receive $5 million and seven million acres of land out West. The majority of Cherokee were not in agreement with the treaty, however, and a petition with

15,656 Cherokee signatures was signed proclaiming it a fraud. On May 23, 1836, the federal government ratified it anyway.

In the next two years only 2,000 Cherokee moved West on their own accord. As it became apparent that the majority would not abdicate their lands and leave willingly, the federal government went into action with steps to begin a forced removal. By 1837 the buildup of military forces in the territory and the construction of the structures necessary to the operation of forced removal were underway by the federal government. On October 5, 1837, Capt. Ezekial Buffington was ordered, along with his company of Georgia Guard, to immediately leave New Echota where they had been stationed and make their way to Canton in Cherokee County to choose a site for a cantonment. He was ordered to build huts and stables for the company of paid volunteers as quickly as he could. Private John H. Wood was quartermaster and commissary for the operation.

The contingent under Capt. Buffington's command arrived in Canton on October 15.

CENSUS OF THE CHEROKEES OF GEORGIA of 1835

Copied at Washington D.C. by

Maud B. Allen, and Mignon A. Holfert

Heads of Families	Total	Heads of Families	Total
COB. CO. ALATUNA CREEK		Robbin Tooks	7
		George Proctor	14
Jos. Proctor & Son	14	Dave	11
Tanna	7	Sultaner	8
Anna Wake	6	Tickler	9
Uchilla		Otter Lifter	5
Hider	7	Elowa	6
Now Hail	11	Poor Bear	10
Susannah	4	Good Woman	2
		Grasshopper	1
CHEROKEE COUNTY ETOWAH RIVER		Thompson	8
		Stealer	6
James Proctor & Son	4	Dog Light	7
Turkey	7	Mushtick	13
Crow	3	Silly	10
Tinka	5	Spaniard	12
Alunahaka	7	Sweet Water	6
Ticannahuisca	17	Kieukan	8
Chicken Snake	6	Stand	9
John	3	Tarripin head	4
John	3	Censkaka	10
Seeds	8	Moses Downing	13
Oo-wa-tee	14	Dan Still	5
Big Horn	5	Doghead	4
Stop	7	Smoke	6
Jake	4	Aaron Downing	4
Nick a jack	6	Sampson	8
Rusty Belly	5	Bear	15
Whiteman killer	10	Zug	8
George	6	S. Water	6
Cloud	4	Sunday	4
Nelly	6	Ned Still	6
Polly	8	Blossom	6
Bears Paw	7	Chuchecha	5

A portion of the 1835 Cherokee Census showing those Native Americans who lived along the Etowah River. The census was ordered by the federal government prior to the Indian Removal of 1838.

The site chosen was on the plantation of Moses Perkins, whose stepson, Newton J. Perkins, was a private under Buffington's command. After the site was chosen, construction was begun on the buildings for the new post. While the exact location is not known, efforts continue to determine the actual site of the fort. According to a 2005 study, the fort could have been located either north or south of the Alabama Road. To the north of the road it could have been in one of two possible locations, one adjacent to Harmony Primitive Baptist Church on Harmony Drive, and the other in the pasture or parking area near the church. However, the study places the more likely location on the south side of the Alabama Road in a field between two streams.

Using timber from the surrounding area, the soldiers constructed officer and soldier barracks, stables for 103 horses, three corn cribs, two block houses, pickets and a forge, according to John W. Latty in his book, *Carrying off the Cherokee*. As soon as the buildings were completed, large quantities of supplies and foodstuffs began to arrive at the new cantonment. By the end of November, what had been

Cherokee women were respected members of their society and handled the running of the household.

designated Camp Buffington was renamed Fort Buffington. In the early part of 1838 the fort was extended and fortified. Men were working feverishly building block houses and picketing or fencing the area. The block houses were constructed of massive hewn logs with openings to allow for the firing of weapons.

Weaponry was secured from a variety of sources to arm the outfit. The number of companies serving at the fort is unknown, but at least several were armed and had ammunition, including bayonets and musket balls. By the end of April, about 90 men were headquartered at the fort. On May 6, 1838, an order was issued explaining how the soldiers were to engage the Cherokee. "Officers and parties of soldiers in pursuit of fugitive Cherokee Indians are directed not to fire upon them… as the object of the pursuit is to apprehend and hold them…and not wantonly or unjustly to wound or kill them."

The other removal station in Cherokee County was known as Sixes and was located in the area of today's Sixes Community. It may have been constructed at the site of Camp Hinar, which some accounts say was a Federal Army camp at the Cherokee town of Sixes during the gold rush set up to oust white miners and later used by the Georgia militia to protect the mines. However, according to some accounts, Fort Hinar could have been constructed in response to the Indian Removal Act of 1830 then later Camp Sixes was set up there. But enough records exist indicating Sixes was used in the Cherokee removal in 1838 that it is probable it was a second site in Cherokee County. It was, however, not thought to be as large or as well-provisioned as Fort Buffington, and was not a stockade.

The roundup started on May 24, 1838, as state militia began going to the homes of the Cherokee and ordering them at bayonet point to pick up what they could carry and come to the forts to await further instructions. Federal officers in charge of the roundup included General Winfield Scott and General Charles Floyd, who headed field operations. Orders given to the soldiers included instructions that the residents living in the area be told not to interfere, "the business of emigration which is about to begin. Any such interference cannot fail to bring on hostilities and lead to the murder of many white families; for as large as the militia force is, a company cannot be sent to protect every white man's habitations, the citizens must therefore perceive the danger and impropriety of taking the business of removing the Indians out of the hands of the United States."

An excerpt from the diary of Nathaniel Frank Reinhardt, the son of Lewis Reinhardt, who moved to Cherokee County in 1834, offers some insight into the roundup. Young Nathaniel was only five years old in 1838 when the events took place and 20 years old when he began the diary that retraced his earlier life. Portions of the diary are included in the Lloyd G. Marlin's *The History of Cherokee County*.

"In this spring, many U.S. soldiers were passing through the country for the purpose of collecting and removing the Cherokee Indians to the West. They frequently lodged at night at Father's. Saw old Foekiller, a neighbor Indian, just after he had been arrested by the soldiers, who were carrying him to Fort Buffington. They treated him rather cruelly which excited my sentiments very much in his favor. The old Indian desired to see Father, who solicited better treatment in his behalf…. After the Indians had been collected by the soldiers and started on their final march off, they came near our house the first night and camped. I caught the measles from a soldier who lodged with us that night and had them severely. One of the neighbors came and stayed the night at Father's from fear of injury by the Indians."

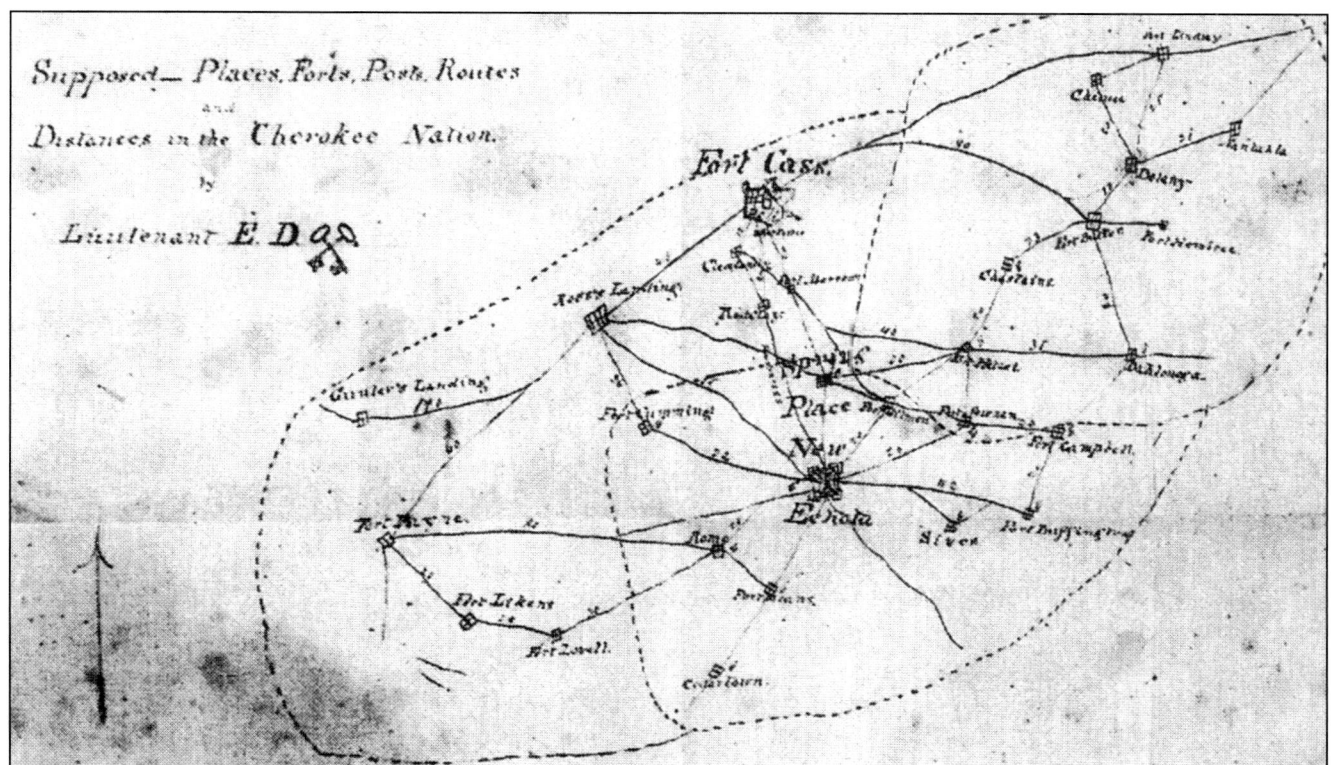

A military map was drawn in 1838 by Lieutenant E.D. Keyes to mark the forts, routes and posts in the Cherokee Nation. Fort Buffington was a major cantonment used by the government for its roundup of Native Americans. *National Archives as reprinted in Carrying off the Cherokee by John W. Latty.*

The Cherokee were also allowed to sell their property before removal. Many of the reports indicated that the Cherokee made no resistance, but did indicate that they were reluctant to leave their homes. Many of them still clung to hopes that John Ross would intervene at the last minute and they would be allowed to go back home.

By May 28, there were an estimated 500 Cherokee at Fort Buffington. Description of the treatment of the Cherokee at the forts varies. While the federal government gave strict orders that food be given to the Indians, it is believed that many were denied enough sustenance. Living conditions were described as filthy and squalid and in the weeks that followed, and the roundup continued, many of those already incarcerated began to be sick, with some dying even before the march began.

One report from N.W. Pittman of Daniel Madison's Company stationed at Sixes said that on May 28, 1838, the company traveled until midnight taking prisoners and leaving guards at the houses of the Cherokee. They rested for a while in the road, and then continued to round up the Native Americans until the company had a total of 92 prisoners. In all as many as 927 Cherokee were taken into custody in the county, with a portion of those sent to Sixes.

Once the roundup was complete, the Cherokee were marched to detainment camps at central location points in Alabama and Tennessee to begin their forced exodus from the lands where only a few decades before they had had clear claim. That exodus was made across nine states and 2,200 miles on foot and in wagons in the months that followed. The first two groups to begin were escorted by the military, but so many deaths and illnesses were reported that the removal was halted until the cooler weather of the autumn months could begin. The latter groups were allowed to migrate along the trail under the leadership of their own Chief John Ross.

Mose Daniel and George Still, two of the names listed among the Cherokee from Cherokee County, led one of the detachments along what would become known as the Trail of Tears. That detachment left an agency area on September 30, 1838, and ended their march the following year on March 2, 1839, at the home of a Mrs. Webber in Oklahoma, used as the principal depot and termination point for the march. Of the 1,035 Indians who traveled with Daniel, only 924 arrived at the end of that long journey. In all more than 16,000 Indians were removed to the West in 13 detachments, with estimates of 4,000 or an even higher number of those who suffered the removal dying along the trail

One letter written to his family by a white man, Daniel Davis, who had been hired by the military as a teamster in the group from Fort Buffington, told of the cold that Christmas as they traveled across Illinois and camped on the Mississippi River. He wrote of deep snow, and ice so thick that they had to break it to water the cattle and horses.

He told of one of the ferries bursting a boiler and killing at least two people and scalding many more. He said that Christmas was not even marked and that it had taken the contingency of Native Americans a month to travel 66 miles.

By mid-June, collection of the Cherokee people was completed and the militia and volunteers were honorably discharged. As the years progressed, the buildings of Fort Buffington were abandoned or removed from the property where they once stood. A block house survived until it was removed from the property in 1895, according to an article in the *Cherokee Advance*. The plan was to put a portion of the old Fort on display at Grant Park in Atlanta as a relic of the past. The newspaper reported, "It is one of the last reminders of the Indians, and will be preserved and treasured as a memento of the history of the country. The old weather beaten building has stood the storm of more than half a century alone, and neglected, but now it is to be vested with historic interest and gazed upon by thousands as one of the wonders of the age." What actually became of the portion of the old Fort is unknown.

An 1889 sketch of the rebuilt Fort Buffington Blockhouse. *Atlanta Constitution.*

The Cherokee Removal from the land they had held for centuries including today's Cherokee County ended a bitter political and human contest over who would control the northern part of the state of Georgia. By the winter of 1838 Cherokee County was mainly devoid of the native people who had once populated its lands. One military report in June 1838 stated, "The Cherokee difficulty is now considered by the people in this country at an end." But their legacy is still remembered in the names of communities, rivers and landmarks throughout the county. Reminders of their lives are still found in the forests they once roamed and along the waterways that once sustained their lives. With the events of 1838 a page was turned forever in Cherokee County's history.

The Cherokee Mine was worked as early as 1854 and was the only mine in the county to employ hydraulic mining techniques in which water was used to wash dirt downhill so the gold ore could be isolated and removed.

Chapter Two

New Opportunities and the Promise of Land

At the start of the new decade in 1840 Cherokee County had grown to a population of 5,895, according to the first official United States census following the removal of the Native Americans. Many of those pioneers who were living in Cherokee County in 1840 migrated into the region in just the two years after the Cherokee were removed in 1838. An earlier 1834 census conducted for the state of Georgia by Absalum C. Avery and Phillip Kroft to determine the "white population" indicated a total of 1,342 "white free inhabitant Citizens in Said County." The 1840 census revealed that within six years that number had quadrupled.

The settlers arrived in their wagons and carts bringing all their worldly goods and their families and sometimes even their slaves with them. Those early pioneers wasted no time in clearing the land and erecting homes out of the hand-hewn logs they made from their timber. They began cultivating the soil, planting the first crops and toiling to feed their families and make a living. Mills were built along the streams and rivers of Cherokee County to grind the corn into grain and turn the farm products into saleable goods. General stores began to spring up at crossroads to provide the farmers with essential goods. Soon towns were growing out of the early settlements. The early pioneers were building homes, starting businesses, and forming the first schools, settling into a way of life that would blossom into the Cherokee County of the future.

Among those earliest settlers listed in the 1834 census were several families who located in Cherokee County before 1830, including John Epperson, who, according to Lloyd G. Marlin, operated a trading post in the county as early as 1815. Other early families in the 1834 census include those of John B. Garrison, R. Frank Daniel, Henry Holcomb and John S. Holcomb, Eli McConnell, John Timmons, and Noble Timmons.

Religion was an important facet of early life in Cherokee County. Missionaries had come into the region, first to minister to the Native Americans, then remaining to care for the religious needs of the settlers. The Methodists sent some of the first preachers into the county. Many of those same early religious leaders also began to educate the settlers and schools began to spring up all across the county. The new settlers were eager to see that their children had a chance to learn. Many of those locating in Cherokee County came from South Carolina, North Carolina and other points north and were well educated themselves. Soon they were importing knowledgeable teachers to lead in the classrooms.

Those early years of the county's history were prosperous ones, offering financial riches as well as the promise of a good life to those who pushed their way into the new county. By 1850 the population had surged to 12,800 permanent residents, larger farms and more elaborate homes than had been seen before were being established on the rich lands along the Etowah River, and Cherokee County was beginning to make its mark as a significant center of commerce and trade within the state.

Gold Mining Spurs Settlement

In the early 1840s it was becoming more difficult for miners to make a living out of panning for gold in the streams and rivers of Cherokee County. Despite less gold being found, many of the miners still clung to dreams of a fortune and continued to pan the streams of Cherokee County throughout the 1840s. From 1838 to 1849 the gold fields in north Georgia yielded about five million dollars in gold, only about one-fourth of the twenty million dollars of gold they had produced from 1828 to 1837. In 1849 when word of the great California strikes reached Georgia the miners left the region in droves.

Mining was still popular as an off-season activity for many of the planters and farmers. After the fall harvest the farmers would head to the hills to mine for gold. Planters in the area bought or leased the gold lands and worked their slaves in the mines. Canton founder William Grisham owned as many as a dozen gold lots.

In the 1850s as placer mining played out, mines to take the gold out of the ground were being erected. Some of those known to be in operation in 1845 included Pascoe's, Cherokee, Oliver, Clarkeston, Glade, Cheynogowah or Worley, Strickland, Sixes, Williamson's and Franklin Gold Mine. Kellogg was another well-known gold mine in south Cherokee County, as well as several others in that area. Other minerals being mined from under the rich earth of Cherokee County were iron ore, copper, titanium, quartz, mica, granite and marble.

John Pascoe established the Pascoe Gold Mines on the Etowah River in the early 1830s. John Pascoe came to America from Cornwall, England, about 1826, along with his brothers Samuel and James. The brothers were copper miners and engineers in their home region of Cornwall. James settled in the Pennsylvania area and died in 1838 in a coal mining accident. Other siblings, including sisters Ann Pascoe and Catherine Pascoe, would immigrate later. Samuel Pascoe worked in the gold industry in Dahlonega in those early years before settling in Cherokee County. John Pascoe eventually began building a large plantation home for his bride on the site in Cherokee County. Before the house could be completed, John died in 1853, poisoned by exposure to mercury during the processing of gold from his mines. Samuel Pascoe then moved his family into the house, which was willed to him by his brother. Samuel Pascoe, a slave owner who later served in the Civil War, made several trips back to England to bring saplings for his plum and apple orchards and livestock for the facility. Half of the house was torn away after his death, but the main portion of the house was left intact. Slave cabins, barns, a ferry, and the mines eventually were torn down. The Pascoe mines were later incorporated into the Franklin Creighton Gold Mines. The house served as the Creighton mine superintendent's home. The structure was later

Mary Jackson Pascoe and Samuel Pascoe. When they married in 1834, her dowry included 200 acres in Heard County, two yokes of oxen and personal slaves. They later had fourteen children.

The Creighton - Franklin Gold Mine was one of the richest and longest running mining operations in Cherokee County.

purchased by the company doctor, who built a store in the office on the property.

Mary Graves Cleveland Franklin was a widow who won a land lot in the 1832 land lottery. A descendant of a prestigious family who came to America in the early 1600s, she was married to Col. Abednego Franklin and had several children before his death in 1815. When she took possession of her land in Cherokee County, she brought several slaves with her. In the 1850 Georgia Slave Owners census, Mrs. Franklin is listed as having eight slaves. Her land proved to have valuable gold deposits and soon after taking possession in 1832 she was mining her land. She also expanded her land lot holding to include adjacent land. The gold mine produced as much as $1,000 per day in gold. Mrs. Franklin began operating a stamp mill to crush the ore and extract the gold. Her son-in-law, Charles James McDonald, who married her daughter Anne, helped to run the gold mine. By 1882 the mining operation and landholdings encompassed about 1,300 acres and was incorporated as the Franklin-McDonald Mining and Manufacturing Company.

In 1893, J.M. Creighton, who was the vice president of the company, bought out the other owners and the name was changed to Creighton Mines. The Creighton Mining Company operated until 1906 when a cave-in destroyed the mine and the Etowah River took back what it had once given up. In the late 1890s, the mine employed as many as 300 workers and a small town known as Creighton Hills grew up in the area with a general store, post office and other businesses to serve the workers who lived in the community.

The "Shingle House" is the last remaining building from the Creighton/Franklin Gold Mine Complex. The complex at one time included the mining plant with large stamp mill, a chlorination plant,

Miners were still working several of the gold mines in Cherokee County in the early 1900s, although many in the area had already played out. Here, miners at the Cherokee Mine include Mr. Freeborn, Frank Tumlin and H.H. (Bud) Hillhouse.

assay laboratory, blacksmith shop, stables, miners' cottages and a dam with two large turbines to generate power for the site. The "Shingle House" was built during the 1880s and was a commissary, offices, post office, boarding house, and a small stamp mill where local residents could sell gold ore. The building has been empty for many years and is a familiar landmark to area residents.

By 1896 as many as 37 mines were still in operation in Cherokee County. But by the beginning of the next century most had played out and gold would only be remembered by the old-timers. Gold fever would become a thing of the past.

Cities Make Their Mark

The earliest settlers in Cherokee County chose well when they put down their roots and selected where to build their homes and locate their businesses. Cherokee County would eventually have five incorporated cities including Canton, Woodstock, Ball Ground, Holly Springs and Waleska. A portion of Nelson is also in Cherokee County. Those towns were some of the most prosperous of the settlements that grew and took shape at numerous crossroads and locales throughout the county. Canton formed as the county seat in 1833, but it would be a number of years before any of the other communities incorporated. However, they all played important roles as the county took shape and grew.

Canton

Much of Canton's early growth and success was based on its location at the center of a rich agricultural region and the ingenuity and resourcefulness of its early settlers. Situated in the geographic center of the county, on a mile-wide curve in the Etowah River and near the best roads of the day, the town was set to take off with development from its earliest days. After being chartered on December 24, 1833, and renamed from Cherokee Courthouse to Etowah by the state Legislature, the fledgling city quickly established as the commercial, social and economic center of the county, earning it the reputation to go with the designation of county seat. Although it served as the economic center of the region, Canton was still a village in the first years of its existence. Many of the early buildings were simple in design and material, made from logs or rough planked wood. The streets were dirt roads and the main town had only a general store, a post office and a few other buildings, according to Marlin's *History of Cherokee County*. Those who first settled Canton began to establish themselves more decisively as the community's leaders in all facets of life in the growing town. Postmaster William Grisham was instrumental in organizing the new school, Etowah Institute, and the new Canton Baptist Church. In 1841 Grisham built his permanent home, a Georgia plain style two-story house that would remain the family home for generations to come. The home featured a porch across the front on both the upstairs and downstairs levels. The grounds had a picket fence as well as a smokehouse and other outbuildings.

Another early settler and leader, Judge Joseph Donaldson, was also a farmer, involved in the operation of the ferry and later in building a bridge across the Etowah River. While his

A steel bridge was constructed over the Etowah River in North Canton following the Civil War. The original wooden bridge might have been burned when Sherman's troops came through Canton, but records of the time are insufficient to be certain.

friend Grisham helped build the Baptist church, Donaldson lent his support to the Methodists. Donaldson was a farmer of note and ran what was designated a large plantation for north Georgia. In the 1850 census he had 26 slaves, which was a large number for a Cherokee County farmer. His home was known as a center for entertainment and hospitality.

Other early settlers of prominence included John P. Brooke, who helped found Canton and was one of the earliest sheriffs of the county. He also served in the state Legislature and was credited with establishing law and order for the early settlers who often found the region fraught with crime and lawlessness. R. Frank Daniel was the first clerk of the superior court and was postmaster in Canton for several years. Daniel was also touted as a man of much moral influence in the town. The first commissioners to govern the town were William Grisham, Howell Cobb, Philip Croft, M.J. Camden and James Burns.

Woodstock

The area surrounding Woodstock was some of the richest agricultural land in the county. Although not incorporated until December 8, 1897, it was one of the earliest towns settled in Cherokee County, with the first settlement established possibly as early as 1825. By 1833 Woodstock had an established federal post office under the direction of postmaster John Winn. How Woodstock got its name is not known, but one theory is that it was named for the book by Sir Walter Raleigh. Another theory is that one of the earliest settlers was named Woodstock. The first mayor of Woodstock was N.A. Fowler.

What is known is that the area had rich land that was attractive to the pioneers pushing into the area. The community grew up around the river, creeks and early roads that brought the pioneers into the area. Several gold mines operated in the area. However, it was agriculture that contributed to the success of the early economy of Woodstock. Several plantations, including one owned by Dr. John Miller McAfee, were located in the community. Dr. McAfee is listed in the 1850 Census of Georgia Slave Owners as having 43 slaves at the time, a considerable number for a plantation in Cherokee County. Dr. McAfee had a 700-acre plantation and another 400-acre farm. The well-known doctor was elected a state senator in the Georgia General Assembly in 1840.

The D.M. Johnston family located to Cherokee County in 1836 from Warren County, North Carolina, settling first in the Hickory Flat community. In 1887 Johnston's son, J. H. Johnston, moved to

Woodstock from Cobb County. He opened a general mercantile store in Woodstock. His wife, Avis Benson Johnston, was a descendant of a pioneer family of Cherokee County. The couple had several children, including Smith L. Johnston, Joseph E. Johnston and Hugh Lee Johnston who continued to make their homes in Woodstock.

Another family that would have long influence on Woodstock was the Dean family. In 1851 William Hiram Dean settled in Woodstock in a log cabin he built close to the future site of the depot but across the road from where the railroad

Woodstock was one of the earliest towns settled in Cherokee County, but was not incorporated as a city until 1897. By the time the city was officially chartered, it was already a bustling center of commerce surrounded by rich farmland and served by the railroad, as seen here in 1910.

tracks are today and south of the downtown stores. Dr. Dean had studied medicine in Augusta, Georgia, and in New York. He traveled the roads around Woodstock by buggy treating patients. He was a doctor in the Confederate Army and upon his return from the war wrote of finding his home still standing, but no pigs or chickens. In 1862 he was ordained the pastor of Enon Baptist Church, the forerunner of Woodstock First Baptist Church. Other early Woodstock families included Dobbs, Paden, Fowler, Haney, Dial, Lathem and Chandler.

One of the biggest boosts for Woodstock's growth and eventual incorporation came in 1870 when the state Legislature approved the railroad being run to the town and on north to Canton and beyond. The Marietta and North Georgia Railroad was designed to access the rich mining areas of marble, copper and iron in North Georgia and to spur and encourage industry and commerce. The first depot is believed to have been built in 1879. The later depot was built in 1912 and became a centerpiece of the Woodstock historic downtown.

Ball Ground

While the heritage of Ball Ground dates to the days of the Cherokees, the city was not chartered until 1883, its growth fueled by the railroad and the marble industry. Ball Ground was the second largest city in the county during the nineteenth century and for the majority of the twentieth century. Until the time Ball Ground was chartered, however, it was a small settlement of agricultural farms, and the town consisted only of a few homes and two country stores. Its early fame lay in its Native American heritage and the legends surrounding its name.

When the railroad came through the county in 1882, Ball Ground was chosen as a site for a depot. That decision changed the future of the town. Land was donated by the families who lived in the area, including Sarah Carpenter, Martha Carpenter, Berty Carpenter, J.C. Carpenter, J.W. Byers, Hester Byers, Ellen Byers, P.H. Lyon, F.M. Waldrup, A.M.F. Hawkins, and Ancil Bearden. These individuals hoped that by establishing a town in the place of the settlement their properties would increase in value. Within two years of the decision to build the depot there, the city had a population of about 296 people in the 1890 census.

Ball Ground was the second largest city in the county at the turn of the century. Here, the town's population turns out for a celebration circa 1900. A city well draws thirsty town people at right.

The Ball Ground Baptist Church was constituted in 1883. Land for the church was donated by the Carpenter family. The church had a prominent location on the hill overlooking Old Canton Road. The Ball Ground Methodist Church traces its original roots at least as early as 1870. M.J. Cavendar donated an acre of land for the church in 1874. The first Methodist Church was a log cabin. Then in 1896 a frame building was erected at the same site. Both the Baptist Church and the Methodist Church were severely damaged by the tornado of 1915, which struck the town.

The oldest home in Ball Ground is the Alfred W. Roberts house, which was constructed in the 1850s. It was built by the original owners as a large two-story farmhouse.

The early government of the city consisted of the first mayor, Capt. Patterson Lyon and Councilmen Dr. A.M.F. Hawkins, W.A. Hayes, R.J. Boling and J.H. Kilby. J.N. Percell was the town's leading law enforcement officer, the marshal. Ball Ground received a new charter in 1911 to broaden the city's powers and allow it to maintain a public school system.

Holly Springs

The area where the city of Holly Springs eventually was located was first settled by those drawn by the promise of gold. The mines and the creeks and streams gave glimmers of riches that drew many settlers to Cherokee County and those mines around Holly Springs continued to be worked into the early 1900s. Holly Springs was established in Gold Lot Number 343. One of the earliest settlers of the region of the county that today is downtown Holly Springs was Richard Ragsdale, who began to mine for gold on the property using the placer mining process, finding gold in the creeks or along the ground. As the lure of gold began to diminish, the harder but more dependable currency of crops and agriculture became prevalent. Ragsdale also began to farm the land, raising corn, cotton, wheat, oats, and tobacco. He was joined by other early settlers whose names have continued to be prominent in the history of Holly Springs and Cherokee County, names like Hillhouse, Roach, and Chapman.

In the 1840s families moved into the area and set up small farms. By 1850 only about seven families comprised most of the population of the area that one day would bear the name Holly Springs. Along with Ragsdale, James Samuel Roach, who was married to a daughter of Ragsdale, Abner Honea, and the Vaughn family were a few of those who originally settled the area. Many of those early settlers were veterans of the War of 1812 and were eligible to receive land for their service

The city was not officially chartered by the Georgia Legislature until August 14, 1906. The town was the last to be chartered in Cherokee County. But for the people who have called it home through the decades, it has always been a special place to live, even before it was officially Holly Springs. How Holly Springs got its name is not crystal clear. There were mentions of some springs that gave the Cherokee and later the settlers their drinking water, but the only known mention of holly trees was by Lloyd Marlin in his 1932 Cherokee County history where he said that at that time only one such tree was still living on the site that gave the city its name.

In the early days of settlement, a recent arrival from South Carolina, Jacob Chapman, started operating a gristmill just north of where Holly Springs is located today. While there were no stores or trading posts in the community at the time, farmers could now have their crops of corn turned into grain. They were becoming more self-sufficient. As the population of Cherokee County grew in the years leading up to the Civil War

Holly Springs was in the center of one of the richest agricultural regions of the county and cotton was a major crop. The coming of the railroad in 1879 made transporting the cotton bales to market more efficient. Here, bales stacked at the depot await transport. The building in the background was later replaced by the E.M. Barrett Store.

other names were added to the Holly Springs community, including among others, McWhirter, McCollum, Pierce, Pool, Hughes, Ferguson, Smith, Bennett and Starnes.

Waleska

The city of Waleska grew out of the work of two early pioneer families, the Reinhardts and the Sharps. Families who first settled the area were of German descent and many like the Clines still remain there today. One of the first settlers in the area was Lewis W. Reinhardt, who came into northwest Cherokee in 1834. Reinhardt, whose grandparents had emigrated from Germany to the United States, was born in North Carolina and later lived in Tennessee. In 1830 he moved to Hall County, Georgia, where he married Jane Harbin. Reinhardt and his family settled on Shoal Creek and built a gristmill and a farm there. He traded with the Cherokee and ground their grain.

In 1835 he built a log cabin on a tract of land on Pine Log Road. Pine Log Mountain is the second highest elevation in Cherokee County. Soon Reinhardt was keeping a tavern and a roadhouse for travelers. An excerpt of a diary of Reinhardt's son, Nathanial Reinhardt, in Marlin's history book relates that in 1837 the family attended a Cherokee ballgame and dance at a Cherokee ball field near Waleska. "I was at a large Indian ballground near Father's. The exercise opened with a game of ball

The city of Waleska and Reinhardt College prospered together in the late 1800s. Here, a battalion drill takes place in front of the administration building on the campus when it was Reinhardt Normal College.

in which the men actively participated. The trees over and around the playground were filled with women, children and spectators looking on."

The younger Reinhardt goes on to relay that 1838 was, "A very cold winter. An immense number of pigeons flocked over the woods; the Indians killed great numbers of them. Father brought me a bowl of Indian connahaynee of which I was quite fond."

Waleska is supposed to have gotten its name out of the relationship the Reinhardts had with their Cherokee neighbors. The story goes that in those years leading up to the Cherokee removal, the Reinhardts were friends with a young Native American girl named Warluske. Her family name was Walaska, which means frogplace or Frog Town in Cherokee. The girl could read and write Cherokee. When she and her family were taken to Fort Buffington to be relocated West on the march known as the Trail of Tears, Lewis Reinhardt renamed his settlement Waleska in her honor and memory. In 1834 Lewis Reinhardt founded the first church in the settlement, the Reinhardt Chapel, a Methodist Church. He was known as a religious and well-respected man and got along with his Native American neighbors, who had great respect for him and his family.

In 1855 another family that would have great influence on the community of Waleska moved in and opened a store and a cotton gin and tobacco factory at the crossroads. Three brothers from South Carolina, John J.A. Sharp, White Sharp and Joseph Sharp were the trio who would make their mark on the region. The three siblings established their homes and business in the years leading up to the Civil War. When they returned after serving in the conflict the economy was in dire straits. One of the largest contributions that the Sharps made to the area was in educational and moral development of those living near them. Colonel John Sharp owned a large number of books which he would loan to the young men and women of the area. He also helped start a Sunday School and other endeavors. That love of learning would eventually help found the college that would become the town's chief attraction.

Nelson

Cherokee County has most of a sixth city within its boundaries. The town of Nelson grew up as a result of the marble industry on the northern border of Cherokee, with a portion of the city in Pickens County. The small city, which has around 1,300 residents, was on the railroad line as it came through Cherokee County in the early 1880s.

According to a history by Luke E. Tate in 1935, as the marble industry developed, the need for another finishing plant caused the Georgia Marble Company to purchase the property of John Nelson, located on the railroad near the Cherokee County line, for this purpose, and the town that sprang up there logically took the former

The Nelson Mercantile Corporation Store, Nelson, Georgia.

The city of Nelson was established as a result of the burgeoning marble industry in the 1880s. The Nelson Mercantile Corporation Store, above, and a saloon and ice house, left, were thriving establishments during the town's heyday.

owner's name. The man Nelson was named for was a farmer and a gunsmith of considerable note.

Since the beginning of the marble industry at Nelson, the stone for many important buildings throughout the country and many beautiful works of art in marble have been finished here. Among the skilled workmen at Nelson were a considerable number from Italy and Scotland, where they had previously been workers in stone, and some remained to become citizens. About 40 Italian workers came with their families to live in Nelson in the early 1900s. They were employed to carve, sculpt and finish Georgia marble from the quarries nearby, and for the most part they remained in the area until the 1940s.

Other communities:

Hickory Flat was one of the oldest settlements in Cherokee County, possibly settled before Canton in the late 1820s or early 1830s. The community was considered for the county seat, but was passed over in favor of Canton. One of the earliest academies, possibly the second school of its type

Hickory Flat is one of the oldest communities in Cherokee County and was considered for the county seat before Canton was chosen. The Hickory Flat Store stood at the crossroads of the community and also housed the Masonic Lodge.

in the county, was located there shortly after the opening of Etowah Academy in Canton. It was called the Hickory Flat Academy. The name Hickory Flat is believed to be a translation of the Native American name for the area. The community built up on the old Cherokee trading route through the region. As Hickory Flat took shape, it developed into one of the most thriving farm communities in the county. The community had several stores and two churches to serve the residents.

Just north of Hickory Flat is the **Indian Knoll** community. The knoll is literally a crest in the middle of rolling farm land where the Native Americans are believed to have gathered. Today a church and a new Cherokee County public school carry the name.

Avery Community lies east of Hickory Flat. A school was established at Avery in 1877 and continued to serve the community for 80 years until 1957 when it was consolidated with Buffington School. The Avery school was on East Cherokee Drive, which was an unnamed road at the time, and was built on land which was acquired from Thompson Moore on July 7, 1877. The school is believed to have been named for a Mr. Avery who resided in the community. The water supply for the school came from a nearby spring and wood was the exclusive heating fuel for many years at the school.

The community also included a general store, a steam-engine-run cotton gin, corn mill, wheat mill, and sawmill, all located on today's Upper Union Hill Road. Cotton was the major crop in the early part of the 20th century in the community. Mt. Zion Baptist Church which was established in 1836 was considered the community church. The Carmichael family was a prominent one in the community. Other families include Gramling, Bobo, Haley, Owen and more.

Big Springs community built up around what was believed to be the largest spring in Cherokee County. Big Springs United Methodist Church on Sugar Pike Road was built near the springs, and a camp meeting was held there for many years. The community was also home to Big Springs School. Both facilities received their water from the spring. The first school was held in a log cabin with Mrs. Hallie Hook as teacher. The community encompassed the area from

Union Hill was originally called Pleasant Hill and the rural community became known for its chicken and cattle business. Following the Civil War the name was changed because A.D. Smith, a Union sympathizer, gave land for a school and church provided they were named Union Hill. The name took. Here, Union Hill School circa 1900-1902, with Lee Johnson on the back row second from right in front of the window, and Florence Atkins Johnson seated in front, fifth from the left with a light-colored bow in her hair.

today's Fulton County line to Antioch Christian Church to Mill Creek Road. The Sims family was one who settled in the area in 1896. Other early settler families of the community were the Nix family and the Payne family. The community had a blacksmith shop run by Taylor Porter, a cotton gin run by Walter Nix and a general store run by Russ Bates. Cotton and syrup cane were major crops of the area. The community also had a post office, which was known as Batesville.

Buffington community grew up along the road east of Canton and around the site of the removal fort from which it took its name, Fort Buffington. For many years it continued to be known as Fort Buffington. Harmony Baptist Church was an early church that served the religious needs of the community of settlers and was in its early days called Fort Buffington Church. Bell's Store was one of the landmarks of Buffington. As the community grew, cotton became one of the leading crops. The two-room Buffington School served the community.

East of Buffington, **Orange** community was one of the earliest centers of commerce for that portion of the county and one of the largest. Sometimes said to be the second community established in Cherokee County, Orange was the site of a post office and general store. The Orange

The early town of White City in east Cherokee County was later absorbed into the Lathemtown and Macedonia communities. *Reprinted from Living, Laughing, Loving in old Lathemtown.*

Store was the hub of activity for the community of settlers. The store was moved to Stone Mountain Plantation in the 1960s as part of the exhibit of structures from the time period. The community also had a corn mill. Orange United Methodist Church continues to carry the name of the community. Eventually, Orange and its neighbor **White City** were absorbed into the later communities of Macedonia and Lathemtown. **Macedonia** is believed to have taken its name from the church of the same name which was established in 1873. Macedonia is taken from the Biblical reference in the book of Acts about a man who appeared to Paul and said "Come over into Macedonia and help us." Macedonia developed a reputation as a community whose residents helped others.

Lathemtown took its name from the family who originally settled the area. Many of the families who moved into the area in the 1830s have descendants who live there today. The W.A. Lathem and Sons General Store was at the heart of the community, and was established around 1906. The Lathem cotton gin, as well as a corn mill, a blacksmith shop and other businesses served the prosperous farm community. Quay Lathem's Mule Barn was another Lathemtown institution. According to family recollections, Mr.

Univeter was planned as a community in the early 1900s by the owner of the property at the time, Ben F. Perry, who built this hotel or dwelling house on the land. The property may have been intended as a resort. Perry later sold the property and it was eventually purchased by Evelyn McCollum Cox and her husband John Heisman. A post office of the same name was located in Univeter and was also a passenger stop for the train.

Lathem and Elbert Tippens of Canton would go to Tennessee and purchase as many as 100 mules at a time along with some horses and bring them back to Canton by train. Then the stock destined for Lathem's mule barn would be driven along Highway 20 by men on horseback. Farmers would purchase their mules in the spring and pay for them after their crops were harvested in late summer.

Another community in the area was **Free Home** at the intersection of Highways 20 and 372, which was known as the Birmingham Highway. The oldest school in the community was established in the 1870s. Captain Delavan Lively, a captain during the War Between the States, owned land near the school in the Cross Roads Militia District. Farming the land at the time was proving

The Francis Marion Purcell House, shown here circa 1914, was a landmark for the Free Home community. Purcell, far left, and family and friends gather during the building of the house. The home later became Free Home Traditions restaurant and gift shop.

hard, and to attract new residents to the area, Lively offered to give free land to anyone who would build a house. The name Free Home derived from that offer.

Toonigh, also known as Lebanon, is a community halfway between Holly Springs and Woodstock. Some say its location gave rise to the name, since it was too nigh, or near, Woodstock and too nigh Holly Springs to be a city of its own. However, another story is that when the train station was brought into town it was put close to the tracks, and one of the workers kept calling out "Too nigh, too nigh," giving rise to the name. John Goff in his place name book said it was named for the Cherokee word *tuni* which meant medicine man or healer. Yet another possibility, according to Hal Brinkley, in his book, *How Georgia Got Her Names*, is another Cherokee word, *tooantuh*, which means spring frog and was the name of a Cherokee chief or leader. However it got its name, it was a prosperous early settlement. The post office's name was originally Toonigh, but was later renamed Lebanon.

Just north of Canton was a community known as **Keithburg,** named for the large Keith plantation, which covered thousands of

Toonigh community is said to have gotten its name because it was too near, or nigh, to Holly Springs and too nigh to Woodstock. Here, people are gathered in 1920 for a June singing at a church in the community.

acres in the area. Keithburg was established in 1882 and was called Mabel at the time. The railroad established a depot in Keithburg and the community also had a post office by the same name. The area surrounding Keithburg contained many orchards, some of them owned by the Teasley family. Cherokee Heights Orchards was owned by the Teasley family had more than 30,000 peach and apple trees in the heyday of the farm. George I. Teasley was an attorney in Canton and served as county school superintendent and as mayor of Canton during his career. Teasley was the grandson of one of the early settlers of Cherokee County, Isham Teasley, who came to the community in 1840. Isham married Mary Maxwell and they had several children, among them William Arthur Teasley, who was also a prominent member of the Canton bar and began practicing law around 1856.

Lathemtown was named for one of leading early settlers, W.A. Lathem, who owned the general store and buggy shop, top right. His home is visible at top left in this photograph of the community circa 1910. *Reprinted from Living, Laughing, Loving in Old Lathemtown.*

Trickem or later Trickum settlement, another early trading post established a few miles south of Woodstock in the earliest days of the county, is thought to have gotten its name from other settlers warning of the merchant there who was running the general store.

Bascomb and **Oak Grove** are two communities that grew up in Southwest Cherokee County around churches and schools. The two communities were close together and in many ways similar so that their separate identities are often hard to distinguish. Bascomb community was on the Bell's Ferry Road near the Bascomb Road intersection. Bascomb Methodist Church was a one-room facility until the 1930s. During the summer baseball games were played on the church grounds. Farmers in the area raised crops of cotton and corn. Farmers would transport their crops to Marietta by horse-drawn wagon. The Oak Grove community was further south and had a gristmill and sawmill owned by W. O. Tyson.

Salacoa in extreme North Cherokee is said to have been named for the Cherokee word for "silk grass" or "bear grass." The name could also mean big corn because the valley and the soil were so fertile. The first settlers originally came from Virginia around 1850, and brought with them knowledge of how to grow tobacco. Families who settled the area included the Mahans, Taylors, Jeffersons, Richardsons and Fergusons, among others. The tobacco production thrived and soon there were several tobacco factories to turn the crop into marketable products. Another family with long prominence is the Dr. James H. Bennett family, who originally moved from Pickens County into Salacoa in 1899. Dr. Bennett was a country doctor, traveling on horseback to see his patients in the rural northwest corner of the county. Later he traveled by Model T. The family eventually operated a store and a cotton gin.

Sixes was one of the original communities in the county, located on Little River to the west of the Cherokee village of the same name. The community contained two notable gold mines, the Sixes Mine and the Cherokee Mine. Also known as Cherokee Mills, in 1876 the area contained three churches, a gristmill, post office and general store, a blacksmith, mining company, seller of liquors, and a school. The population was 150. A biography of Elijah Hillhouse from *The Standard and Express* published in 1872 recalls Mr. Hillhouse conducting a "singing school" at the Sixes schoolhouse in 1838. Although many historic sites in Sixes were destroyed for the making of Lake Allatoona, descendents of the families remain with such names as Hillhouse, Cantrell, Woodall, Anderson, Wooten and Reece.

Sutallee is the Cherokee word for Six or Sixes, and was the name of an early settlement in northwest Cherokee County. The early settlement had a post office and was a few miles northwest of the site of the former Cherokee village Sixes Old Town which was located on the waters of the intersection of the Etowah River and the Little River. The Fields, Gramlings, Knox's and others established early farms in the Sutallee area. The home of Joseph Knox was built in the Sutallee community in 1837 and was believed to be one of the first homes built in that district.

Beasley's Gap is located north of Waleska and is named for John and Jane Beasley who settled the area in the early 1800s. They gave their name to the gap between Pine Log Mountain and Garland

Mountain where the sparsely populated community was formed. The gap developed slowly as settlers came into the area looking for land. Cotton became the major crop and grew well in the fields found along the gap. Some who made the area their home included the Davis, Poole, Debord, Garland and Blalock families.

The community children attended Midway School which was a one-room schoolhouse four miles up into the gap. Oak Hills Baptist Church was formed in 1875. There was also a water-powered gristmill in the gap. The gap was known for its rock formations and natural spring which flows from Pine Log Mountain.

Mica School was located in the northeast corner of Cherokee County near Stancil's Store. The original schoolhouse was on the Old Federal Highway. The school was replaced twice. After the school was closed, the school bell used at Mica was donated to the Cherokee County Board of Education and placed on the central office grounds in Canton.

The community of **Mica** was located about eight miles east of Ball Ground and sprung up as a result of the gold rush in the area. Kenneth Krakow in his *Georgia Place-Names* says Mica was named for the gold and mica mines in the area. Stancil's Store was established in 1912 in the area and continues to serve the community. Nearby **Ophir** community is believed to have received its name from the biblical reference meaning "land of riches," used because the area was rich in gold and minerals.

Many of the early names were derived from the militia districts, which under Georgia law each county was divided into following the War of 1812. The practice continued for several decades and was in existence when Cherokee County was first established. Men in each district were expected to serve in the militia, and its chief objective was to deal with difficulties arising with the Native American inhabitants. Some of the militia districts took their names later from the towns and settlements that were located within them. Names of the districts in Cherokee County included Salacoa, Harbins, Clayton, Ball Ground, Conns Creek, Canton, Mullins, Cross Roads, Little River, Hickory Flat, Lick Skillet, Woodstock, Bells, Wildcat, Sixes, and Fair Play. The militia districts were also used as divisions when a census was taken and for elections.

A list of post offices in Cherokee County in 1895 reveals a number of names of communities, some which eventually were forgotten, and some still in use. Laughing Gal and Field Brothers post offices were located in the Fair Play district along with Sutallee. Payne and Kelpin were in the Bells District. Greeley was located in the Salacoa District and Bullock's Barn was a post office located in the Woodstock district. Owl Hollow Mills was in the Wildcat District where Holly Springs and Toonigh were located. The Sharp Top post office was located in Clayton community. Ophir and Boling were in the Cross Roads District. In the Conn's Creek District there were four post offices, McConnell's, A.C. Conn, Laredo and Mica.

Education Important to Settlers

From the earliest days, those who settled in Cherokee County wanted a good education for their children. Academies and tuition schools were being formed almost as soon as the first log cabins and houses were going up. Tuition schools, or subscription schools as they were also known, were founded by itinerant teachers who were paid by the parents of the students who attended. The prospective teacher presented himself to the parents of likely students, and if he got enough interest and enrollees he would conduct the school for the annual session. Tuition was usually one or two dollars per month. Many of the teachers were young men, or sometimes women, who wanted to go on to college and were using their skills to earn money for their own education. Academies were generally for the more well-to-do, had several teachers and offered a broader range of subjects. A good education could be had, but usually only for a price. For those who could not afford tuition, parents who could read and write taught their children themselves using whatever limited books and resources they had.

The Etowah Institute was an impressive two-story school on the site of the Canton High School on Academy Street in Canton which later served as a Cherokee County Board of Education office.

One of the earliest schools in the county was the Bascomb School which started around 1830 in a log cabin, according to the late Glenn Hubbard, who grew up in that community. Early Cherokee settler William K. McCanless, the millwright, assisted in organizing the school. In those early years the school, located in the southwest portion of the county, was a three-month institute, but later expanded to seven months, five in the winter and two in the summer.

The first state-recognized school in Cherokee County was the Etowah Institute in Canton, which was chartered by the state Legislature in 1833. The first classes were taught by Joseph Knox, an early settler of the Sutallee community. Mr. Knox, according to Marlin's *The History of Cherokee County,* was the first school teacher in the county and might be a descendant of the Reverend John Knox of Scotland. He married Malissa Brooke, daughter of John P. Brooke, one of the three founders of Canton. The original wooden building was built on the site that would later become the location of the first Canton High School on Academy Street. One fact about the school is that in 1844 Joseph Emerson Brown would come to the town and teach at the institute. Brown, who is discussed in subsequent chapters, later became the governor of Georgia and led the state during the Civil War years.

Hickory Flat Academy was chartered by the state in 1838, and was the second recognized school in Cherokee County. The academy was built on a flat area where several hickory trees grew and was located between where the old Hickory Flat Store and later Hickory Flat Elementary were built. The first trustees were George Gunby, Thomas Johnson, John McConnell, John B. Garrison and George Tyler.

Another early school was Little River Institute which was located about four miles from Woodstock on the old Alabama Road. Founded prior to the Civil War in a spacious two-story building, it also served the community for years following the war. For a number of years P.D. Wheelan was the schoolmaster. A native of Dublin, Ireland, Wheelan had studied for the priesthood, but later chose teaching as a career because he was known as an independent personality and did not believe himself suited for the cloth.

The Hickory Log School was opened for the African-American residents following the Civil War in 1870. The school was named for Hickory Log Mountain and Hickory Log Creek and was actually constructed of logs. The first teacher was Michael Byrd. Other early teachers included Abe Brown, Georgia Keith and Elias Keith.

Early Mills Fuel Settlement

The Etowah River and its many tributaries, creeks and streams gave the early settlers more than just water. Industrious early businessmen began to construct gristmills along the streams in Cherokee County to harness the flow of the water and grind their corn and wheat into flour and cornmeal, as well as into feed for their animals. As many as fourteen mills are believed to have existed at one time in Cherokee County, and perhaps even many more as records are incomplete. Few old mills survive today, but many of those that once operated are still remembered in legends and names of places and areas in the community.

One mill whose foundation can still be traced is the Brick Mill, later called the Scott Mill, which was located just east of Canton on a creek with steep rocky waterfalls. Thomas Clark Mason and Tyre B. Davis were millers who moved to Cherokee County from nearby Cass County, now Bartow, in the 1860s. The two built a three-story structure out of red brick, which gave the mill its name. The duo ran their gristmill and general store there until around the turn of

Brick Mill, which was later called Scott Mill, was just east of Canton on a creek with steep rocky waterfalls. The three-story structure made of red brick operated first as a gristmill, then a distillery.

the century. Then in 1897, in a land swap, a gentleman by the name of A.J. Scott took over the mill and operated a government distillery in it. It was renamed Scott Mill. Both names still exist today as road names in the area where the old mill once provided surrounding farmers a place to grind their crops into food and to buy the supplies they needed to operate and to live.

Another mill whose name and memory still remains was known as Cherokee Mills and was located on Little River about a mile from where it runs into the Etowah River. In the early days of the county, the property was owned by three men, J.P. Brooke, Daniel Mitchell and G.W. Jones, who later sold it to John H. King. King kept the property for five years, and then sold it in 1840 to Farrow Stegall. It is believed that during the years King owned the property he constructed the dam and mill on it, although few records of that time remain. For the next 75 years, through the Civil War and beyond, various owners operated the mills, which included a store, gristmill and sawmill.

Much later the property was sold to Joseph M. Brown, who followed his father Joseph Emerson Brown to serve as governor of the state of Georgia. The younger Brown improved the mills and continued to operate them for the next decade. However, the store was sold to other owners. In 1927 the entire property was sold to Georgia Power Company, but the mills

Cherokee Mills was located on Little River and was once the site of a post office. The property had a gristmill, store and sawmill in operation for many years. One of the owners was Joseph M. Brown, a governor of Georgia. The property was eventually sold to Georgia Power Company to make way for Lake Allatoona.

continued to operate until the 1940s when Allatoona Lake was constructed.

The role played by textile milling in Cherokee County's history was started by a family who emigrated from Manchester, England, to the United States in the mid-1800s. First settling in New Jersey, the family made its way South to finally settle in Talking Rock around 1870. There they established their first cotton and wool yarn mill, along with a gristmill. The Atherton family would continue to have an influence on the local economy for years to come, as they invested in Cherokee County as well as its northern neighboring county.

The Shoal Creek Cotton Mill was built near Waleska in 1874 by William C. Atherton,

Sorghum mills such as this one owned by William Dozier Husty made good use of the sorghum cane grown in the fertile bottomlands in Cherokee County. Husty can be seen beside the cooker. Sorghum was a popular sweetener before and after the Civil War when it was difficult to get cane sugar or molasses. Later sorghum was a popular ingredient in the making of moonshine.

whose two brothers, James Atherton and Thomas Atherton, also were involved with the mills in Pickens County. By 1875 the mill in Waleska employed seven workers and was operated by Atherton, Keith and Co. It is believed that it produced yarns. By 1880 the mill employed about 16 workers, with the youngest being about 11 years old. Females were the predominant workers and many employed there were under the age of 16. In 1883 the mill was sold to Elias A. Fincher, the son-in-law of James Atherton. It ceased operations around 1896.

However, the mill in Waleska was closely tied to another mill in southwest Cherokee

The Rope Mill Dam, now in ruins, is the site of Rope Mill Park near Woodstock. For many years the mill located there was a major contributor to the economy of the region and the rope produced was widely distributed.

County that would continue for a number of years. Known during its history as the Little River Mills, the Dorn Rope Mills, the Cherokee Cotton Mills and the Woodstock Cotton Mills, the operation is remembered still by those whose families were involved. The mills, which over their lifetime would produce yarn and later rope, grew up on a site of good water and had their earliest beginnings in a gristmill.

Located near Woodstock, the Little River gristmill was in operation as early as the late 1830s and took full advantage of the rock falls of the waters for which it was named. In the early days the mill was used to grind corn into feed and meal, but by 1875 it was also the site of a woolen mill and a sawmill. The gristmill was producing about 257,000 pounds of cornmeal a year and 9,520 pounds of feed.

At that time the mill was operated and owned by members of the Joel Haley family, but in the 1880s it was sold to James A. Atherton. Atherton was also still operating the Shoal Creek Mill. His daughter, Emma Jane Atherton, married Elias Fincher, who worked with his father-in-law in the mills. The two men together operated the newly acquired property, known as the Woodstock Cotton Mills at that time. The younger couple later inherited the mill from Atherton when he died in the mid 1890s.

Shortly after the turn of the century, the Finchers sold the mills to a man named J.S. Dorn, who is said to have paid for them with gold coins and was remembered as a man of great energy and drive. The old mill buildings, where about 25 people were employed, including some children, were at that time constructed out of wood, but Dorn replaced them with brick buildings. He, his wife and their six children lived in the old home on the property for a number of years. In 1925 a flood broke the original brick dam, which Dorn then rebuilt. He also enlarged the mill at that time to allow for increased production

By then the mills were producing rope which was wound into bales, hauled to Woodstock by wagon where it was shipped out by rail. The rope had a reputation of high quality and was sought after by cotton producers who needed it for their machinery. In those years, as many as 2,000 bales of rope per year were being produced.

In 1928 Dorn sold the mills and land to a development company which in turn sold it to Georgia Power Company. Woodstock residents Joe E. Johnston and Smith L. Johnston leased the land from Georgia Power for the next 20 years and operated the rope mills until after World War II. The mills produced rope for plows and wells during that time, but during the war the rope produced was used for military tents. By that time the mill employed around 30 people.

In 1948 the United States government purchased the property where the mills were situated as it prepared for the construction of Lake Allatoona. The rope mill, dam and mill houses were removed in 1952, and according to accounts, on the last day the mill ran the workers walked the narrow raceway wall and opened the sluice gates for the last time, a symbolic gesture that marked the end of an era for them.

Early Churches Bring Settlers Together

One of the first orders of business for many of the early settlers was a place to worship. In the earliest days circuit preachers would come to homes or arbors to offer the word of God. In 1830 before the county was chartered at least one church congregation, which would later become Bascomb United Methodist Church, was meeting in a log cabin. It is believed that early pioneer W.K. McCanless was instrumental in starting Bascomb Church at his mill which was about a mile west from the present-day lo-

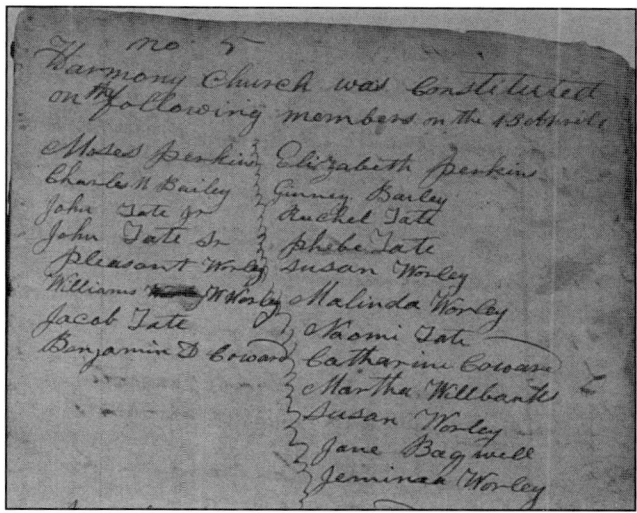

cation of the church. Within a short time, the church relocated to a log cabin on the present site of the church on Bascomb Carmel Road. The log structure also served as a school in those early days. The church is said to be named for Henry Bascomb, an orator and bishop at the time of the church's founding. A frame church was later built to replace the original log structure.

Before many years, other churches would begin to organize and meet in all corners of the county. Records indicate that one of the earliest, if not one of the first places of worship to be constituted, was the church that later became the Canton First Baptist Church. Two missionaries for the state Baptist Convention joined with 10 members on Aug. 23, 1833, to begin the church, which was originally called Ararat Church. Those first members were Daniel Butler, Julia Burns, Elias Putnam and his wife

A page from the early records of Harmony Baptist Church shows a list of the original members when the church was constituted on April 13, 1839.

Faith Putnam, William Grisham and his wife Susan Grisham, Moses Perkins and wife Elizabeth Perkins, and James Wilson along with his wife Mary Wilson.

They adopted a constitution, Gospel order and a list of rules of decorum. The early leaders of the new church decided to make it a sovereign church, answerable to no board or convention. They called themselves the Baptist Church of Christ. That early church met in the homes of its members, and it was not until 1840 that a church building was constructed. The original church was housed in a frame building with one large room and is believed to have been at the corner of Jarvis Street and Gainesville Street. The church building had many uses and functions for the early community, including being used as a place for the

A committee was formed in 1881 to build a new Canton Baptist Church on land deeded to the church by former Governor Joseph E. Brown of what was then his garden lot. The new church was constructed of brick and faced the courthouse, which at the time was on the square in Canton.

Methodists to meet, as a school and as a library. In 1872 it began to be used as a courthouse as well.

In 1862 during the Civil War, the church listed a total membership of 58 with 43 white and 15 black members. After the war, the African-American membership was listed as freedmen and freedwomen rather than as colored, but in 1871 all the black members were issued letters of demission to join a segregated church which had formed. The two earliest African-American members are listed as Mary Scott and Elias Decatur Keith.

Like many of the early churches, the church at Canton observed communion seasons and held foot washings, revivals, and union meetings with other churches. For many years the Canton Baptist Church held its baptisms in the Hightower Ferry on the Etowah River just south of town. A Sunday School was established around 1859.

In 1881 the Canton Baptist Church decided to build a new building. The committee to come up with a plan included Jabez Galt, R.T. Jones, James R. Brown, William Ellis and J.L. Coggins. Ex-governor Joseph Brown deeded the lot for the new building, which was known as his garden lot, in 1882. A building was constructed in 1883 facing toward the courthouse, which was on the square in the center of town.

The church's growth mirrored that of the town of Canton, as it changed from an agricultural community to a thriving manufacturing town, and by 1900 the church had 97 members.

The Woodstock Methodist Church, shown here in 1910, was organized around 1889 with the help of J.H. Johnston. Johnston, a lifelong Methodist, was chairman of the board of stewards at the church where he belonged for almost half a century.

In January 1901 the church celebrated the beginning of a new century, looking forward to accomplishing good in the community. In the early years of the new century, revivals continued to be held, and the church was remodeled so that it faced Brown Park. A tower was added to call the community to worship. On February 14, 1914, a New Testament, an association minutes, a list of the membership, a copy of the *Cherokee Advance* and a little bouquet of violets were placed in the corner stone of the tower in a special ceremony of prayer. The blessings were believed to help the church to continue in that location for decades to come.

Ten miles to the south of Canton another church formed in 1837 with 12 members. Enon Church, the forerunner of First Baptist Church of Woodstock, was constituted on October 13 of that year in a settlement near Little River and Rube's Creek. The name Enon is said to mean "full of springs." Those early members included George and Martha Crawford, John, Elizabeth and Susan Black, George Blythe, David Guess, William and Isabell Sims, S.D. and Jane Rolen and Asinith Strickland.

This church was used by the congregation of Enon Church from 1891 to 1913 after it became Woodstock Baptist Church. The church was built in town near the depot and was destroyed by fire in 1913. The only items saved were the seats and the Bible.

By 1848 Enon Church had grown to 42 members and by the 1850s showed a membership of 125. Much of the records of the early church are dominated by disciplinary activities, including cases of stealing, adultery, swearing and dancing. Disciplinary actions included admonishments and sometimes exclusion and a request to leave the fellowship of the church. The church membership also found time for revivals and for worship, quickly establishing the church as the center of the community.

Settlers in other areas of the county were also losing no time in finding a place to worship. Sharp Mountain Baptist Church was chartered in 1836. New Bethel Baptist Church was organized in 1837 in the Sixes community with about seven members. Hightower Baptist Church on Highway 369 is also among the oldest churches in the county, with records dating back to as early as 1835. It is believed that some of the graves in its cemetery are those of Indians and slaves.

Canton United Methodist Church was officially chartered in 1842 with several of the county's most prominent settlers involved, but it may have been meeting even before that time. The land for the building was donated by Judge Joseph Donaldson. An original structure was soon replaced with a small frame building and then in 1850 a

The members of Canton First United Methodist Church constructed this building in 1850 and it served the congregation until 1925 when it was removed to make way for a new brick church complete with beautiful stained glass windows.

beautiful church building was constructed on the same site. The brick building that served the congregation for more than 50 years was built in 1925 and the city's most prominent cemetery, which included Riverview, the city cemetery and eventually the Jones family cemetery, grew up around it. At around the time that Judge Donaldson donated the land for the church, he also gave the land for the cemetery. It is not believed that the cemetery was a part of the church. The first documented burials at the cemetery are in 1844 and are infant Susan Moss and Mary Dickerson. There is evidence that a stacked stone gravesite located in the cemetery is that of a Cherokee Indian chief, whose burial would probably have taken place

This is the second church constructed by Hickory Log Missionary Baptist Church. The church was replaced in 1957 with a new brick building.

before or at the time of the 1838 removal of the Native Americans. There are five known graves at the cemetery of people who were born in the eighteenth century. Nehemiah Garrison, a captain in the War of 1812 and who later lived in the vicinity of Fort Buffington, is buried there. Garrison also participated in the removal of the Cherokee to the West in 1838.

In 1863 the first church established for the African-American population was the Allen Temple Church in Woodstock. A faithful group of the community met first

under a brush arboreal they constructed. The group included Baptists and African Methodist Episcopalians. The new church took its name from Deacon Allen Dial. The original trustees of the church included Miles McAfee, Giles Haney, James Fowler, Will Dean and a Sister Benson. The school for the African-American community was on the same property. The church was located near the center of what is today's historic downtown Woodstock. In 1909 the original church was replaced with a new building.

The old St. Paul AME Church was located on North Crisler Street in Canton.

That facility was a white frame church that had no running water or electricity. Then in 1977 a new church building was constructed. Later the church moved to a new site of 32 acres. Today the church has more than 1,000 members.

In 1872 the African-American population in Canton established the Hickory Log Missionary Baptist Church under the direction of the Reverend Levi Greenlee. The first church was constructed of logs and built on land donated by one of its organizers, Philip Keith, who also became one of the first deacons of the church. Other early members and organizers included William Brown, Abe Brown, Bolis Nicholas, and Sydney Roberts. Hickory Log Cemetery was also established at around the same time. The Reverend Silas Smith was pastor. In later years, the Reverend Robert Ralph Freeman led the church in the building of the new facility. The present location on Elmwood in North Canton was established in 1957. Today under the leadership of the Reverend Robert Holmes the church remains a vibrant part of the community.

Camp meetings were another important aspect of the early settler life. In 1838, the same year the Cherokee were removed, Holbrook Camp Meeting was founded. Families would come to the camp meeting held for 10 days in late August and tent, which meant living in one-room cabins built in a circle around the arbor where the preaching took place. The present-day arbor is believed to have been built around 1845. In those early days the arbor was lit by kerosene lanterns during the services each night. Those who came to the camp meeting brought all they needed for the duration of the revival, including their milk cow, live chickens for Sunday dinner and a wood stove on which to cook. Everyone in a family slept in the one room on pallets. Services were held three times a day, morning, afternoon and evening, with both a Baptist and a Methodist preacher giving the message.

Along with Holbrook Camp Meeting, there is mention of

Holbrook Camp Meeting was established in 1838. Services were held each day for about 10 days in August each year. Those attending would stay in small cabins, or tents as they were called, built around the Arbor where the services were held. This Arbor was built as early as 1845. *Reprinted from Living, Laughing, Loving in Old Lathemtown.*

camp meetings in Waleska, the Shiloh community and Little River district. Minutes of Canton First Baptist Church indicate that church once considered a camp meeting, but whether it actually started or not is unclear. The Shiloh Camp Meeting is said to have been one of the largest, set on a ridge, and continued into the 1880s. Early settlers who made Cherokee County their home, mostly migrating from North and South Carolina and Northeast Georgia, found opportunities to worship in a variety of locations across the county, and most were of the Baptist or Methodist denominations.

As the settlers established themselves and their families more permanently onto the land they now claimed as their own, the communities they were building began to flourish and prosper. Opportunities were expansive and the residents of Cherokee County were looking forward to a bright and promising future. But even as they worked to settle into their new homes, events were on the horizon that would bring unexpected change.

Elias Earle Field was one of the most respected planters in Cherokee County at the time of the Civil War. The Field family was among the earliest settlers and Field owned 3,000 acres of some of the richest land in the county. He served in the state Legislature and was a leader in the Confederate cause.

Chapter Three

Civil War Sweeps Through Cherokee County

Just as it did for the entire South, the four painful years of Civil War constituted a pivotal point in Cherokee County's history. Cherokee County was on a track to prosperity when the winds of war began to blow. Georgia was among the wealthiest states in the nation at that time and Cherokee County was a flourishing financial hub in the state. In the years leading up to the clash between the North and South, Cherokee County emerged as an agricultural center, with wheat and cotton topping the roster of cash crops. In the 20-plus years since its incorporation, Cherokee County had begun to establish itself as an important center for commerce and business. Those who originally settled the county were prospering and their investments in the lands and resources of the area were paying off. The war ended those claims, leaving the county, the state and the entire South negatively impacted economically for decades to come.

The county was reduced in size during the 1850s when land was transferred from what was then Cherokee County by the state Legislature to help create Pickens and Milton counties. That decision also reduced the population, which the 1850 census placed at 12,800 people. By 1860 the population of Cherokee County was placed at only 11,291 residents. The city of Canton claimed 200 people inhabiting the county seat.

In the years leading up to 1861, the breath of secession blew through towns and cities across the South, bringing the stirrings of war in its wake. With the election of President Abraham Lincoln in 1860, Southern states moved rapidly to call conventions to consider secession. A state convention was called by the Georgia legislature for January 16, 1861, in Milledgeville. Counties throughout the state held their own conventions prior to that to elect delegates to

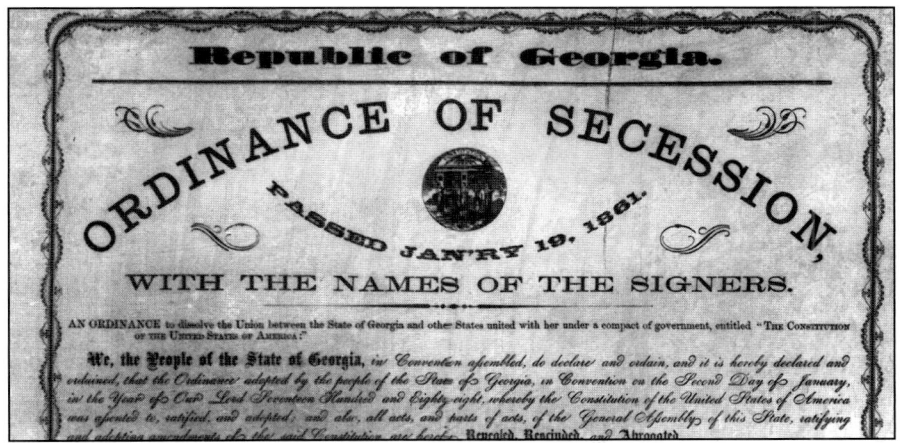

The Georgia Ordinance of Secession was signed by three men for Cherokee County, Elias Earle Field, John McConnell and William Arthur Teasley.

SCHEDULE 2.—Slave Inhabitants in *the 13th Division* in the County of *Cherokee* State of *Georgia*, enumerated by me, on the *26* day of *Nov*; 1850. *Wm P Kennedy &c* Ass't Marshal

NAMES OF SLAVE OWNERS.	Number of Slaves.	DESCRIPTION.			Fugitives from the State.	Number manumitted.	Deaf & dumb, blind, insane, or idiotic.	NAMES OF SLAVE OWNERS.	Number of Slaves.	DESCRIPTION.			Fugitives from the State.	Number manumitted.	Deaf & dumb, blind, insane, or idiotic.
		Age.	Sex.	Colour.						Age.	Sex.	Colour.			
1		2	3	4	5	6	7	8	1		2	3	4	5	6	7	8
1 *John & Lewis* ✗	1	30	f	m				1 *Mariah S Harrison*	1	32	f	m			
2	1	11	f	m				2	1	37	f	m			
3	1		f	m				3	1	35	f	m			
4	1	4	f	m				4	1	20	f	m			
5	1	95	f	m				5	1	14	f	m			
6	1	4	f	m				6	1	14	f	m			

A page from 1850 Cherokee County Slave Census has the owners recorded along with the ages and sex of their slaves, but not their names. John Lewis and Mariah Harrison are noted here as owning 64 and 20 slaves respectively. The majority of Cherokee County slave owners in 1850 had fewer than five slaves.

send to the capital for the assembly. Cherokee County selected three leading landowners, Elias Earle Field, John McConnell, and William Arthur Teasley, Sr. as representatives to the convention. The august body of men debated the issue for two days before voting 208 to 89 to adopt an ordinance of secession.

The flag of the Cherokee Brown Riflemen who were named for Canton resident and Georgia Civil War Governor Joseph Emerson Brown. The flag is now held in the Chicago Museum of History.

On January 21, the three Cherokee County residents signed the ordinance of secession in a lengthy signing ceremony with leaders from across the state. With the decision made to secede, it would not be long before the war began in earnest.

As the South prepared for the conflict, Cherokee County answered the call, pouring men and resources into the cause, despite the sentiment of some parts of the county to remain committed to the Union. While most farmers in Cherokee County did not own a large number of slaves, many did own a few. Among the larger land owners slavery was more prevalent. About nine percent of the county's population at the time of the war was made up of slaves and about 150 people were slave owners in Cherokee County. Unlike the larger land owners and the city dwellers, the farmers of the hill country in the north region of the county scraped their living out of the ground with only their sons and sometimes a hired man or tenant farmer to help. Those who did own slaves often used them as house servants or to work their farmlands and mines. Those dynamics helped set up a split in sentiment, with wealthier landowners favoring the war, and the farmers and residents who did not own slaves and who viewed the impending war as a rich man's conflict opposed.

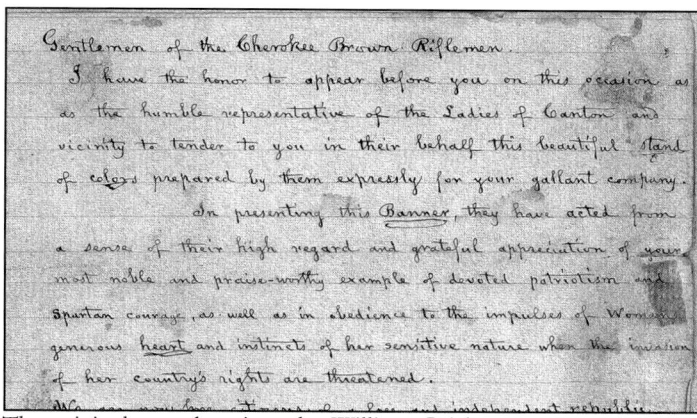

The original speech written by William Grisham in 1861 and spoken by Susan Elizabeth Galt, his granddaughter, to the Cherokee Brown Riflemen as they marched to war. The speech is on display in the Cherokee County Historical Society office.

Regardless of the differing views, Cherokee County men of all ages rushed to enlist for the Cause. Although there were mixed sentiments in Cherokee County about the war, heavy support was given to the war effort. Those who were not sympathetic to the plight of the larger slave and landowners feared the impact to the economy. Patriotic fervor for the South often won the day. While the war did bring economic ruin to much of the South, Cherokee County recovered more quickly than most other areas of the state, although the years of Reconstruction were hard ones for the county. Part of the reason that the county saw a rebound was that the farmers in the hilly and mountainous areas of North Georgia and Cherokee County were more self-sufficient, living mainly off their farms, and survived by bartering for the goods they could not produce during the tough years during and after the war. Before many years after the war the cotton crop was once more producing yields and a new system of farming the land was emerging.

Cherokee County Responds to the Call

Sometimes called the War of Secession, Civil War was officially declared on April 12, 1861, beginning what few in the South at the time believed would be a long and bloody conflict that would end in defeat. As shots were fired on Fort Sumter in the Charleston bay by Southern troops, outfits in Cherokee County were beginning to form and equip for battle. Among the first companies to answer the call was Cherokee Brown's Riflemen, also known as Company F of the Second Regiment, a group of about 100 men under the leadership of Capt. Thomas E. Dickerson. Around 23 companies from Cherokee County responded to the need for men to fight for the South. In all about 1,800 men from Cherokee County enlisted, more than any neighboring county. Cherokee Georgia Mountaineers, Cherokee Dragoons, the Cherokee Avengers, and other colorful names marked the regiments of men. The Canton Infantry, or Company B, went out under the command of Capt. John B. Garrison. Company D or the Cherokee Home Guard stepped out under the command of Capt. William T. Dowda. Men from every corner of the county signed up to fight, leaving behind their families and their farms to battle against the government they were once a part of. Men like the Cherokee Repellers and the Salacoa Silver Grays gave the Rebel battle cry as they charged against those who were once their fellow countrymen.

Elias Earle Field, one of the signers of the Ordinance of Secession from Cherokee County, was middle-aged at the time of the war and could not actively serve in the Confederate Army. Like many wealthy Southerners, he helped raise a company to serve, christened the Field Guards in his honor, which reported to the front. While Field

The flag of the Cherokee Dragoons, which was Company C of Phillips' Legion, Calvary. The flag is now held at the Kennesaw Mountain National Battlefield Park.

himself remained at home, he believed that as a member of the secession convention he should do everything he could to support the war. With that in mind he served in the Confederate Commissary Department to support the armies in the field.

An article in the September 14, 1861, issue of the *Cherokee Mountaineer*, a newspaper published in Canton at the time of the war and reprinted in the *Cherokee Advance* in November 1915, offers insight into the sanguinity and anticipation that accompanied the more somber reality of the conflict which eventually took more American lives than any war in the history of the United States. The newspaper had on its masthead: For President - Hon. Jeff Davis of Mississippi, For Vice President - Hon. Alexander H. Stephens of Georgia, and For Governor - Joseph E. Brown, Cherokee. The newspaper was a two-page sheet which was mostly filled with poems about the war, political opinion and advertisement from local lawyers including Judge James R. Brown, Col. W. A. Teasley, James Jordon and Samuel Weil of Canton. The publisher and editor was W. J. Sloan.

The article headed "New Volunteer Company" told of the company, which was outfitted by founding father Judge Joseph Donaldson, leaving Canton for the war:

There is now a new Volunteer Company just organized in this county, and named in honor of our esteemed fellow-citizen Judge Donaldson. On Thursday morning last, this gallant company met in Canton and went into an election for Commissioned officers, which resulted in the election of N.J. Garrison, Capt., E.G. Grambling, 1st Lieut., H.D. Freeman, 2nd Lieut., and W.J. Jordan, 3rd Lieut.

After the election closed, the company, by special request of Judge Donaldson, marched to his house for dinner. The Judge, in his unbounded patriotism, had, at his individual expense, prepared to receive them in this manner; and on their arrival, they found a spacious table laden with the most choice dishes ever tempted the eye of an epicure. On the arrival of the company, at Judge Donaldson's, they were marched into the yard in front of his dwelling, where large quantities of cool water, as well as refreshments of stronger nature, were amply provided.

After a short time, dinner was announced, and the company marched to it in good order, and we have never seen better order prevail than did during the repast.

When dinner was over, the audience again adjourned to the yard, where they were entertained for a short time with an eloquent address by Dr. T.G. Underwood. The doctor at times gave vent to his feeling in the most thrilling sentences and with every lineament of his features gleaming with "the thoughts that live" he broke forth in strains of the wildest pathos.

We have not often listened to him; but, if we may decide, his hearers up to this time never received from him a better effort.

Enoch Milton Benson of Woodstock and a member of an old Cobb County family had this charcoal drawing done around 1862 1863. He died in the Civil War. He is believed to have lived in the Noon Day Church area

After Dr. Underwood had concluded, Misses Sue Galt, Annie L. Wilson, Fannie Vernon, and M.A. Donaldson were in turn called for, and each responded in a brief but telling manner. The young ladies, each and every one, acquitted themselves with honor to the occasion and to themselves: and the gleaming eye told plainer than words could tell, that under these gentle appeals, uttered in soft, winning accents every man in that noble company resolved to return in victory or return nevermore.

While too much praise cannot be bestowed upon each of the above-mentioned young ladies, we cannot forbear to notice the cool calculating delivery and speech and the wonderful presence of mind evidenced by Misses Wilson and Vernon. The brilliant sentiments to which we listened on Thursday last will never retain a place at fond memory's shrine, and if in our life there be an Oasis in the desert of our toils, surely last Thursday was the day.

Miss M. A. Donaldson stated to the company that, for lack of previous notice, no banner yet had been provided for them; but as soon as practical, a banner would be made and forwarded to them.

Dinner, addresses, & c., dispensed with, the company formed into line for departure, when three cheers were proposed and given for Judge

Donaldson. The company halted its passage through Canton, where the parting of the company from friends and relatives presented a touching scene. Soon the company was again in lines and took up the line of march for Camp Stephens near Griffin. On their departure three cheers were given for the company and three cheers for the citizens of Canton and vicinity. We cannot close without referring to our high appreciation of the men composing this company, may victory crown them on every battle field.

As the war droned on, Cherokee County farmers and those left behind by their husbands, brothers and fathers began to experience the hardships of lack of food and farming supplies. The bright enthusiasm which greeted those men who had marched off into battle soon faded to worry about the future and the difficulty of day-to-day existence. A letter to a soldier written by his wife on October 10, 1862, printed in the *Cherokee Mountaineer* and later reprinted in the *Cherokee Advance* tells the story.

My Dear Husband: I seat myself this morning to write you a few lines to let you know that we are all well as common, hoping this will find you well and in good health. I have not herd(sic) from you over a month and I am getting uneasy about you and I thought I would write you, but I don't know whether you will get it or not, but I will send it any way for I hear there is a chance to pass letters now and I hope I will get a letter from you tomorrow for I would give anything to hear from you, I am lonesome today for it is a wet cold day and you know how lonesome it is when it is such a Sunday, for I am lonesome enough in the week when I am at work or trying for I can't work with any heart for thinking about you for I don't know whether you are alive or not.

Times are hard here. Everything is out of reason. New corn is bringing from one Dollar to two. Bacon is 40 cents per pound and pork is 20 to 25 cts per pound and beef is bringing from 8 to 10 cts per pound butter is 2 dollars a pound only papa sells it for 1 dollar a pound and dry goods is not worth talking about buying them for calico is selling at one dollar and a half a yard and everything else as high according and factory thread cannot be got at all, and if this war holds on much longer I am afraid the people will suffer, but I do hope and pray to God that it will soon come to a end and that all that are a live will have the pleasure of getting home to their friends for I know it would be the greatest pleasure to me if you were spared to get home again and that is my prayer to God daily to keep you safe until this war is ended and I do hope that he will answer them for I think I would be willing to stay home all the time if you were here, but if you never get home I will pray to God to take me and the children for I don't want to live in this world without you in it.

There are several of the folks been killed and wounded lately. Bill Honey is

John Keller Moore, pictured here in 1850 with his wife Frances Independence Garrison Moore and sons David and Arobias, enlisted with the Cherokee Rangers in 1863 at the age of 48. He returned safely from the war and did not die until 1886, when he was 69 years of age.

killed. Tyre Davis is at home, he is wounded in the arm, D. Coker is wounded in the hand, he is at home. Bob Wyley was killed. Captain Garison(sic) is at home, his thigh is broken and it is a wonder they did not all get killed for Mr. Davis said there was 80 thousand Yankees fought 15 thousand of them all day.

So I will quit this. Mr. Kinnett, the children want to see you, they have not forgot you yet, they talk about you every day. Every time Jackson eats he wants to send you something to eat, and I hope you will be at home by the time I have the hogs fat to kill and eat them. I think I will keep most of them and bacon them if I can get some salt to salt them, but salt is so high and hard to get, I have never drawed anything yet but they say we can draw half a bushel of salt paying $1 but it looks like a long time before we get it.

Mr. Kinnett I have got that jeans for your clothes made, it looks like I cant send them to you I am afraid you are suffering for clothes and shoes I want you as soon as you get this letter to sit down and write me all about whatever you need and about everything you can think of. Lee, Nicholas, Cades and papas families are all well except mother, she has been sick over a week I don't know what is the matter with her unless she is taking fever and the family was up at camp meeting. There was 14 or 15 joined the church but it was no satisfaction to me to be there. So I will close by saying write as soon as you get this. So I remain your true wife till death,

Jacob A. Chapman was a Confederate soldier from Holly Springs. He was in the McAfee and Donaldson Guards, captained by Nehemiah Garrison. Chapman enlisted in 1861 at the age of 18. He died of disease while serving in Virginia the following year.

Louisa Kinnett
To Ralph Kinnett

Louisa did soon receive a letter from her husband letting her know that he was still alive. In her response to him a month later she talks about how he wrote her that he was struggling with lack of supplies and the fighting conditions. She wrote, "I would be half mad too if I had to go off and fight for my country and get nothing for it. I am sorry you are barefooted I wish I could send your boots and clothes to you before now but I have not had a chance. But I will send them this week by Captain Caniel. You said if they did not do better I might look for you home. I would be glad to see you coming home. I would give the world if I had it to have you home."

Later in the same letter she wrote, "Papa got a letter from John Owens last Friday and he said there was great prospects of peace being made and that is the chat here, but I am afraid it will be just talk, but I hope and pray it will be the case."

Unfortunately, the talk of peace was premature and the war would drag on for several more years, before General Robert E. Lee surrendered on April 9, 1865. Then finally those men who still fought for the South came home.

While the majority of families in Cherokee County made tremendous sacrifices for the war, there were those who silently and defiantly sided with the Union, a development that occurred throughout the South in almost every community. In Cherokee County, the fierce independence of the mountain region people, sometimes called the hill people, coupled with a disdain for the rich

Ben McCollum originally enlisted in the Confederate Army as a private in Company F, 2nd Regiment Georgia Infantry on April 18, 1861. He was discharged the following year, but he then traveled to Virginia where he reenlisted.

neighbors and their slaves made those who did not sympathize with the South quietly committed. As the war dragged on and the conditions at home became worse, those against the war became more committed and perhaps a little louder in their sentiments. Spurred by neighbors to the north in communities where Federal tendencies were stronger, such as Pickens County where the federal flag still flew, those dissenters grew in volume and in sound. It would not be long before there was an ugly answer from those who held the South in high regard.

As the battles grew closer the home guard began to take on more and more duties. Some of the self-appointed enforcers fought guerilla warfare against the Yankee forces moving into the area. Others became vigilantes who enforced an unwritten law of their own.

Governor Joseph Brown was organizing his state militia and The Cherokee Legion was the local unit whose role it was to protect those in the county from invading Union soldiers. Most of the home guard were humane in their treatment of those living in the community, but a few became little more than outlaws themselves, hanging those they believed were sympathetic to the North and taking all that they owned.

One of the guard groups formed to protect the state from the invading northern army had deep roots in the Holly Springs area. McCollum's Scouts was under the direction of Benjamin McCollum who according to most reports was around 18 years old or perhaps younger when the war broke out and who enlisted at that time, but quickly returned back home. He may have been discharged because he was not old enough to serve, but accounts differ. He re-enlisted and served with General Lee and returned home on furlough in 1864. He raised a regiment of about 25 men as part of Joseph Brown's home guard to fight against the Federal soldiers and also to enforce punishment

Ben McCollum's 1864 Commission as Captain in the Black Horse Calvary of the State Militia.

against Union sympathizers, especially those believed to be spies for General Sherman. As Sherman made his way through the region, his Union soldiers traveled into Cherokee County to raid farms and ultimately to burn and pillage. McCollum's Scouts and other vigilantes would shoot at the soldiers, attempting to disrupt their supply line. They also hanged or shot and killed those local residents believed to be spies for the Northern forces.

Times were so tough and supplies were so low, that Governor Brown issued quantities of salt and other commodities to the women who were heading the households and to discharged soldiers who had been wounded. The list for Cherokee County was dated July 24, 1863, and contains about 750 names. During those dark times many of the women left at home did not know how they could continue to feed their families.

Just a month before Thanksgiving in 1864 General Sherman was preparing to begin his March to the Sea. The order to burn Canton was issued from Cartersville where Sherman was camped on October

30, 1864. A detail of 250 men along with forage wagons was dispatched to Canton by Brigadier General John Smith and ordered to allow the citizens to remove what they could and then to burn the town.

While details of what happened when the troops arrived in Canton are unclear because of the turmoil of the times, it is believed that at least half of the town was burned, including the courthouse, most businesses along Main Street and the bridge over the Etowah River. No one knows exactly why the order was given, but theories say that it was because the war governor of Georgia, Joseph Emerson Brown, had his home there. There is also a theory that it was because of the activities of Benjamin McCollum and his men.

> **HDQRS, THIRD DIVISION, FIFTEENTH ARMY CORPS,**
>
> *Cartersville, Ga. October 30, 1864*
>
> Col. T. T. Heath
> *Commanding Fifth Ohio Volunteer Cavalry:*
> Colonel: A detail of 250 men go out with the forage wagons at 6 a.m. tomorrow, starting from Division quartermaster's office. You will take all your available force, and move with them. When they get out as far as it may be necessary to go, you will take eight wagons and proceed to the houses of Doctor Payne, Widow Edwards, and Warren's; load them with their effects and families, and return to the infantry escort without delay, after which you will proceed to Canton. You will permit the citizens to remove what they desire, and burn the town, after which you will proceed to Cassville and make the same disposition as at Canton.
> By order of Brig. Gen. John E. Smith:
>
> **S. M. BUDLONG,**
> *Captain and Acting Assistant Adjutant-General.*

The orders to burn Canton were given on October 30, 1864, according to this copy of the military document. Residents of the town were to be given time to remove their belongings before the homes and businesses were burned.

The Canton home of William Grisham, which was built in 1841, was spared. Family members say it was because the family had Masonic ties and the Union soldiers, many of whom were also Masons, respected that fact. Other homes may also have been left standing as the soldiers moved through the town setting fire to houses along the street.

Joseph Brown Makes His Mark

They called him "Young Hickory" when he was a rising lawyer with a bright political future ahead of him. Joseph Emerson Brown was destined for the highest office in the state during one of the most turbulent and challenging segments of history, the Civil War years. He was not a native son, but he became the most famous person to hail from Cherokee County. His achievements are remembered by some with pride, others with shame, and to this day there is controversy surrounding his legacy. Joseph Emerson Brown served four terms as governor of Georgia and was one of the most powerful and prominent men of his day. Following the war he became one of the state's most wealthy men during the new industrial age that followed Reconstruction.

Joseph Emerson Brown was born on April 15, 1821, in Long Creek in the Pickens District of South Carolina. When he was still a young boy his family moved to a farm in the Gaddistown area of Union County, Georgia. Until he was 19 years old, young Joe Brown worked on the family farm and peddled firewood in nearby Dahlonega. Of that time he said, "My only education was that I could read and write, and I had been in arithmetic as far as the rule of three."

In 1840 Joe Brown was ready to seek further education and he and his younger brother James enrolled in Professor Pleasant Jordan's Academy in the Anderson District of South Carolina. They traveled there with only a change of clothes, a plow horse and a yoke of oxen to barter for tuition and board. While his brother quickly threw in the towel and returned home, Joseph Emerson Brown toiled the next three years at the academy to glean all he could in his lifelong quest for achievement.

Joseph Emerson Brown served four terms as governor of Georgia including during the Civil War.

After completing that phase of instruction and with the influence of family friends such as William Grisham, Brown moved to Canton in 1844 and took charge of the academy where he undertook to teach and use the salary he received to pay the rest of his school debt. During the winter of 1844 and 1845 he tutored the children of Dr. John Washington Lewis of Canton, the man who became one of the most important influences on young Brown. Brown spent his spare time reading law and preparing for the bar. In 1845 he was admitted to the bar, but did not begin a practice. Instead, once more, he took a bold step and took a loan from Dr. Lewis to attend Yale School of Law. After a year at Yale, Brown returned south and began his practice before the Georgia Supreme Court in March 1847.

In December 1846 another important event happened in the life of Joseph Brown. He met his future wife, Elizabeth Grisham, niece of William Grisham and daughter of a Baptist minister, Joseph Grisham and his second wife Mary Steele Grisham. They met when he was on a visit to West Union, South Carolina, where her family lived. The Grishams were old friends of the Brown family. The young Brown was quickly smitten with the lovely and stately Elizabeth and he traveled from Canton to see her twice more that spring before proposing. In keeping with the times they set a quick wedding date of July 13, 1847, her twenty-first birthday.

The couple was feted at a grand wedding in South Carolina followed by a wedding feast that included a multitude of cakes, pies, turkeys, and four young pigs. Some of the cakes were described as "steeple cakes two feet high with ornaments on top." Cookies were baked by the bushel and as many as 27 cakes remained uncut after the day long feast. After a wedding trip through familiar areas of north Georgia, including Dahlonega, the Browns were ensconced at the home of William Grisham while their own home was built. In the fall the couple traveled back to South Carolina and Mrs. Brown remained with her family until 1848 when Brown brought his wife to her new home on Marietta Street in Canton. The couple would live there until they left for the state capital of Milledgeville following Brown's election to governor. It would remain their official home until it was burned by Sherman's troops late in the ensuring war. The site of the home was later donated by the family and designated Brown Park. Mrs. Brown's dowry from her family at the time she moved to Canton included a slave named Celia and Celia's two children, as well as household goods including two feather beds, kitchen furniture and crockery. Elizabeth's parents presented them with a six-horse wagon to travel in and a smaller wagon to transport her dowry. Mrs. Brown's parents soon moved to Canton to be close to their daughter.

Canton was still a small frontier community, too small to be included in the census, so some records are not available. In the 1840s only about 6,000 people lived in Cherokee County. In the years that followed the couple had five children, Julius Lewis Brown, May 31, 1848; Mary

Elizabeth Grisham Brown, lower right, was the wife of Joseph Emerson Brown and the niece of William Grisham. Here, she is pictured with her son and his wife, Elijah Alexander Brown, standing, and Law McBride Brown, left. Elizabeth Street in Canton was named for Mrs. Brown.

Virginia Brown, January 3, 1850; Joseph Mackey Brown, December 28, 1851; Franklin Pierce Brown, April 15, 1853; and Elijah Alexander Brown, September 4, 1857.

Brown's abilities as a lawyer quickly propelled him into a prosperous legal practice, where he won the respect of all who came into contact with him. Just as quickly, he began to amass the beginnings of what would become a sizable fortune in real estate, agricultural lands and city lots. Many of the acres he purchased were rich in mineral deposits. But Brown sought higher goals. By nature, he was a politician and he had a touch with the common people. It was no surprise then in 1849 he was elected to the state Senate representing Cherokee and Cobb counties. During the ensuing years of his term in office, he would meet many valuable state leaders. He had no problem debating some of the greatest minds of the day in state politics on the issues of slavery and states rights. After returning home to Canton from his time in office, Brown continued to practice law and closely follow the political scene.

During that time, Joseph Brown's brother, James Rice Brown, married Dr. Lewis's daughter. Joseph Brown's land holdings continued to increase and he purchased more slaves to work his considerable farmlands. Joseph Brown also speculated in copper mines and invested the profits he made on more land. In 1855 Brown became a candidate for judge of the Blue Ridge judicial circuit. Brown won the election and began a new phase of his career on the bench in the courtrooms of North Georgia. There he quickly won a reputation of severity tempered with dignity. Throughout North Georgia Judge Brown began to be marked as a potential state political leader.

It was in 1857 that Brown's career took yet another turn that would change his course and thrust him into the eye of the storm that became the Civil War. Without his knowledge Brown's name was submitted for governor at the turbulent state Democratic Convention by some of his political friends. Many political forces were in play at the convention, but none of the front runners and favorites could garner a majority. As the convention wore on, the sentiment that someone from Cherokee county should be chosen began to prevail. The name that was put forward was Joseph Emerson Brown. Delegates called him a man of sound principles, clear head and unquestioned ability. They stressed his character, his judgment and his age. At the end of the day the vote was unanimous.

Brown was harvesting wheat at his home in Canton when a friend, Samuel Weil, rode up on horseback to inform him of his nomination. In the days that followed, Brown moved quickly to placate the splintered factions from the turbulent convention. He pledged support for the principles adopted at the state convention and praised the Democratic Party for its achievements. But he would give no promise on the matter of political appointments. On the

The family of Joseph Emerson Brown donated the property for a park where the governor's Canton home stood before it was burned by Sherman's troops. Members of the family attended the Brown Park dedication in 1906. Governor Brown's brother, Judge James Rice Brown, is at left wearing a hat. Judge Brown lived at the Brown farm near Canton.

state level, Brown was the object of some political satire and sometimes called the plowboy judge and of the mountain boy. But the reality was a far different story. Brown would prove himself a shrewd leader capable of swimming in the most perilous political waters.

Brown accepted and began his historic journey to the governor's mansion.

On November 6, 1857, Brown was sworn in to his first term as governor. The couple had their sixth child on April 26, 1859, a fifth son named Charles McDonald Brown. Brown already had his sights on reelection. Governor Brown won the seat a second time and was sworn in that November 1859. The family continued to spend the summers in Canton, according to some records. In 1860 Brown's net worth was put at $44,790, and he owned 13 slaves, five in Milledgeville and eight in Canton.

In 1860 the questions of secession, slavery and state's rights were coming to a boil and by January 1861 when South Carolina

United States Senate,

WASHINGTON, D. March 20th, 1883.

Mr. Elijah A Brown,

Atlanta, Ga.

My Dear Son:

I wrote you some two weeks or more ago, asking you to buy a good corn sheller and send it up to me at Holly Springs, so that Wiley can get it and carry it out to the plantation. I have sold my corn to McAfee and can not get it shelled. I have had no reply to the latter and suppose either you did not get it, or in the hurry of business you have not been able to attend to it. I wish you would go to an agricultural store and get a good sheller, and ship it to me care D E Wiley, at Holly Springs. McAfee is wanting the corn, and the delay will soon be in the way.

Affectionately & c.

Joseph E Brown

Joseph Emerson Brown was serving in the United States Senate when he wrote this letter to his son Elijah A. Brown asking for his help in purchasing farm equipment.

withdrew from the Union it was inevitable that Georgia would quickly follow suit. On January 16, 1861, under Governor Brown's leadership and with his full backing and support Georgia seceded from the Union.

Back home in Cherokee County, Governor Brown's popularity was strong as he vowed to raise one million dollars across the state for the cause. Governor Brown urged the people across the state to help with manpower, money and supplies. In the midst of the turbulence Brown also faced the political decision of whether to stand for a third term for governor, something that was rare in the state's history. Perhaps it was not his decision alone. The constituency was clamoring for him to continue to lead. He was called "the man for the place" and "the man for the times." Despite political opposition from his enemies his popularity continued to be strong with the people and he was re-elected to a third term in November 1861. He would be elected a fourth time in 1863, an historical accomplishment that spoke of his popularity with the people, if not all the politicians.

Following the war, Governor Brown was arrested for calling an emergency session of the state Legislature to discuss the condition of the state and its people. He was taken to Washington, D.C., where he was imprisoned, but his captivity was short lived. He was released June 20, 1865. Upon his return to Georgia, Brown stayed in the governor's mansion until that December when Reconstruction Governor Charles Jenkins took office. During his last months in office he joined with the Republicans, which caused him to be unpopular for what people thought was his abandonment of his principles for self-profit. When he left Milledgeville, he moved to Atlanta. The home he had loved in Canton was gone, burned by General Sherman, and he did not want to rebuild.

Brown's political career was far from over. In 1868 he was appointed chief justice of the state Supreme Court. Brown was also on his way to being an extremely wealthy man, having purchased thousands of acres of land across North Georgia and even in other states. He heavily invested in mining and the railroad, investments that in Reconstruction times would become more and more valuable. Questions surrounded his loyalty to the South and his close relationships with the Carpetbaggers. Even so, Brown was appointed to fill an unexpired term in the United States Senate in 1880. That fall the state Legislature elected him to a full term. In 1884 he was reelected to another term. In 1890 due to health issues he retired from public life.

Of their children, their son Joseph Mackey Brown, who was born in Canton, is the best known, serving two terms as Georgia governor in 1908 to 1910 and again in 1912 to 1914.

Although there is no doubt about the influence and historical significance of Joseph Emerson Brown and his political career, there are few buildings or infrastructures in the state named for him. Brown Park in Canton where his home once stood still bears the name of its famous resident. There is a monument erected in 1928 on the capitol grounds in Atlanta of him and his wife, funded by the Brown family. The monument boasts two inscriptions that say much about the couple. "Joseph Emerson Brown was governor of Georgia, Patriot, Statesman, Christian. Born April 15, 1821, Died November 30, 1894. Governor of Georgia four terms 1857-1865. Chief Justice of Supreme Court of Georgia 1868-70. United States Senator 1880-1891. Founder of Charles McDonald Brown Fund at the University of Georgia." The other inscription reads "Elizabeth Grisham Brown Wife of Joseph Emerson Brown. Born July 13, 1826. Died December 26, 1896. Devoted Wife Loving Mother Loyal Patriot. A Christian obedient to God."

In 2005 the Cherokee County School Board considered a plan to name a new high school for Joseph Emerson Brown, but the outcry against the proposal killed the plan. Many of those who spoke against the school naming in honor of the late governor from Cherokee County cited the ties to slavery and political stands, as well as Brown's actions while governor as reasons that it would not be correct to name the school in his honor. However, newspaper reports at the time stated students who were asked to contribute ideas on the naming of the school and who wanted it named similarly to the middle school in the area were unhappy with the Cherokee County School Board's plan to ignore their proposal. A public middle school in Atlanta does carry the name of Joseph Emerson Brown Middle School.

Reconstruction Brings Tough Times

With the end of the war in 1865, under President Andrew Johnson's reconstruction plan, Georgia adopted a new constitution that repealed secession, abolished slavery and called for the election of a new slate of state officers. In April 1866, President Johnson declared peace restored in the war-torn country. But while the war was officially over, the reality was perhaps different. The South had been brought to her knees economically and would take many decades to even begin to recover. Many of the husbands and fathers who left to fight for the South did not return, crops were almost non-existent, and few had any money to buy goods or start over on their farms. The freed slaves were willing to work

Captain Joseph Miller McAfee returned from the war to become one of Canton's most successful merchants and businessmen in the years following Reconstruction. His home, pictured here circa 1881, was one of the town's most prominent residences. It later became the Central Hotel and was located where the Hotel Canton was later built.

for less than the returning soldiers when jobs were available, although pressure from vigilante groups made it hard for those who did hire the former slaves.

In Cherokee County, those who could began to quickly rebuild what had been burned by Union troops, and the farms that had been stripped by soldiers for provisions began the slow process of replanting.

While it is unknown exactly how many buildings and homes were left standing in Canton, the residents hastily began to build anew and attempt to get back to business and life as usual once peace was declared. According to Marlin's *The History of Cherokee County,* Joel Lewis Galt was one of the town's most significant merchants in the years following the end of the war. Galt, who was born in South Carolina in 1817, was a son of prominent settler Jabez Galt, who moved his family to Cherokee County in the 1830s. The older Galt built the town's first brick building, a mercantile store in 1839. In the years following the end of the war, Joel Galt built up the business and made it successful during the Reconstruction time.

Aggie Keith, at left, pictured here circa 1890-1900, was a slave on the Keith farm, one of the largest plantations with three thousand acres between Canton and Keithburg. Three of Aggie's four children were born in slavery. Son Amos, standing next to her, was born in 1866.

Also shortly after the ending of the Civil War, another merchant, a veteran of the conflict, came to Cherokee County to start another mercantile business. Capt. Joseph Miller McAfee started with a capital investment of $200 in those dark days after he served with Stonewall Jackson. McAfee was successful with his endeavors and soon helped build up business in the county seat. McAfee was active in farming, milling, ginning and building and in 1874 built the town's first hotel, a brick building in downtown Canton where the Hotel Canton later was constructed.

In 1870 yet another prominent merchant came to Canton, Benjamin Franklin Crisler. The *Cherokee Advance* later wrote of Crisler after he made his mark in Cherokee County as a successful merchant that "His example to the community has been one of consistent Christian living and the embodiment of the highest ideals of careful conduct. He has always been keenly interested in the things that were for the betterment of the town, and when a question of moral nature arises he is always to be found on the right side." Crisler was born in the part of Cherokee County that later became Milton County. He was only a teenager when war broke out, but he enlisted and served with General Lee's army in Virginia. He was twice wounded, and at the age of 21 was honorably discharged when the war ended in 1865. He returned to Canton and worked until he could put together 40 bushels of potatoes to sell and give him a stake to start his own business. In 1870 he established a general mercantile business, and eventually a tannery and a shoe and harness shop.

Charles Marshall McClure was an additional merchant who helped get Canton back on its feet in those difficult Reconstruction years. McClure also served as ordinary of Cherokee County courts, was a preacher and a teacher and active in the community.

Cashing in on Cotton Crops

When the war ended in 1865, Georgia's cotton crop was at 20 percent of what it had been before the onset of the Civil War in 1861. Like most rural areas, Cherokee County farmers faced a bleak economic outlook as they tried to replant and get on with their lives. In Cherokee County, cotton was an important cash crop. Those farmers who had used slave labor prior to the war now had to find a new way to work their fields. It was not long before a new system began to evolve — tenancy farming. Also known as sharecropping, under the system those laborers with no land of their own worked on the land of others and at the end of the season the landowners would pay them a portion of their crops. The system developed with the theory that it would benefit both parties, the landowner who was cash poor and land rich and the laborer who had no land but could work and hopefully clear enough at the end of the season to purchase his own land. The reality was that most of those who worked the farms of others never got enough ahead to leave the system.

A farmer takes his cotton to the Blankenship gin in Hickory Flat to prepare it to sell.

The sharecropping system developed after the federal government's attempts to insure employment for former slaves through the Freedmen's Bureau, a social program designed during Reconstruction to negotiate labor deals between the newly-freed black population and the white landowners. There was talk of taking land from the white landowners and giving plots to the former slaves, but most land was returned to its original owners. Neither the former slaves nor the landowners were willing participants in the Freedmen's Bureau negotiations. Some farmers were unwilling to hire the former slaves, even though they might be willing to work for less than their white counterparts. With the coming of the Night Riders and other vigilante organizations in the early 1900s, those farmers who did hire African-American workers were often tormented. But despite the perception that sharecropping was a black institution, sharecroppers of all types of poor Georgians were working the land for others.

Woodstock resident Glenn Hubbard wrote of the sharecropping system in Cherokee County in the early twentieth century in his memoir paper, "Before Allatoona." While the system had evolved somewhat at that time it was still much the same.

Workers pick cotton at the Galt family field in Canton in the early 1900s. Canton Cotton Mill, seen in the background, was a major procurer of the cash crop grown in much of Cherokee County at the time.

"Generally there were two types of families. One was the landowning family and the other was the tenant family. In reality the difference in the two families was not as great as one would expect.

"The farm owner family usually had a farm purchased on credit terms. This family would plant, cultivate and harvest a crop chiefly of cotton. Cotton was the cash crop. Most of the proceeds of this crop were used to chiefly pay the interest and sometimes a small amount of the principal of the farm indebtedness.

"The tenant farmer cultivated a portion of the landowner's farm on a sharing basis in one of two ways. One way was

that each party would share one-half of the expense of seed, fertilizer, etc., and each to receive one-half of the harvest. The landowner would furnish the land, living quarters, livestock and equipment. The tenant would furnish all the labor. This was known as 'farming on halves.' The other sharing arrangement was for the landowner to furnish the land, living quarters and one-fourth of the fertilizer. Then the tenant would furnish the livestock and equipment as well as the balance of the fertilizer. At harvest time the division called for the landowner to receive one-third of the cotton and one-fourth of the corn, the balance to remain with the

The Field Plantation was one of the largest farms in Cherokee County, comprised of more than 3,000 acres. The home, shown here circa 1910, housed several generations of the prominent family. Miss Lucy, center, was a former slave who stayed with the family after she received her freedom. Miss Lucy helped to raise the children of E. Earle Field Jr. after their mother died following the birth of the couple's fifth child.

A copy of a claim filed by Philip Keith in 1871 asks the U.S. Government to reimburse him for a horse, bridle and saddle which he owned and Union troops commandeered on a raid from Cartersville during the Civil War. He received $150 for the claim.

tenant. This was known as farming on the third and fourth."

Hubbard tells that the landowner rarely moved, and farms were known by the name of the owner. "Most of the time the landowner had somewhat of a better living than the tenant, although neither party fared very well financially." Most people had little cash, Hubbard says.

April, May and June were the months when the work of preparing, planting and cultivating the crops took place. Even small children helped, if by only carrying jugs of water into the fields for the workers. July and August were the leisure months of year, known as the time after "laying by" of the crops. During these months the children attended school and the parents tended to the chores of canning and preparing for the upcoming cold months. September and October were the time of harvest, and the children would be out of school to help with the cotton-picking.

"Each child looked forward to at least one ride on a wagon load of cotton to the cotton gin and to seeing the process of the machinery separating the cotton fibers from the seed," Hubbard wrote of his life in Cherokee County.

In Cherokee County around nine percent of the population before the war was comprised of slaves. In the years following the end of the war, several African-American communities emerged around Canton, one known as Pea Ridge between Canton and Waleska, one closer to Canton called Nineteen Community and one called Stumptown close to the downtown Canton

area and so named because of the trees that were cut down to build the houses.

In a published paper funded by the Georgia Department of Transportation by Garrett W. Silliman and Lori C. Thompson, a history of how the land ownership could evolve is given from an oral history of Frankie Shepherd collected by the researchers. The account tells that the main plantation family of the area was that of Keith.

"After Emancipation, a former slave from the Keith Plantation acquired a large amount of land. His name was Phillip Keith. It was told that he was bought in South Carolina with two other women who were rumored to be his wives. The land encompassed the area of North Canton to Pea Ridge to School Road. He donated land for the school – which was originally Hickory Log School. He also donated land for the Hickory Log Baptist Missionary Church and owned land where Keith Field was located. There are still many descendants of Phillip Keith in Canton living on the original Keith land." Deed records of the transaction donating the land for the church are not available, but that could be because of the volatility of the times in which the transaction took place. Phillip Keith is mentioned in the *Cherokee Advance* on his death in 1889 as being a respected citizen who was well thought of by all who knew him.

In the years after African-Americans received their freedom they valued education for their children. Students at the Olive Vine School in Waleska during the twentieth century include, back row, Julia Mae Washington, Jessie Mae Dean Watts and Thomas More. Second row includes L.W. Washington, Virginia Washington, Louise Harris Gearing and Betty Jane. Front Row includes Juanita Moore and Bonnie Washington.

The Hickory Log School, which was originally located just beyond the Hickory Log Church according to *Public Education in Cherokee County*, was built of logs. The school was reorganized in 1913 and met in the Hickory Log Church until 1916 when a new Hickory Log School was built on the location of what would later become Ralph J. Bunche School.

Education was extremely important to the former slaves in Cherokee County. Cherokee County educator H.A. Bell wrote of the movement to educate those who had just achieved their freedom. "The newly freed slaves of Cherokee County shortly after 1863 possessing an insatiable thirst for an education started small community movements. Many of these movements in duration were as flickers in the night. They may be characterized as nomadic with myriad political, financial and social upheavals."

To sustain the "burning desire for an education to make a literate citizenry, a number of schools were organized and classes begun including Burnt House Ridge, Briar Patch, Mineral Springs, Sardis, Free Negro, Olive Vine, and Hickory Log. Those early schools for the former slaves were held under brush arbors and in tents for a two month term in the summer and a three month period inside churches in the winter. Although there was little money to fund the schools, tuition fees were paid by the parents and trustees administered the funds to the teachers. The trustees were considered powerful guardians of the educational process as those who formerly were denied an education sought to obtain one. Eventually the school term expanded to six months."

Mining for Copper

In the years leading up to the Civil War and after the lure of gold had begun to fade away another mineral surfaced that would beckon with the promise of riches. Copper mining was not new to North Georgia when in the mid-1850s construction on the main shaft of the Canton Copper Mine was begun. The mine was located on what would later become known as Copper Mine Hill in Canton.

At the time the land on which Canton Copper Mine was located was partially owned by Joseph Emerson Brown, who had just been elected judge of the Blue Ridge circuit. William Grisham was a part owner of the property at the time as well. But the two quickly sold their interests for a substantial profit based on the initial findings of a sizeable vein of mineral ore. By 1860, a large number of miners were listed on the census, some of them with familial English origin. But as with many of the industrial endeavors of the time, the mining operation was closed down in 1861 because of the war. By 1870 only one person in Cherokee County was identified as a miner. There are no definitive reports on how much copper was ever recovered from the mine, but it never proved as successful as hoped.

The mine did not reopen after the war and the property and equipment were eventually sold at sheriff's auction in 1868. The property was sold in the 1870s to James Rice Brown, Governor Brown's brother, with a portion being purchased at a later date by W.A. Teasley. The mine was worked for another mineral, pyrite, as well as copper, lead and other metals sulfides. In 1900 William Rich and Herman Rich purchased the Canton Copper Mine. The two men, who were cousins of the owner of Rich's Department Store in Atlanta, became ensnared in a long legal battle over the purchase price. Litigation lasted for almost 15 years but the two men did operate the mine during that time. Isham Elrod

The Canton Copper Mine operated from 1856 until around 1919. *Ink drawing by Hoy Cook.*

was in charge of the mine. Elrod had originally worked in other minds around the area including the Franklin Goldmine. He and his wife Tina Jane Kirk of Holly Springs eventually built a house on the property. Over the years as the family grew the house was enlarged. Isham Elrod died in 1921 and the Rich family subsequently transferred title of the home to Tina Elrod.

In 1918 the Canton Copper Mine was flooded. Eventually the main shaft caved in, the hole where it had been was filled, and homes were built over the old site.

Donaldson's Furnace

A substantial portion of the wealth of Cherokee County before the Civil War was found beneath the ground, and plans seem to have been in play for the county to have a central role in the industrialization of the region. Several of the most influential political and industrial leaders, including Joseph Emerson Brown, Dr. John L. Lewis and Mark Anthony Cooper were instrumental in the development of the iron industry in the area. By the 1840s, the rich agricultural lands, forests, waterpower and minerals all combined to make Cherokee one of the most attractive areas for investment and development. Cherokee County's mineral wealth has been described as among the richest in the state, including iron ore, marble, quartz, copper, titanium, granite and, of course, gold. Descriptions of the Etowah Valley are rich in detail about the iron ore deposits that were traced along the hills and came to the surface at intervals, giving hint of vast quantities of excellent raw material to turn into iron, the ingredient needed for battleships, railways, cannons and weapons.

In the years before the war, Jacob Stroup was a pioneer of furnaces and operations throughout the South. His son, Moses Stroup, was associated with construction of the Etowah works. Neighboring Cass County, today's Bartow County, had a successful iron manufacturing operation with several furnaces built along the Etowah River and its tributaries for the purpose of turning the iron ore into metal. The smelting process and iron manufacturing in the neighboring county were run by the pioneer ironmasters, including the Stroups, who constructed a furnace on Stamp Creek which still stands today. There was also a rolling mill there, one of only two in Georgia. The industry was in its prime in Georgia in the mid-1850s, with seven charcoal furnaces, four forges and two rolling mills. However, the North was still the leader in iron production during those years. With the devastation wrought by the Civil War, the South would not enjoy another opportunity for iron production.

Judge Joseph Donaldson was listed as the wealthiest man in Cherokee County in the 1860 census, with a net worth of $68,000. His home, which was built on the Etowah River near Canton in 1856, was considered a showplace. Donaldson was born in South Carolina, along with his wife, Malinda, and as noted earlier was among the first settlers and founders of Canton. The couple had five children. By the 1849 census, Donaldson owned 165 acres of first quality land, 385 acres of second quality land and 1,930 acres of third quality land.

This iron furnace is believed to have been constructed by Judge Joseph Donaldson, one of the county's wealthiest landowners leading up to the Civil War. Donaldson probably constructed the furnace in the 1850s, but indications are that it was never used.

One section of land Donaldson purchased was a tract near Shoal Creek in the Fourteenth District, Land Lot 23. Donaldson acquired the property out of a sheriff's sale for the sum total of $12 in 1837 and retained possession of the land until his death in 1892. Over the years Donaldson also purchased mineral rights for several tracts of land in the iron rich Etowah Valley area. Neighboring Cass County, today's Bartow County, had a successful iron manufacturing operation with several furnaces built along the Etowah River and its tributaries for the purpose of turning the iron ore into metal. The smelting process and iron manufacturing in the neighboring county were run by pioneer ironmasters, among them Jacob Stroup, who constructed a furnace on Stamp Creek that still stands today. There was also a rolling mill there, one of only two in the state of Georgia.

Not far away, it is believed Donaldson was planning to produce iron at a furnace constructed sometime between 1859 and 1865. Construction of an iron furnace on Shoal Creek would have been advantageous in the years of the Civil War with the market for pig iron at a high pitch in the South. A study of the Donaldson Furnace done for the U.S. Army Corps of Engineers in 1987 shows the structure located on a narrow shelf near Shoal Creek and at 900 feet above sea level. The site consists of the furnace, a charging platform and an old road bed, and the study concludes that the furnace was never used. The furnace is constructed of sandstone from the area,

iron pipe and earth, and the front is partially collapsed. The furnace was almost completed and then abandoned, according to the study. Reasons for the abandonment are believed to have been the outcome of the war, the destruction of the armory in Cass County by Sherman's troops where the iron would have been sent for manufacturing, or possibly that Donaldson himself lacked the resources at the time to complete the furnace. For whatever reason, the furnace was abandoned before it was ever put to use.

The remains of the furnace still stand today in the Sutallee Trace area. It serves as a reminder of the Civil War days and the period immediately preceding it when the county was on the brink of industrial success. While the years immediately following the war were challenging and it appeared unlikely the local economy could find a firm footing, in the coming years Cherokee County would once again prove its resilience. Once more fortunes would be made and industry would grow as the county moved in a new direction.

With the coming of the railroad in 1879 Cherokee County was transported into a time of renewed pros-perity as Woodstock, Canton, Holly Springs and Ball Ground and smaller communities along the way were connected to the outside world. Goods such as marble, cotton, cloth and rope could reach a broader market much more quickly. Here, a train in front of Roberts Marble Company in Ball Ground is loaded and prepared for departure.

Chapter Four

County on Track for Era of Expansion

The coming of the railroad to Cherokee County in 1879 ushered in a new period of growth and prosperity. As in the past, transportation was a key ingredient to the dawning of a new time of economic success for Cherokee County. Once more the unique location of the county and the forward thinking and perseverance of its leaders and residents helped propel the community forward. Just as they had throughout the county's history, the rich natural resources such as the Etowah River and the abundance of minerals including marble played a significant role in the county's economy following the bleak time of Reconstruction. As the new century drew near and began, positive changes occurred that would set the course of financial success for many years to come. An industrial age was beginning, and while it did not replace agriculture as the

The 1874 Cherokee County Courthouse was located on the present square in downtown Canton. The courthouse fell into disrepair and finally burned in 1927, making way for construction of the white marble courthouse on the other side of the square. The Central Hotel next door was later removed to allow for the larger Hotel Canton.

county's main source of revenue, it instead offered new opportunities and a solid base for Cherokee County. The people of Cherokee County rose to the task of rebuilding and contributing to the strength of the county. Both those who had made their home within its borders since the earliest days of settlement and new leaders who located in Cherokee County in the waning days of the 19th century would help chart the course toward the future. Residents would see opportunities in business, education and modern advancements such as medicine. Financial institutes were established by community leaders with the objective of multiplying that wealth and using its strength to position Cherokee County as a force within the state. From those who worked with their hands and their backs laying the tracks and constructing the new factories to the owners of the land and the buildings on it, families across the county benefited from the new age of prosperity.

In 1880 the population of Cherokee County was once more on the increase, after experiencing a decline following the Civil War. The census that year showed 14,325 residents made their home in the county. By 1900 a total of 15,243 people lived within its borders. Twenty years after the Civil War ended, an article in the *Atlanta Constitution* commented about the county seat. "Its backwoods atmosphere is gone and Canton is a town of new and modern appearance. Most of the buildings are brick." After the fire which claimed so many structures during the war, residents were now building to last with a renewed optimism. From 1880 to 1890 the population of Canton almost doubled from 363 to 657 residents, and by the turn of the century the town had grown to just over 2,000 residents, the increase spurred by the opening of a new cotton mill which offered the prospect of jobs. Cotton production was high in Cherokee County in those years leading up to the new century. The county had one of the highest per acre yields in the state. The work force, those resilient farmers and hard-working laborers who wanted a better life for their families, was a strong resource not to be overlooked. New avenues of transportation, ambitious leadership and a strong labor force were all factors which set the county on the road to a brighter future.

Railroad Transports Prosperity to Cherokee

Mls.	STATIONS.
0	.......Etowah........
32	........Farner.........
43	.......Ducktown......
48	.......Copperhill......
61	......Blue Ridge.....
77	........Ellijay........
87	......Whitestone.....
97	........Jasper.........
102	...........Tate.........
105	........Nelson.........
109	.....Ball Ground.....
120	........Canton........
126	....Holly Springs....
132	......Woodstock......
144	.......Marietta......

Table 58. ETOWAH AND MARIETTA.

The Louisville and Nashville Railroad purchased the rail line through Cherokee County in 1902 and had several stops a day at some of the county's cities.

The Marietta and North Georgia Railroad line to Cherokee County was completed in May 1879 and impacted the area more than perhaps any single thing had before, opening the county to unparalleled commerce and growth. The journey to get rail service into Cherokee County was a long one with many delays and false starts. The final completion of the line to the towns of Cherokee County was just one of many stops on a long journey to bring rail service to North Georgia and beyond, which had many failed attempts before success was ultimately achieved.

The Civil War had halted earlier efforts in their tracks. In 1846 plans were laid to run a rail line into Cherokee County as part of the Etowah Railroad which would have connected industrialist Mark Anthony Cooper and partner Moses Stroup's ironworks with the Western and Atlantic Railroad. But that project did not materialize. The Etowah Railroad Company acquired a charter in 1847 with plans to run their rail line up the river and perhaps close to Donaldson's ironworks in Cherokee County, then further north to Dahlonega. However, the only section of the rail line that was completed was in Cass, later Bartow County, along the north part of the Etowah River. That rail was abandoned after Federal troops destroyed the ironworks in 1864 during the war.

The next try to bring rail to Cherokee County occurred in 1854 when the Ellijay Railroad was incorporated and an effort was made to bring the railroad from Marietta to North Georgia, but that attempt also derailed. In 1859 a group of Cherokee County residents including James Rice Brown, William A. Teasley and James Jordan met at the county courthouse to formulate plans to bring the railroad into the county, but yet again the plan was diverted, this time by the onset of the war a year later.

Finally in 1870 the Georgia Legislature agreed to fund the railroad expansion for the Marietta and North Georgia Railroad line. While the state authorized $15,000 per mile of rail in funding, the local communities were also required to raise money. Stock was sold and Teasley and Brown were among those who purchased the shares.

In May 1879 the railroad was linked from Woodstock to Canton

By 1884 four trains a day were stopping in Canton. Here, the Canton Depot was a busy spot in the early 1900s as passengers took advantage of the railroad to visit the area, helping to boost the economy and make Canton a popular destination to visit.

Ball teams could take the train to their games in the days before automobiles and paved highways became commonplace. Here, the Ball Ground Baseball Team poses at the Ball Ground Train Depot circa 1912. Webb Hawkins is holding a child and other children and fans can be seen looking out the windows. George Walter "Buff" Howard is standing, second from the right.

and in November the "Little Mary," the first engine to bring a load into Canton, chugged up the line from the south. A large group of residents was on hand for the historic moment and it is reported that they cheered as the train arrived, turned around and returned to Marietta. At that time the train line ended in Canton. Two years later it would be extended to Ball Ground and that town saw its first train arrive in May 1882. By January 1884 the rail line was completed to Ellijay in Gilmer County and by 1887 the tracks extended on to Murphy, North Carolina.

Several contracting companies, many of them local, worked on building the rail bed through Cherokee County. Wallace, Haley and Company, as well as R.F. Maddox and Company; Field, McAfee, Tate and Company; and J.M. McAfee and Company had a hand in preparing the line. The line was originally built as narrow gauge, but was converted to standard gauge in 1889.

By 1884, four trains a day were running to Canton, and the town and surrounding area were billed as a resort area with a grand hotel featuring 25 rooms and splendid accommodations at good rates. The hotel was two-story brick and a fitting monument to the growing town. Canton at that time featured wide tree-lined streets and boasted about 700 residents. The city's growth helped contribute to the need for more government and voters went to the polls to choose Canton's first elected officials. At the first municipal election on January 7, 1882, five council members were elected including Benjamin Crisler,

Henry Newman, Odian Galt, Benjamin Perry and J.P. McConnell. Galt was chosen as the city's first mayor.

In an article in the *Cherokee Advance* in 1915 recounting the county's accomplishments and progress, some of the people who impacted the economic climate following Reconstruction were noted, among them J.M. McAfee and R.T. Jones. "Capt. J.M. McAfee, a hardened hero of man's struggles, came here from Forsyth and began his business career. He put up the first brick buildings in the town and he kept on putting them up until he has put up more structures of this kind than any other man in the town. His buildings were for business purposes and developed one side of a well-rounded town only." Jones was commended for his contributions to industry which the newspaper noted helped make Canton the place it became. "To these two men must be given the credit of hav-

Thomas Wilburn "Bud" Hubbard and his family made their home circa 1905 on Lower Sweetwater Road, about two miles from where Allatoona Lake was later constructed. The home was typical of the day when built by Hubbard's father, Patrick Hubbard in 1854. The house had six rooms, three on each side of a centered hall, with a kitchen attached to the rear. Family members included, from left, Isabella Hubbard, Eliza Rebecca Kolb Hubbard, Margaret Hubbard, Cosby Hubbard, Thomas Wilburn Hubbard, and Boyce Hubbard.

ing built more businesses, houses, factories, hotels and churches than all other men who have affected the history and growth of the town."

Woodstock was also significantly impacted by the railroad, which opened the unincorporated town to its neighbors to the south and allowed farmers and businessmen to more easily export local goods and crops. The Woodstock Depot that stands today was built in 1912, but it is believed that an earlier depot stood not far away. At the time Woodstock was incorporated in 1897 the city had about 300 residents, and a depot was mentioned as a point of reference when the city limits were set. By the time the new depot was built the name and ownership of the railroad had changed.

In 1887 the railroad company consolidated with the Georgia and North Carolina Railroad and the line was completed to Murphy, North Carolina. The name was changed to the Marietta and North Georgia Railway. Then in 1890 the line became a part of the route from Atlanta to Knoxville when the Knoxville Southern Railroad completed the track into Tennessee. In early 1891 the company encountered financial difficulties that forced it into receivership and finally in 1896 it was sold. It became the Atlanta, Knoxville and Northern Railway until six years later when in 1902 the Louisville and Nashville Railroad purchased the line. Later the Georgia Northeastern Railroad acquired the southern portion of the line. It was under the L&N ownership that the Woodstock Depot was built.

The coming of the railroad gave the businessmen in Woodstock a means of more easily and readily selling their goods including the rope produced at the rope mills near the town and the bales of cotton from surrounding farms. Cotton suppliers and buyers constructed five cotton warehouses near the railroad tracks in Woodstock. An article in the *Atlanta Constitution* claimed, "Woodstock is one of the best cotton markets in North Georgia. The buyers here receive from the farmers of the neighboring territory something like six to seven thousand bales each fall. Not always does one find good cotton markets in good towns, for some very good towns have very poor cotton markets, but always when you find a cotton market that draws men and trade to the town, you find a com-

The railroad played a major role in the success of commerce in Cherokee County. The Amicalola Marble and Power Company railroad ran between Ball Ground and Harrington Quarry near Marble Hill transporting marble to the cutting companies. Calvin Farmer, fifth from left, was an engineer of Amicalola Marble and Power Company, seen here somewhere between 1905 and 1910.

munity that is on the high road prosperity and that is destined to grow to be much larger than it is today."

The town was portrayed as a major industrial point following the coming of the railroad. The Little River Cotton Mills, which were some of the oldest in the state, begun in 1827 and expanded in 1836, benefited from the new railroad. The Little River Mills produced rope and were under the leadership of John S. Dorn. According to the Atlanta newspaper, "The Little River Mills is a part of Woodstock, and is the most important part of its industrial life, forming also one of the important parts of the town's trading territory." In addition to the rope mills, Woodstock Oil and Fertilizer Company's plant, the Runyan Marble Company's plant, and the Watson Marble Company's facility would be located there. In 1888 J.H. Johnston started his mercantile store in Woodstock.

J.H. Johnston established a mercantile store in Woodstock in 1888. The store served the community for decades. Johnston and his sons were leaders in the community and involved in a number of business operations, including the rope mill, cotton brokerage and banking. J.H. Johnston, from left, Joe Johnston, Smith Johnston, Hugh Lee Johnston, along with Sam Dawson, Margaret Durham, Emma Barnes, Mrs. Tom Fowler, John Hillhouse and Roy Freeman in front of the store.

Leading resident J.H. Johnston was born in Cherokee County in 1855, the youngest son of D.M. Johnston and Elizabeth Johnston, who had located to the Hickory Flat area around 1836 from North Carolina. The couple had five sons, one of whom was killed while fighting in the Civil War. Following Sherman's march and the end of the war, the family moved to Cobb County when young Johnston was 11. Before moving back into the Woodstock area in 1887, J.H. Johnston married Avis Benson, a descendant of Cherokee County settlers, in 1877. The couple had several children, including Smith L. Johnston and Joseph E. Johnston, who both played a leadership role in the growth and success of Woodstock. Other children included W.A. Johnston, Ava Elizabeth Johnston, Hugh Lee Johnston and

Jack H. Johnston. Smith L. Johnston married Florine Dial, another descendant of early Cherokee County pioneers, and had several children including Smith L. Johnston, Jr., who eventually took over his father's banking and business interests in Woodstock.

In Holly Springs, residents finally had a convenient way to go north to Canton or south to Marietta, mail was delivered by

A cotton gin was constructed in Holly Springs following the coming of the railroad. Farmers could bring their cotton to town and, once it was ginned and bailed, it could be shipped by train to buyers.

train each day and merchants and businesses could more easily get goods. As with other stops on the train's route throughout Cherokee County, Holly Springs was given the opportunity to grow. Holly Springs resident John Ragsdale sold the railroad companies much of the property they wanted for right-of-way near the town, and in 1878 construction of the tracks began through the Holly Springs area. As with other cities in Cherokee County, the railroad helped bring new opportunities for industry and for the farmers of the area. Before the coming of the railroad, farmers had difficulty getting their crops to market. Once the railroad in Holly Springs was operating, the difficulty they had once had in transporting their crops was greatly reduced. Since farmers were producing more, they began bringing productivity to a level not enjoyed since before the Civil War. Production of corn was high and the cotton crop had a significant increase. A cotton gin was constructed in Holly Springs shortly after the railroad came through the town. A loading dock was built near the tracks and cotton bales could be loaded directly onto the freight cars of the trains serving the area. A local sawmill was built around 1884, helping area landowners turn their timber into lumber and more readily sell it.

The city of Ball Ground also experienced an era of unprecedented growth once the railroad came to town. With the help of the marble industry the city reached a heyday of economic prosperity. Ball Ground was the second largest city in the county at the time and offered its residents a progressive and impressive environment. The post office was one of the busiest in the nation. The town boasted a number of prosperous businesses and stores. Other small communities also felt the impact of the new rail system and began to thrive.

Canton Cotton Mills and the Jones Family

In 1879 a pivotal event almost as impacting as the coming of the railroad happened in the history of Cherokee County when one man decided to make Canton his home. Robert Tyre Jones, Sr. and his wife, Susie Walker Jones, moved to Cherokee County from Newton County in middle Georgia. Mr. R.T., as he was known, was 30 years old at the time and his list of accomplishments included working on his family farm, studying at a business college and receiving training as a bookkeeper. He was prepared and ready to meet his future.

The coming of the railroad played a role in Jones' decision to move to Cherokee County, according to family papers and a published account in *Eminent Georgians*. Jones' relative by marriage, Robert F. Maddox, Sr., was the president of the new railroad being built in North Georgia. He advised Jones that it was a good time to take a look at Canton as a potential location to establish a business. Jones made the trip to the small town in North Georgia on the Etowah River and found everything he needed for his plans. Within a year he and his wife and infant son had made the move that would be the last of his life.

That was the beginning of great things for Mr. Jones, and for Canton and all of Cherokee County. While the greatest achievement and impact to the community would not happen for more than 20 years in 1899 when he founded Canton Cotton Mills, Jones made his presence known in every facet of business in the community in the years both before and after that milestone. In the two decades leading up to the building of the cotton mill R.T. Jones made a tremendous impact on the business, financial and social life of Canton. His first local business was Jones Mercantile Company, which he founded with $3,000 he had managed to save, a large sum of cash for the times. During his 20 successful years in the general merchandise business he became well respected by all who came in contact with him. A major portion of his business was with the farmers. He received their crops of cotton in return for the staples and merchandise they needed to live on their farms.

Mr. R.T. joined the First Baptist Church of Canton and by 1881 was a deacon in the local church. His strong religious convictions and moral ethics were well known by all who worked with him or knew him socially. He remained a deacon there for 56 years and was Sunday School superintendent for 49 years. The *Cherokee Advance* reported, "It is really inspiring to see him on Sunday morning meet the men and women from the counter, the shop, the mill and even nearby farms and lead them in the study of the Great Book of Life." More

For the 35th anniversary sale of Jones Mercantile Company in 1914 residents and farmers flocked to downtown Canton for the celebration. R.T. Jones, above, came to Cherokee County in 1879 and started the mercantile business which he operated for 20 years before founding Canton Cotton Mill.

than 600 people were in attendance at Sunday school under his leadership. Over the years he also gave substantially financially to the church, helping construct a new church in downtown Canton in 1925. That same year the two largest Bible classes at the church were consolidated and named the R.T. Jones Bible Class in honor of Mr. Jones.

As his business success grew, so did his influence and in 1892 he, along with a group of other leading businessmen, started the Bank of Canton. In 1893 R.T. Jones became the president of the bank. In the years to come, although he was not a majority shareholder of the bank, it would become known locally as "the Jones bank." He later purchased Georgia Marble Fin-

Numerous members of the Jones Family, including the children and grandchildren of R.T. Jones, occupied leadership roles in business and the community in Cherokee County. Annual gatherings at the home of the family's patriarch in Canton would bring together the many siblings and their families. This 1908 Christmas dinner is attended by, from left: Robert Permedus Jones, Clara Thomas Jones, Bobby Jones, P. W. Jones, Mary Foute Jones, Sue Jones, Rube Jones, Louise Jones, Miss Lil Coggins Jones, Eleanor Jones, R.T. Jones, Sr., Jim Cross, being held, Jack Jones, Louis Jones, Sr., Albert Vaughn Jones, May Reynolds Jones, Emily Foster Jones Brooke and George Brooke.

ishing Works. R.T. Jones also served as mayor of Canton and on the City Council. R.T. Jones was also a part owner of the Hotel Canton on the square in downtown.

Mr. R.T. and his wife Susie had eleven children, seven of whom lived to adulthood and four who died in infancy. Their oldest child, born July 18, 1879, in Newton County just before they moved to Canton, was Robert Permedus Jones, who grew up to be an attorney in Atlanta and was the father of famous golfer Bobby Jones. The second child was Paul Walker Jones born July 15, 1881. He later married Mary Foute and in time ran the mercantile company for his father. Third was Emily Foster, born October 27, 1882. She grew up to marry George W. Brooke. The fourth child was May Reynolds Jones, who was born October 4, 1884.

Albert Vaughn Jones was born August 7, 1886. He is remembered for helping to organize the Continental Marble and Granite Company in Canton and for being president of the *North Georgia Tribune*. He married Ella Grady Perry, daughter of Ben Perry, who founded the *Cherokee Advance*.

The next child to survive to adulthood was Louis Lindley Jones, Sr., who was born March 24, 1890. At the time of his birth no one could have predicted that it would be this child who would succeed his father in heading the mills. But upon his graduation from Canton High School in 1905 and graduation from Virginia Military Institute in 1912, he immediately became involved in the family business. In

1912 he married Jessie Pearl Turner of Dawson County. In 1915 Louis Jones was elected secretary of Canton Cotton Mill and in 1916 at age 26 became superintendent of the mill. In 1917 he became a director of Canton Cotton Mill and in 1926 he was named general manager. Then in 1932 he was named vice president of the two mills.

The last child that R.T. Jones fathered with his first wife was Jack Walker Jones, who was born July 4, 1894, and later became a dermatologist in Atlanta. Dr. Jones married Elizabeth Coggins, the daughter of Augustus Coggins.

Susie Walker Jones died April 17, 1899, just months before the opening of the Canton Cotton Mill.

Mr. R.T. Jones' second wife was Lilly Coggins Cross, the sister of Augustus Coggins. They had four children, including Eleanor Frances Jones, who was born May 25, 1902. She grew up to marry Dr. Albert Clayton Reid. Next was Rube Coggins Jones, who was born August 31, 1903. He would marry Nina Thompson of Canton. Rube Jones was active in the cotton mill operations, and later the Ford Automobile Agency in Canton.

The third child of R.T. Jones' second marriage was Louise Jones, who grew up to marry John Wood, a prominent attorney and Ninth District Congressman. The youngest child of Mr. R.T. was named for him. Robert Tyre Jones, Jr., was born July 11, 1907 and later married Sarah Law. He owned the Main Street Garage and Chevrolet Agency in Canton.

The Jones family home was a beautiful, substantial white Victorian house in downtown Canton behind the Jones Mercantile Company. The home, which was later torn down after Jones' death, was in those days the center of family life, filled with friends of the children, site of family dinners and holiday celebrations for the many children and grandchildren, and hub of social life for the community. Family members reminisce about the Christmas celebrations where the family would gather and each child would get a gold coin until gold was recalled and replaced with paper money in the Roosevelt era. To the right of Mr. Jones' house was the home of his son Paul and wife Mary and across the street his sons Albert and Louis and their families occupied two homes.

Grandson Ben Perry Jones writes in a family history that "Papa," as Mr. Jones was called by his children, liked to play the cards most evenings. As Ben's family ate dinner, the telephone would ring and his mother would say "That's Papa and he wants us to come over and play Rook."

"I suspect these telephone calls were not considered mere invitations, but were more likely akin to commands. At exactly 7:30P.M., no matter where they were in the game, Granddad would leave the game and go to bed. I'm sure he needed the sleep, as he arose every morning around four or five A.M.," Ben Jones wrote.

As a child his grandfather seemed stern, unsmiling and generally unapproachable, but as Ben grew up his opinion somewhat changed. "I see him now as a dedicated Christian, as a great leader and organizer, and as a man with much business acumen. He was a compassionate, caring, honest man of high integrity – a good family man who was always willing to cooperate with and to help other people and worthwhile causes."

While R.T. Jones built a legacy in family and in business, his greatest contribution to Canton and Cherokee County was the founding and success for decades of Canton Cotton Mills. As a mercantile owner and a good businessman, he was able to see the potential the town offered: good labor force, readily available raw materials, rail transportation, the Etowah River, all factors that made Canton the ideal location for a textile mill. Once he had the vision, it was not long until the mill became a reality. On December 2, 1899, Canton Cotton Mill was chartered and capitalized at $100,000 with R.T. Jones as the largest shareholder and many other local business leaders involved as stockholders. Ninety percent of the shareholders were from Cherokee County including prominent people like W.A. Teasley, Sr., Thomas M. Brady, William Galt, J.M. Price, G.I. Teasley, W.J. Webb, Samuel Tate and Benjamin Franklin Perry. Several stockholders of the mill were also directors of Bank of Canton.

Construction of the original Canton Cotton Mill, later known as Mill Number One, was begun in 1900 and built out of local bricks made from red Georgia clay from the banks of the Etowah River. It had a marble foundation given to the mill by stockholder Thomas M. Brady. The mill had 160 looms and manufactured cotton sheeting.

The first year was not a successful one financially and many of the stockholders were concerned about their investments. R.T.

R.T. Jones founded the Canton Cotton Mill in 1899. Here, employees line up in front of the original mill, circa 1900. Whether these are all employees or some are family members is not known. It was not until after 1906 that Georgia's Child Labor Law forbade the employment of anyone under 10 years old.

Jones made an offer to buy out anyone who was not satisfied and also took over day-to-day operation of the mill after spending a few months visiting similar operations across the South. By the following year the mill was making a profit.

In 1902 a dye house was built and in 1903 Canton Cotton Mills began producing denim, soon becoming a leader in production in the South. However, denim made in the Northeast United States was considered superior and Mr. Jones wanted to make his product competitive. That led to major investment of machinery and expertise, and capitalization increased to $200,000. That investment paid off and the white-back denim produced by Canton Cotton Mills beginning in1905 developed a reputation of being some of the finest in the world. During 1909 and 1910 loom capacity was doubled and the capitalization rose to $300,000.

In 1923 Mill Number Two was built in North Canton and was completed the next year, putting 750 looms and 23,000 spindles in operation. The new mill employed around 600 workers and provided better working conditions. Enhancements to equipment continued in the ensuing years with a finishing range added to give the cloth a better appearance. In 1935 Sanforizing machines were installed.

Many families spent generations working in the mills. As in many mill towns across the South, housing was provided for the workers in mill villages. The original mill village, later known as Mill Village Number One, was across from the first mill. A new mill village was constructed in North Canton beginning in 1923 and was viewed as a model for mill towns everywhere. The village across from the new Mill Number Two was modern in both appearance and function, with such features as indoor plumbing and modern baths, closets and pantries, and four to six rooms to accommodate families of all sizes. They offered free water and electricity, and eventually paved streets. A school was also constructed and funded by the mill. Canton Cotton Mills paid for the operation of North Canton School but it was actually operated by the Cherokee County Board of Education. It, too, was modern, with 13 classrooms serving grades one to nine, and offered a gymnasium, library, home economics room and music room for students.

Mr. R.T. Jones died in 1937 and his son Louis Lindley Jones took over operation of the mill. The death of R.T. Jones at age 88 left a large void in the community. But he also had helped build a solid foundation for the next almost half-century of economic achievement in Canton and all of Cherokee County. One of his famous quotes perhaps sums it up best. "No man ever accomplishes anything really worthwhile alone. There are always two additional forces at work – other people and Providence."

Louis Jones, Sr. built on his father's legacy, continuing the production of denim that clothed millions of workers of all types across the nation. He fathered four children with his wife, who was known as Miss Pearl. On November 27, 1913, Louis Lindley Jones, Jr. was born; Sarah Baldwin Jones was born on March 5, 1916; John Turner Jones was born Dec. 25, 1918; and Pearl Turner Jones was born on May 4, 1920.

Marble Industry Shines Bright

Although cotton was king in Cherokee County, Georgia marble was the undisputed queen of the region, with a number of finishing companies established in the county in the late 1880s and continuing to have an economic impact until the mid-1900s. The marble found in the Cherokee County region and north in Pickens County was calcite marble, which was originally limestone formed from marine creatures and altered through temperature and pressure into the crystalline marble. Because the marble found in North Georgia is low in moisture absorption and because it is strong, it is considered ideal for architectural use. Throughout Cherokee County there are examples, from the Bank of Canton to the foundation of the Canton Cotton Mill to the white marble courthouse in downtown Canton, of using the beautiful material for buildings.

While Cherokee County contained a vein of marble from Ball Ground to north of Canton, the largest lode of the mineral was in neighboring Pickens

This postcard depicts the Creole Quarry of the Georgia Marble Company in Tate. The section of the quarry is 90 feet deep. Marble quarried by the Georgia Marble Company was used around the world on monuments and buildings, including the Lincoln Memorial in Washington, D.C. Much of the marble was finished in nearby Ball Ground.

County near Tate and Marble Hill. Samuel Tate and his family established the Georgia Marble Company in 1884. Marble had been mined in the area since the 1830s along Long Swamp, and with the coming of the railroad to Ball Ground it was economically attractive to invest in the business. Soon the marble quarries in the area were flourishing. By 1900 marble quarrying and finishing was considered the region's number one industry. As many as 500 workers were employed in the marble finishing industry in Ball Ground. At least four finishing companies flourished in Ball Ground.

Georgia marble can be found on buildings of note throughout the Southeast, the United States and in Washington, D.C. North Georgia marble was used on the Lincoln Statue at the Lincoln Memorial

in Washington, D.C., as well as the Pan-American Building, the Corcoran Art Gallery and the Columbus Fountain. In Atlanta the local marble was used on the Hurt Building, Emory University and the Citizens and Southern National Bank. Other buildings of note where marble from the area was used include the New York Stock Exchange and McKinley Memorial in Niles, Ohio, as well as the Maine Monument in Havana, Cuba.

The Roberts Marble Company was founded in Ball Ground in 1898. With good quality marble and granite so close at hand, and the town ideally located in the quarry region of Georgia, the company quickly took off. Roberts Marble Company was started by Alfred Webb Roberts. Later all of his sons but one would be involved in the business locally.

Alfred Webb Roberts   Georgia Ann Coggins Roberts

According to company literature, the Roberts business was founded on the principle "From Finishing Plant to Cemetery," with the goal to provide quality at a reasonable price. Many of the marble finishers stayed with the company for their entire career, and the company pointed with pride to the beautiful memorials they created. As the company grew it established a showroom in Atlanta, and the company was called one of the largest and best equipped in the United States. The company had a sound reputation nationwide and monuments made in Ball Ground could be found in every state in the Union.

Alfred Webb Roberts did not limit his endeavors solely to the marble industry although that is certainly where he made an indelible mark. He was also successful as a merchant, cotton broker and banker and was heavily involved in real estate dealings in the county. With his marriage in 1879 to Althea Georgia Ann Coggins, he was linked to one of the most prominent families of the time in Canton. Georgia Ann was the daughter of Alfred Burton Coggins, a merchant and successful businessman in Canton. Coggins had served in the Confederate Army with Roberts. Roberts was 35 years old and Georgia Ann was 19 at the time of their marriage.

Georgia Ann also had several brothers and sisters of prominence, including Lilly Coggins Jones, who was married to R.T. Jones. Roberts was the principal cotton buyer in Ball Ground and, using his family connections, sold his cotton to the Canton Cotton Mills among other mills. Another of Mrs. Roberts' siblings was Frank Coggins who owned the Continental Marble Company in Canton. Perhaps the best known, though, was her brother, Augustus Coggins, who owned the Crescent Farm on the Etowah River, a 350-acre estate of prominence.

In 1887 A.W. Roberts and his wife Georgia Roberts moved into what would become the family home in Ball Ground. The home was built about 1855 and was originally constructed in the Plantation Plain Style. The Roberts later renovated it for the Victorian period as it is shown here about 1910.

Alfred Webb Roberts was also a successful merchant and owner of the A.W. Roberts and Sons Store in Ball Ground, a general store that sold everything from groceries and staples to clothing and farm tools. Farmers and the hill people of the area would come to the general mercantile store once or twice a year to stock up on the supplies they needed. The store served the area for almost 80 years. Roberts had a reputation as an honest and caring citizen and community leader.

The couple's home overlooked the town that meant so much to them and their family. Built in 1855, the couple moved into the home in 1887. Originally built in the Plantation Plain style, the house was renovated into a Victorian residence by the Roberts family. The steps leading up to the front of the house are marble, and there are marble sidewalks, benches, urns and birdbaths featured on the grounds of the house. Roberts took pride in the landscaping of the family home.

The children of Mr. and Mrs. A.W. Roberts included Martin Clyde Roberts, born 1880; Judson Brown Roberts, born 1882; Alfred Roy Roberts, born 1885; Augustus Paul Roberts, born 1887; Carl Weldon Roberts, born 1890; Lou Bernice Roberts, born 1896; and Aaron Webb Roberts, born 1898. All of the sons worked at Roberts Marble Company except Aaron Webb Roberts, who established a marble business in Dallas, Texas.

Roberts Marble Company workers helped make the marble finishing business opened in Ball Ground in 1898 by A.W. Roberts a success.

Alfred Roy Roberts managed the marble works in Ball Ground for 45 years.

Other marble finishing companies to operate in Ball Ground were the Ball Ground Monument Company, Southern Marble and Stone Company, and Consumers Monument Company. Ball Ground Monument Company was established by outside investors with Ben F. Perry, Jr. as the president and general manager. Perry was also mayor of Ball Ground and a councilmember. The company is believed to have transferred ownership in the 1930s to the Roberts family. Likewise, Southern Marble and Stone Company was begun by outside interests and later sold to the Roberts. Southern Marble's operations were located one mile south of town. Carl W. Groover and Clyde Brady formed Consumers Monument Company in 1911. The company was significant in the economic development of Ball Ground. Groover was president of the company for 60 years. Georgia Marble Company eventually acquired several of the other companies in the area, including Blue Ridge Marble Company and Southern Marble Company.

One of the earliest marble finishing companies in Cherokee County was the Georgia Marble Finishing Works, which went into business in 1892. Thomas M. Brady had worked in Cobb County as a marble finisher before starting his own company in Cherokee County. Take a walk through Riverview Cemetery and the Brady monument stands as a reminder of the man and his talents. Sam Tate of neighboring Pickens County helped Brady start his company, which quickly built a stellar reputation for the carvings and monuments he produced. Among his best known is the Lion of the South, a Confederate memorial at Oakland Cemetery in Atlanta which was dedicated in 1894. Georgia Marble Finishing Works also did the original marble work on the Bank of Canton building, bidding $299.95 for the job.

Thomas M. Brady was a leading citizen of Cherokee County, serving as mayor of Canton, as councilman and a member of the board of education. He was a director and original stockholder of the

The Cherokee Marble Works was in Canton, which like Ball Ground had a thriving industry finishing the stone quarried in north Cherokee and Pickens County. Jesse McClain, who later served as mayor of Canton, is second from left.

the Bank of Canton. In 1904 when his health deteriorated and he wanted relief of the burdens of management, Brady sold two-thirds interest in his business to R.T. Jones, Sr., and E.A. McCanless. In 1907 Brady died of a heart attack. McCanless, who became manager of the company, was born in Salacoa, grew up on the farm, and received little formal education. The *Cherokee Advance* wrote of McCanless, "He was trained to hard work on the farm, doing any and everything that came his turn. He received what formal education he got in the common schools of the county." McCanless went to work for the marble finishing company in 1900, where at various times he was in charge of the office, was bookkeeper and cashier. In 1905 he became manager of the company. The newspaper said that the facts speak strong words of tribute to the ability of Mr. McCanless for the size of no institution is greater than the length of the shadow of the man in charge of it. With new management in place, a new and larger plant with more advanced equipment including electric cranes was built in 1906 and 1907 and capacity was doubled.

In 1911, the plant was destroyed by fire but again a new facility was constructed that once more increased capacity. By 1915 the Georgia Marble Finishing Works employed 140 workers and had a capital of $100,000. An article written at the time about the company said: "This is an industry which has helped make our town and county and put wealth in our coffers, and our people are interested in its past and look forward to its future with fond hopes that it will continue to add to the growth and wealth of this section."

The article went on to say: "The business of this great plant is sawing and finishing marble for shipment to dealers in all parts of the United States and Canada. The class of its work is second to none; it has a reputation of being the promptest shipper of monumental marble in the South and bears the distinction of being the largest plant in the South doing strictly wholesale monumental business." The plant was operated day and night to keep up with the demand for its product.

Within a decade of Brady opening Georgia Marble Finishing Works in 1891, the success of his business would lead to several other finishing companies in Cherokee County. Among the many other marble companies that

Green stone quarried in Holly Springs was transported by train to be used on buildings around the country, including the Atlanta Train Terminal. While called marble, the stone taken out of the ground in Holly Springs was actually a type of serpentine.

sprung up in Cherokee County were Continental Marble Company and Cherokee Marble Works. Continental Marble Company and Coggins Marble Works were owned by B.F. Coggins or Frank Coggins as he was known. In April of 1914, Coggins Marble Company was destroyed by fire. The plant was located south of the L&N Depot about one-half mile, and according to newspaper reports, made a big fire lighting the country for considerable distance around. "This was one of Canton's most appreciated and growing manufacturing plants and does a large business throughout the South in retailing monuments, wire fencing and other works of an artistic nature. Mr. B.F. Coggins, the president of the concern, is one of the most progressive young businessmen of our town and has succeeded in building up one of the largest retail businesses in this section." The plant was a total loss and a large amount of marble was ruined by the blaze, as well as finished work in the plant that was ready to be loaded and shipped. Although the company did not have adequate insurance, Coggins vowed to rebuild. "Frank is what we call a game businessman and will raise from the ashes of this fire a larger and better plant than ever."

Holly Springs benefited from the rich mineral resources of Cherokee County as well and enjoyed an economic revitalization as it became more industrialized. A green stone, which was serpentine, was quarried in the Holly Springs area in the 1880s. The green "marble" as it was called, was not of quality to be used on exteriors but was beautiful if not strong and used for decorative purposes. It was utilized for the interior of the Atlanta Train Terminal and in other commercial buildings in the area. The green stone was cut and finished in Holly Springs. The finished product was then transported by rail for use around the state and even further. The quarry was located about a mile from the finishing plant and the town. The stones were hauled by mule teams and wagons. The main quarry was a traditional pit, which was a large hole in the ground with nearly vertical walls and was operated on and off for more than 60 years. Another nearby quarry, which may have been older, was a sheer cliff and two shafts sunk into its wall. Extracting the stone from the quarry was difficult, especially with the lack of mechanical machinery for use in the job. The stone was raised from the quarry in the earlier days by a system of pulleys and a steam engine.

Reinhardt Opens New Book for Education

The years following the Civil War brought a new emphasis on education in Cherokee County and the state. In 1868 the state's newly adopted Reconstruction Constitution included a provision for the state's first public school system to be established. The first school funded with public dollars in North

Cherokee County was known as "Swayback" and opened in 1873 two miles north of Waleska under the instruction of teacher Miss Julia Crawford. The one-room school attracted many pupils from among the area's families. Ten years after the opening of the public school, the residents of the north Cherokee community saw a new academy which would include college classes open in Waleska. Reinhardt Normal College was opened in 1883 by Captain Augustus M. Reinhardt and John J.A. Sharp.

Within three years after Swayback School opened, Joseph M. Sharp was conducting classes there. Sharp was one of three brothers who came to Cherokee County around 1855. Their father, John Sharp, had emigrated from Germany to America following the American Revolution.

Military companies were established at Reinhardt Academy in 1893 and, in 1897, military training became mandatory for all able-bodied male students except those preparing for the ministry. In 1891 the school was chartered as Reinhardt Normal College by Georgia Legislature. Here, a group of Reinhardt Cadets enrolled at the school in Waleska around 1900.

When brothers John James Augustus Sharp and White Sharp arrived in Cherokee County from their family home of Walhalla, South Carolina, they quickly established themselves as successful businessmen, and opened a store, a cotton gin and a tobacco store in the northern Cherokee County community. Brother Joseph Sharp pursued education and teaching as his career.

When the Civil War came along, John J.A. Sharp served under General Robert E. Lee, achieving the rank of lieutenant colonel. When he returned home following the war, he found a region sunk in economic despair. A life-long proponent of education, he saw the need for the people of the area to get a good education to help them better face the future. John Sharp had married Mary Jane Reinhardt, the sister of another man who had a dream for better education for those in his community of Waleska. The two teamed up to realize their dream.

Reinhardt Normal College.   Pub. by R. M. Donehoo.

By 1900 Reinhardt Normal College had an enrollment of about 215 students. The school's chapel and administration building, shown here circa 1907, burned down in 1911. When the school was rebuilt after the fire it was renamed Reinhardt College.

Captain Augustus Reinhardt grew up in the rural Cherokee County community of Waleska, served in the Civil War and later went on to be a successful attorney and real estate investor in Atlanta. But he wanted to help start the school to honor his father, Augustus Reinhardt. Gus, as he was known, was the son of Lewis Warlick Reinhardt and Jane Harbin Reinhardt, who settled in Cherokee County in 1834. Augustus Reinhardt was the sixth of their eight children and was born in 1842. Lewis Reinhardt was a successful farmer who operated a mill on Shoal Creek later known as William Ward's Mill. He operated a house of entertainment for travelers at property he purchased on old Pine Log Road. By 1840 the older Reinhardt was leasing out his land to a tenant farmer. A proponent of education, he sent his children to a subscription school. His farm is where the city of Waleska was located, as the Sharp brothers and others began to build around him.

Captain Reinhardt enlisted the aid of the North Georgia Conference of Methodist Churches to establish the new school that year when it met in Dalton. He asked them for help in finding a strong preacher and teacher to lead the school. While he worked to find support, Sharp bought a sawmill and began to make lumber for the new school.

The school opened in a one-room frame building on Cartersville Street. The school began classes in January 1884 and was officially chartered in 1891. By 1900 the school had an enrollment of 215 students.

In the early days the school served all ages, with students from primary grades through college attending that first school year in 1884. About 40 or 50 students enrolled the initial year, and that was considered a large enrollment for the small community of only 100 residents. Most students were not prepared to take college classes, so the academy in the early days mainly served primary and high school students. The tuition was kept low so that even needy children could attend. The first teacher was James T. Linn, to whom Reinhardt agreed to pay a yearly salary of $1,000. Linn was sent to the new school through the efforts of the North Georgia Conference of Methodist Churches. He was a graduate of Emory College and known as a person of great magnetism and force.

Reinhardt's campus gradually took shape over the ensuing years as new buildings were added, including dormitories, a gymnasium and homes for faculty members. The school evolved and offered students such activities as a glee club, debating societies, military training and a basketball team.

Reinhardt continued to serve as a high school until 1956 when Cherokee High School opened and it merged into the new public high school.

A line of dedicated men led Reinhardt College as president down through the generations. President Ramsey Colquitt Sharp, the son of Reinhardt founder John J.A. Sharp, took the reins of the school in 1901. Financial demands plagued his tenure, with too little money and too many expenses piling up a debt that threatened the future of the school. He persevered for 15 years, but in 1916 his health was such that he retired. However, in 1921 he returned to the position to try for another five years to bring financial stability to the college. The school was thriving in attracting students, but tuition alone was not enough and he spent much energy looking for private funds. One donor was Samuel Dobbs, an Atlanta philanthropist who continued to support the college for many years. Dobbs gave money for a new vocational building.

In 1927 William Branton took over as president. Educated at Peabody College in Nashville and Columbia University in New York, the first thing Branton tackled was to get the school accredited as a junior college. Branton remained president for 17 years, helping expand the college with new dorms and an expanded library. Reinhardt was established as a major educational asset for Cherokee County which would continue to enhance the lives of its residents.

Canton High School Offers New Opportunities

With the enlightenment of the new 20th century, the leaders of Canton wanted a better education for the young people of the community. While the Etowah Institute had served the city and its students well for decades, now was the time to provide a new high school that could offer a more competitive and thorough education for those who would be the business and civic leaders of tomorrow.

The idea of Canton High School was first floated in 1912 by newly elected Canton Mayor E.A. McCanless and his city council, R.O. Fincher, C.T. Darnell, E.M. Rudasill, J.W. Chamlee, R.T. Jones and W.K. Moss. It was these men who decided to appoint a school board to construct and staff a new high school. They chose one of the most respected and educated men in the community, Dr. N.J. Coker, to be the chairman, L.A. McClure was chosen as secretary and treasurer and D.D. Towers, G.B. Johnston and C.L. Parmer were asked to stand as members.

The school board in turn selected a man known as an outstanding educator, W.C. Carlton, as the superintendent for the new high school, and in 1914 the lovely brick building with white columns on Academy Street in Canton was built. It housed all eleven grades. Canton High School had all the most modern features of the day: a large auditorium where each morning opening exercises were held, a home economics department, and music and expressions teachers. Classes were soon offered in Latin, French, geometry, as well as literature and the sciences. There was also a drama department.

The new Canton High School also had everything it needed

Canton High School, built in 1914, had modern features including a large auditorium, a home economics department, and music and expressions teachers. Classes were offered in Latin, French, geometry, literature and the sciences. The new Canton High School was the first accredited school in Cherokee County.

Canton High School had a long legacy of winning girls basketball teams. The Girls Basketball Team of 1916 included, from left, Lucille Coker, Rene White, Edna Williams, Elizabeth Archer and Bertie Perry.

to become the first accredited school in Cherokee County. Since it was the only accredited high school in the county, students from all parts of Cherokee were soon attending. The L&N Railroad ran a morning and afternoon train north and south and gave students monthly discounts. Students came from Woodstock, Ball Ground, Holly Springs and Nelson to attend Canton High School. Each morning those students would walk up the hill from the depot to the school and each afternoon board the train to return to their homes.

The high school enjoyed great athletic success. Superintendent Carlton chose the school colors of green and gold and the Canton Greenies were born. From the beginning the high school earned a reputation of great basketball players. Track was also a popular sport for the school. In those early years, the boys played basketball on an outdoor court behind the high school. In 1922 a new gymnasium was constructed for the students' use. And in 1925, Canton High fielded its first football team, which played its games across the Etowah River on the baseball field there.

Athletics was not the only field bringing home trophies. The school's literary teams quickly built a reputation, and students won many district and statewide competitions in debate, music, theater and declamation.

The original building was constructed to hold about 300 students, but as the school's reputation grew and the city and surrounding county population expanded, more space was needed. In 1923 construction on additional classroom space was begun across the street from the original school and in 1924 grades seven to eleven moved into the new building when it opened. Within a few years a new auditorium was built and other amenities including the library and administrative office were added.

In 1924 Professor J.P. Cash became Canton school superintendent. As with past educators in Canton, Cash was a man of great reputation and helped Canton High School to become one of the best and most respected in the state. He was a man known for demanding the best from his teachers and his students. After an illustrious career, he retired in 1939.

While Canton High School took a leadership position in providing an education for county and city residents alike, other schools in communities across the county provided solid educations for students as well as the new century ushered in an era of expansion.

At the turn of the century the leader of the county school system was called commissioner and that post was filled at the time by Commissioner John D. Attaway, who headed the system from 1886 to 1907. Benjamin Franklin Perry then served one year from 1907 to 1908. In 1908 Jabez Galt was the first county school superintendent, and he served until 1911 when T.A. Doss took over the reins. Zach Collins served the county schools as superintendent from 1924 to 1928.

Public schools came to Woodstock in 1908, with the support of Mayor N.A. Fowler and Councilmen W.W. Benson, J.H. Johnston, James Lathem, Mark Paden, and Dr. Will L. Dean. A few years later, a new school was completed on a hilltop lot purchased from Dr. Dean. Professor Tom Doss was the superintendent of the Woodstock schools.

In 1902 a young man named E.T. Booth began his teaching career just across the line from Cherokee County in neighboring Cobb. At the age of 20, the young school teacher already showed promise in the little one room schoolhouse in Benson, his hometown. But it would be in Cherokee County that he reached his full potential as teacher, educator and administrator.

After spending the next 12 years attending seminary as well as teaching, preaching, marrying and raising a family, in 1914 Mr. Booth was offered a job by the Woodstock board of trustees to teach at Woodstock School and-he taught for two years. He then returned to Cobb County, but just after World War I, Professor Booth re-turned to teach at the accredited grade school, which housed students from grades one to 10. Mr. Booth served as principal until he was named school superintendent for Cherokee County in 1937. Students who graduated from Woodstock School went on to Canton or Marietta to receive their diploma from an accredited high school. Mr. Booth is quoted as saying that of the 110 students he taught, 105 went on to high school and 102 went to college. Mr. Booth is credited with helping many exemplary scholars

Woodstock Academy was established in the 1870s and was built on land that belonged to W.H. Dean. It replaced a school that had been located behind Woodstock Baptist Church.

along the way, including Dr. Eugene T. Booth, who became a Rhodes Scholar, was a professor of physics at Columbia University and played an important role in the research to obtain fissionable uranium at Oak Ridge, Tennessee.

In those early days of the 20th century, students brought their own lunches to school. There was no running water, and buckets of drinking water were placed in each schoolroom, along with a dipper. Heat was provided by pot-bellied stoves, and the teachers and larger boys brought in the fuel and kept the stoves stoked. While the facilities were primitive, the education was anything but, with students under Mr. Booth being taught algebra, Latin, and composition, among other subjects. The schoolhouse stood until 1939, when it burned in a fire of unknown cause.

County Government Evolves and Changes

Oversight of Cherokee County government and collection of taxes were handled in the early days of the county's history by the justices of the Inferior Court. Five justices served concurrent terms in the office during the years of 1832 to 1868, when the position was abolished by the state Legislature. There was also a clerk of the Inferior Court during the years that the office was active. In 1850 an amendment to the state Constitution created the office of ordinary. When the Inferior Court was abolished the duties of overseeing the county government in Cherokee County were transferred to other officials, primarily the office of ordinary. Other officials who helped serve the county included the tax receiver and the tax collector as well as the county surveyor, the coroner, the county physician and the sheriff. In 1932 the offices of tax receiver and tax commissioner were combined into that of tax commissioner.

From 1908 to 1910 a board of five commissioners, which included four commissioners elected from districts and the county ordinary, oversaw the management of the Cherokee County government.

J.M. Satterfield was elected ordinary in 1913 to fill an unexpired term and was thrust into what the newspaper of the time called the foremost position in Cherokee politics. "He ran a short and remarkable race and won by a handsome majority, made few promises to friends further than to say that he would to the best of his ability handle the finances of the County and treat every man and every section of the County with all fairness possible." The newspaper reported that Judge Satterfield was handling the finances of Cherokee County remarkably well and that his economic skill meant that very little money would have to be borrowed in 1914.

Then in 1915 a legislative act changed the makeup of the county's government to that of a sole commissioner of roads and revenues. The new post of commissioner was created to manage the county's taxes and property, care for the roads and bridges, levy taxes and other government duties. The first commissioner of roads and revenues was Robert Olin Fincher. He was followed in 1920 by William Joseph Satterfield. Fincher won another term in 1924 and then in 1928 James H. Holcomb of Ball Ground took office.

The new Cherokee County Courthouse was built 1927-29 out of white marble and cost $150,000 to construct. The building was designed by A. Ten Eyck Brown and became an icon of the community.

Coker's Hospital and Doctors of the Day

One of the most well-known names in the medical community of Cherokee County through several generations is that of Coker. Dr. Newton Jasper Coker, who lived from 1868 to1939, founded the first modern hospital in Cherokee County in 1923. The first Coker Hospital was located on East Marietta Street across from the Grisham-Galt House.

Dr. N.J. Coker opened his medical office in Canton in 1910 upon completion of medical school. He was a surgeon and a medical doctor. Dr. N.J. Coker's roots were deep in Cherokee County, and his family was among some of the first settlers. His maternal great-grandparents, Moses and Elizabeth Perkins, were charter members of the First Baptist Church of Canton in 1833.

In 1893 he married Mary Effie Carmichael and they had five children. Their son, Dr. Grady Newton Coker, followed his father's footsteps into medicine and became one of the most well-known and respected doctors in the state, with a medical career that spanned more than 50 years. He helped his father in

Coker's Hospital in Canton was founded by Dr. Newton Jasper Coker to provide good medical care for the community.

Nurses at Coker's Hospital, the first modern hospital in Cherokee County opened in 1923.

the establishment of the county's first hospital, and later in building the new Coker Hospital in 1934 on land east of Canton on the hill overlooking Jeannette and Muriel streets. The new hospital would serve Cherokee County and the surrounding area as the only hospital for the next 29 years. Many residents of Cherokee County were born at Coker Hospital, and many treated there for a variety of illnesses. Coker Hospital was for many years the only hospital between Marietta and Copperhill, Tennessee, and served thousands of North Georgia patients for, as the newspaper said, "about every medical ill known to man."

Dr. Grady, as he was affectionately known by many of his patients, went on to operate the Canton Tumor Clinic in cooperation with the Georgia Department of Public Health, offering help to cancer patients regardless of ability to pay. Dr. Grady Coker also was active in the community and served as the mayor of Canton and one term in the state House of Representatives and three terms as state Senator. Dr. Coker was a member of the Board of Trustees at Reinhardt College. He also owned NeJasCo farms, where he kept a herd of Guernsey cattle and a herd of Black Angus cows. Dr. Grady Coker and another leading long-time doctor in Cherokee County, Dr. Charles R. Andrews, founded the Coker-Andrews Clinic in Canton. Dr. Andrews practiced medicine longer than almost any doctor in Cherokee County.

A doctor with a gift for healing and for ministry left his indelible mark on Woodstock and South Cherokee County. Later his son would follow him into the field of medicine and the two would practice side-by-side for many years. Dr. William Hiram Dean came to Woodstock in the early 1850s after attending medical lectures at New York University and graduating from the Medical College of Georgia. Dr. Dean was born in Covington, Georgia, in 1824 and grew up in DeKalb County. After graduating from medical school, he practiced in Newton County for one year before moving to Woodstock around 1851.

When Dr. Dean moved to Cherokee County he settled into a log home, which was not far from the plantation of Dr. John Miller McAfee, who had recently retired from the practice of medicine. Other doctors, including Dr. John Boring and Dr. Jim Boring, as well as Dr. W.H. Perkinson, also attended to the medical needs of the south Cherokee County area in those days.

After moving to Woodstock, Dr. Dean soon married his life partner, Emily Benson, of Cobb County. The couple had two children and quickly established themselves in the community, where they were active as members of the Enon Baptist Church. In 1862, Dr. Dean was ordained as a minister and became pastor of the

Dr. W.H. Dean was a doctor and a preacher in Woodstock and south Cherokee County before and after the Civil War. He served as a surgeon in the Confederate Army before returning to private practice.

church, but continued to practice medicine as well. During his years as pastor of the church he baptized as many as 800 people.

However, his life work was the practice of medicine. He covered as many as 200,000 miles of country road on horseback, as he tended to the healthcare of his patients. He traveled the roads delivering babies, treating gunshot wounds, sewing up injuries and caring for the sick. His son, William Lemuel Dean, later joined his father in the practice of medicine. The older Dr. Dean helped his son set up his practice by giving him his medical library, medicines and supplies.

Local author Juanita Hughes writes in her book, *Set Apart: the Baptist Church at Woodstock, 1837 to 1987*, "Dr. Dean, beloved of his congregation because he was also their physician, was no different in this respect and like other preachers of his day, he served many churches. Noonday, Sandy Plains, Carmel, Canton, Olive Springs, New Bethel, New Hope, Salem, Roswell, Shoal Creek and Mill Creek, all list him as their pastor."

Dr. Dean also served during the Civil War as a non-commissioned surgeon in the Confederate Army. Mrs. Hughes writes, "He related in later years his relief on returning home that his house still stood, although the hogs and chickens were gone. He suffered losses within the church fellowship, as noted by him in the church minutes. The beloved church clerk, T.W. Putnam, was killed in battle."

Dr. Dean's grandson, Linton Albert Dean, owned and operated the Dean Drug Store for 75 years. The store opened in 1906 by Dr. W.L. Dean, who was in poor health at the time he applied for the permit to open the pharmacy. Soon after opening the new pharmacy Dr. Dean died at the age of 49. Linton Dean was only 20 at the time, but took over operation of the store which began to sell general over-the-counter remedies. The store would be a city mainstay for the next 75 years.

One man remembered in Cherokee County as a country doctor was Dr. W.O. Rhodes. He was born William Oscar Rhodes in 1883. He studied at Pearson School in Birmingham, Alabama, where he met his future wife, Mattie Land. They were married in 1900 when he was 17 and she was 15 years old. After five years of marriage, he decided to attend medical school and took his life savings and attended the Georgia College of Medicine and Surgery. They then moved first to Holly Springs, then Woodstock, and finally to Hickory Flat community because he heard that area needed a doctor. It was there where he would ultimately practice for the rest of his life.

Dr. Rhodes built a house in Hickory Flat with his office adjacent to the living quarters where he saw his patients. He usually did not charge for a routine office visit. He did have a medicine which he formulated that was prescribed for stomach ailments. The good doctor charged for the medicines. Also, there was a $25 charge for delivering a

Dr. William O. Rhodes moved his practice to Hickory Flat because he heard the community needed a doctor. He and his wife, here in 1918, traveled the road in his Model-T during the flu epidemic, often staying the night at the homes of the sick. He was one of the first to abandon a horse and buggy in favor of the automobile.

Dr. John P. Turk was a prominent doctor in Canton who was retained by the Georgia Marble Company, which charged each employee a small fee to help pay the good doctor for his visits to the employees when they were sick.

baby. It is said that he delivered more than 4,000 babies during his years as doctor. Those who could not pay bartered with chickens, eggs or even a piece of furniture.

The doctor's wife would man the four telephones in the home, which gave patients the ability to easily reach the doctors. In the early days he made his calls in a horse and buggy, but as soon as possible he bought a Model-T automobile. During the flu epidemic he and his wife traveled to the patients, often staying overnight to tend the sick.

Dr. Rhodes and his wife also were instrumental in building the Hickory Flat school and went around the community raising funds for the project. Dr. Rhodes continued to practice in the community for 59 years right up until his death in 1969.

Another country doctor of note was Dr. J.P. Saye, who practiced in Ball Ground. Dr. Saye was born on March 29, 1860, in Woodstock, and following a tumultuous childhood put himself through medical school at the Georgia Medical College. Dr. Saye married Angie Boling in 1911 and the couple had two sons, Maynard P. Saye and Dr. Ernest B. Saye.

Dr. Saye's office was in his home in Ball Ground. Like doctors of the day, he visited his patients night and day in his horse and buggy, often with his wife by his side. She was quoted as saying that her husband often went down on his knees to pray before making house calls to extremely sick patients. He was also known to have an old secret Indian remedy for appendicitis said to be successful. He later drove a Model-T Ford and then a Model-A Ford for his house calls. He continued to make house calls most of his life, even when younger doctors did not. Dr. Saye's first wife died and he later remarried, but is buried with his first wife in the Ball Ground Community Cemetery.

Another doctor remembered for making the rounds was Dr. Samuel Harbin, who was born in Cherokee County in 1873, the son of pioneer stock. Dr. Harbin attended Atlantic Eclectic Medical College before beginning his practice of medicine. He was a familiar sight in his horse-drawn buggy as he served the needs of his patients in and around Canton. He was one of the most prominent physicians of his time.

Dr. John Thomas Pettit practiced medicine in Canton for 39 years and was an active member of the community, familiar to all the residents. Born August 24, 1869, in Cedartown, Dr. Pettit went on to graduate in 1910 from the Atlanta School of Medicine, which later became Emory University. He married Alma Quarles of Cherokee County in 1910. In addition to serving as a family doctor and successful position in Cherokee County, Dr. Pettit faithfully served his community in the Canton Rotary Club and as Canton mayor for two years. He and his wife

Dr. J.P. Saye, whose home, above, was in Ball Ground, practiced medicine in the community for years. He was also known for a secret remedy he had for appendicitis that it was said came from the Cherokees.

had two daughters, one of whom, Rachel Palmer, was a popular and well-loved elementary school teacher in Canton

Another doctor from Canton who became prominent was Dr. John P. Turk. He was born in Canton in 1879, the son of another doctor, John Milton Turk and Virgin Florine Shockley. John Milton Turk had become a doctor following a measles outbreak in Calhoun County, Alabama that had killed seven of their ten children. Almost every descendant of this Turk family became a doctor due to this tragedy.

In 1907, John P. Turk married Mary Elizabeth Scott, the daughter of Aquilla King Scott and Malissa Tryphena Brooke. They had four sons, John P. Turk, Jr., Aquilla Scott Turk, William Brooke Turk, and Tully Robert Turk. In 1915, Dr. Turk went to work for the Georgia Marble Company and served the community until his death in 1944. The Georgia Marble Company would retain 50 cents, later increased to a dollar, from each employee and used this as payment for Dr. Turk for the unlimited visits by families to his office.

Potter Makes His Mark

In the early 1900s folk potter Edward Leslie Stork moved to Cherokee County and began a business that would produce hundreds or even thousands of clay churns, pitchers, bowls and jugs that would leave a lasting legacy in the county's history. E.L. Stork was born into the business and learned his craft from his family in South Carolina before moving to Georgia and eventually permanently locating to Cherokee County. He moved to the Orange community around 1910 and by about 1915 owned 120 acres. It was on this property that he built his kiln and got the clay that would be shaped into the Southern folk pottery for which he is remembered.

Stork Pottery was described in writings by John A. Burrison, included in a paper by Mary Free, as "the usual utilitarian household items used locally – churns, pitchers, jugs and flowerpots, E.L Stork was sensitive also to the tastes of an expanding tourist market, …and possessed the artistry and inclination to pursue this market…..He made fancy urns and flowerpots which rested on a stand, with applied clay decorations turned out from homemade molds." Stork Pottery also included miniature souvenir churns and sets of tableware, including cups, saucers and plates.

While some folk potters made face jugs, Stork was known for his ring jug, which has a neck and loop handle at the top, and an oblong foot which allows the jug to stand at the base. Stork made the two concave halves separately on his potter's wheel and joined them while they were still damp to form a circular tube. He used a shiny light olive glaze on the pieces.

He had a stamp that he had made himself that he used to mark his pottery. He would also take a stick and mark the number of gallons that the piece would hold. Sometimes Stork would date his piece. He used a glaze that he special ordered from Michigan. When he had made enough pieces to fill the kiln, he would fire the kiln and let the pieces process for

Edward Stork, a potter who made thousands of pieces out of clay, lived in the Orange community with his family, above. Stork pottery is highly collectible, especially the ring jug which was a signature piece, above right.

two to three days. Once they were complete, Stork would load them on his wagon and take them to Canton, Ball Ground and into North Georgia to sell.

In 1925 Stork died and while there were some efforts to keep his pottery operation going, they failed. Many collectors still look for the pottery made from Cherokee County soil with the unique design of the day and the era.

Life of Gus Coggins a Fascinating Tale

The life of Augustus "Gus" Lee Coggins is one of the most dramatic stories in the annals of Cherokee County history. Gus Coggins was a farmer and livestock dealer who produced what were considered some of the best horses and mules in the country, as well as fine herds of cattle. As the *Cherokee Advance* put it, "He deals in livestock on a large scale and raises them for the benefit of his county and to demonstrate to his fellow men that there is money in the business." The story of Gus Coggins is also the story of Crescent Farm, the racehorse Abbedale and the battle against the dark forces of the Night Riders. The beautiful brick home he built overlooking the Etowah River known as Edgewater Hall and the Rock Barn which survived the test of time are both memorials to the life of Gus Coggins.

Augustus Coggins, here circa 1900, married Daisy Ryman and settled at the Crescent Farm in Canton.

Controversies surrounding Gus Coggins were many. His practice of hiring of African-American workers was unpopular in North Georgia and led to violence and destruction when several of his barns were burned. That was also a factor in his eventual financial ruin. He also lost a fortune when the mules he was selling for the Great War in Europe could not be shipped overseas because of blockade efforts of the Germans. Then, the bank he was involved with in Cherokee County failed and many people lost their deposits. At that point Coggins was considered financially ruined, but rumors persisted that he had emerged from the crisis as a rich man and moved out of state with his fortune. However, most evidence indicated that instead he moved away from Cherokee County to escape the dislike and persecution he faced in his hometown and that he actually died practically penniless.

The Coggins family moved to Cherokee County following the Civil War at a time when lawlessness was rampant in the far reaches of North Georgia. Later, those same negative forces would play a part in the downfall of a man who at one time was one of Canton and Cherokee County's most beloved citizens.

The main house of Augustus Coggins' Crescent Farm, known for its race horses, was called Edgewater Hall and was a Georgian Revival-style residence designed by noted architect Francis Smith and built in 1922. An earlier Victorian dwelling on the property was home to Coggins in the early 1900s.

Coggins' father, Alfred B. Coggins, was a Confederate veteran. He returned home to Gilmer County following the end of the conflict that brought devastation to the South. Gus was born in 1868, one of nine children. The older Coggins wanted to find a new hometown that offered a better educational opportunity for his family and a more law-abiding community in which to do business. After moving to Canton with his young family, Alfred

Coggins quickly established himself as a leading merchant in Cherokee County. As his children began to come of age, they too began to make a mark for themselves in the community they chose as their home and none more so than son Gus.

In 1894 Coggins married Daisy Ryman of Nashville, Tennessee. Her father was the owner and operator of the Ryman Steamboat Lines and constructed a large auditorium in Nashville familiar to millions of people as Ryman Auditorium. Around the time of his marriage, Coggins leased the 350-acre property known as Crescent Farm, which was situated on the top of the hill called Mount Etowah. The Native Americans once walked the lands that later became Crescent Farm, following paths that crisscrossed the land down to the flat rocks that jutted out over the river. There the Cherokee fished the waters of the river. The first settler to build on Crescent Farm was James McKinney, who purchased the property in 1840 from Felix Moss. It became known as the McKinney plantation. The property then sold to Robert F. Maddox, who built the first frame house on the land in the 1880s. He was one of the men instrumental in bringing the railroad to Canton. From newspaper clippings of the time it appears that the home was used as a summer villa for the Maddox family. The original house was a one-story Victorian-style home with porches on three sides. Maddox sold the house and farm in 1887 to his partner Major Campbell Wallace. Coggins purchased the farm in 1903, after leasing it for several years.

Coggins originally lived in the Victorian house and his daughter Elizabeth Coggins Jones was born in the house in 1899. She later told of the homeplace, which opened on the north side onto a court, and on one side of the court was the kitchen and the other side the carding and quilting room.

The Crescent Farm was a working plantation under the management of Coggins with department heads managing each segment of its operation. A white overseer was in charge of the crops and planting, according to family members. But many of the other managers and workers were African-Americans. Many workers who had formerly been slaves were hired by Coggins, who had a reputation for being a keen businessman. Pete Green, an African-American man who had an imposing appearance was in charge of the mules and the livestock. Another African-American, John Heard, was in charge of the vegetable garden, orchard, personal riding horses and family buggy and surrey. In addition to the farm managers, Coggins hired a large workforce of former slaves and freed men.

Coggins, who also owned livery stables in Canton and in Atlanta and had a mule brokerage business, constructed a number of wooden barns for his operation. Many of those barns were mysteriously destroyed by fire. The first Coggins barn to be destroyed by fire was in February of 1900. The race horse named Queen Nab was destroyed in the fire. Queen Nab had won the Derby in Macon in 1891, capturing a purse of $6,000. She also won races in Knoxville and at the Georgia State Fair in 1891. The cause of the fire was never known. The *Cherokee Advance* reported, "It has often been said that you cannot get a horse out of a burning building, but Hannah, Mrs. Coggins' buggy horse, broke out of her stable, jumped over the lot fence, and ran all the way over to town, and had to be carried back to the farm. Queen Nab, the mare that was burned, was one of the best race horses in the state, and was considered the best animal in the barn."

Crescent Farm Stable, also known as the Rock Barn, was constructed in 1906 by Gus Coggins after several of his wooden barns burned.

In 1906 Gus Coggins built the Rock Barn to house his fine racehorses. The barn was rock on the lower level and brick on the gable portion, with an open latticed gabled end. Marble sills were at each window. The cross-hatched timber gable permitted air to circulate through the hay stored in the loft. The rocks used for building materials were dug from the Etowah River. While no one knows for sure, many theorize that Coggins chose the materials he did for his barn so that it would not succumb to the dangers of fire and the threat of the Night Riders.

In 1915 at a time when the Night Riders were becoming bolder, another fire destroyed one of the barns on the property and this time they claimed credit for the act of terrorism. According to reports in the Atlanta newspapers the Night Riders were charged with destruction of the property, valued at $75,000 after an unsigned note cautioning employers of former slaves to cease from the activity. The fire killed 162 of Coggins' mules and burned 15,000 bushels of corn.

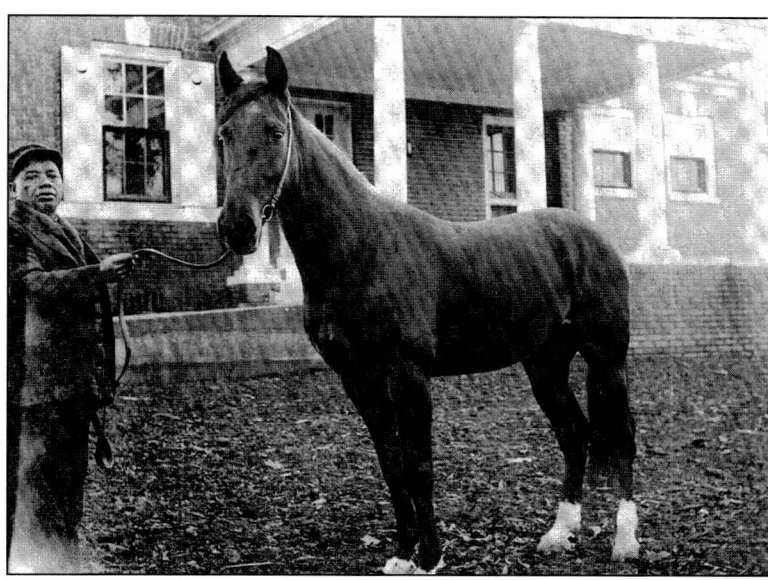
Pete Green holds one of Crescent Farm's notable horses, Little Sled, in front of Edgewater Hall.

Fire struck again in 1917 when the Coggins home, the stately Victorian, was destroyed. A third barn used to house the mules was burned in the early 1920s. Although the house fire was not believed to be the work of the Night Riders, at one time or another almost every building on the extensive property burned to the ground.

In 1922 Coggins rebuilt his home, this time out of brick to last. Designed by Atlanta architect Francis P. Smith, the Georgian Revival style home withstood the test of time. The beautiful structure originally contained five bedrooms, three baths, a living room, sunroom, breakfast room and kitchen. A lovely walnut staircase graced the foyer and eight fireplaces kept the residence warm. In addition to red brick, locally quarried marble was used as accents throughout the structure. He called the new family home Edgewater Hall. It was during those years that Crescent Farm established an even more impressive name in racing circles with Abbedale, its world-class pacer. Abbedale, born and raised in the Rock Barn, is listed in the Harness Racing Hall of Fame in Goshen, NY. Abbedale also earned recognition in *Harness Racing*, a book by Phillip Pines.

Both the Ku Klux Klan and Night Riders were active in Cherokee County during this time. However, the Night Riders were a vigilante group and the Klan an organized white, Protestant supremacy group. This is the cover of a Kloran handbook for one of the members of Canton Klan #70. Woodstock also had an active chapter (#164) during 1920s.

But even as Coggins was rebuilding, events were converging together that would end in his financial downfall. Just at the time when the most devastating fire destroyed most of his livestock, the cotton market began to fall. Cotton was a major crop of Crescent Farm. Coggins and his brother had received government contracts to supply Allied troops in Europe with mules during the World War.

But the German U boats, which controlled the shipping channels, blocked his efforts to transport the livestock, and when the war ended in 1918, he was left with a large surplus of mules. Just at that time the automobile began to gain in popularity and the market for horses and mules was adversely affected.

Then the Bank of Cherokee, of which he had served as president, succumbed to economic factors of the day and closed its doors, out of business. According to his daughter, Elizabeth, Coggins tried to broker a deal to sell Crescent Farm and pay off his debtors. That fell through and all of Coggins' holdings, including his farm and home were sold at auction. Coggins left Cherokee County for a number of years, but prior to his death in 1952 his daughter brought him back to Georgia to stay in her Atlanta home. Elizabeth noted that 120 people came to visit him the first Sunday after he arrived. He died of leukemia several months later at the age of 84 and was buried in Canton.

In 1914 the local newspaper had written, "Gus Coggins probably has more friends than any other man in the county. The people he has not accommodated in some way are scarce in this community. He is bighearted to the last degree, and always responds to the call of the weak and suffering. He owns stock in every church and school house nearly in the county. His greatest pride is that he makes money but that he doesn't make it all for himself."

The events of Gus Coggins life dramatically depict the history of the times in which he lived. He would probably be proud that the acreage that comprised Crescent Farm in its glory days later became home to Cherokee High School, Canton Elementary School, the National Guard Armory, and numerous other businesses. The Cherokee County Board of Education donated the Rock Barn to the Cherokee County Historical Society and it now serves as an events facility as well as preserves the past.

Great War Touches Cherokee County

The first signs of the impending World War whose talons of hate and destruction would eventually claw at the very soul of the country began to be seen in Cherokee County through news reports in the *Cherokee Advance*. On October 13, 1916, the main headlines of the newspaper stated, "Germany U-53 Gets Six Ships." The article told of how the submarine arm of the Imperial German Navy "ravaged off the eastern coast of the United States with four British, one Dutch and one Norwegian steamer sent to the bottom of the ocean or left crippled off the Nantucket Shoals." The war, which at one time had seemed so far away, began to appear much closer.

In the summer of 1917 as the United States prepared to go to war with Germany, in the quiet streets of Canton men were lining up to sign on for military service for their country. Within a month of war being declared by President Woodrow Wilson, more than 135 men had signed up to serve from Cherokee County. Canton led the state for communities of its size with enlistments. In all, around 500 men from all across Cherokee County served in the Great War. Sixteen men from Cherokee County died in the war, giving the ultimate sacrifice for their country. The first man to die from the community in the war was Thomas M. Brady, Jr., son of the marble finisher. He was buried in his family plot at the Riverview Cemetery in Canton.

In January 1918, President Wilson called on all industries to have a five-day moratorium on operations to conserve fuel for the war effort. In Cherokee County, Canton Cotton Mills, Georgia Marble Finishing Works, Coggins Marble Company and others shut down to make their contribution to the fight for victory.

Henry G. Gibbs from Ball Ground fought in World War I. He returned home and passed away of lung disease in 1926.

War bonds were sold by most of the banks in the county. Following the war, bonds for the Victory Fund were sold by the local banks to help speed the economic recovery of the county from the depletion of the war efforts. It was reported in a local newspaper advertisement for the bonds following the end of the war that in Cherokee County "We have many things to be thankful for. We have won a great victory. Only a few of our boys paid the ultimate sacrifice; our country is prosperous, and we are sure our people who have so nobly supported every cause presented them in the interest of our country will now gladly come forward and crown Cherokee's record of honor with a full victory in the sale of the issue of Government notes."

The Peace Day Parade in Canton in 1918 was a time of great celebration. Here, crowds rejoice over the end of the war on Main Street in Canton in front of the Crisler-Green house on Main Street. The home was later demolished.

The July 4th celebration in Brown Park in Canton the year following the war drew a record crowd of 8,000 citizens to honor the veterans who served in the war. A parade, speeches, a dinner for the veterans and games including races and a slow mule race were part of the day's events.

With international affairs settled, and the new century well underway, Cherokee County was poised for the highs and lows of a heyday of growth and prosperity in the roaring Twenties, followed by the depths of the Great Depression.

PARTS
WILL NOT BE EXCHANGED
OR TAKEN BACK
AFTER 9 DAYS

Roscoe Spears and Griffin Roberts built a one-story red brick commercial building on East Marietta Street in 1917 for a Ford dealership. A stone plate names the building as the Old Ford Building and it is now used as office space. Here, Grady Price and Roscoe Spears greet the public in the parts department.

Chapter Five

Best of Times and Worst of Times

The early 1920s were a time of great prosperity for towns throughout Cherokee County, despite the threat of the boll weevil, low prices on king cotton and high prices on almost everything else. The World War was over, the country was optimistic and the South had survived the economic upheaval of Reconstruction. In 1920 about 18,653 people called Cherokee County home, and over the next decade the population would grow slowly to about 20,003, according to United States Census figures. While the number of people did not increase substantially, the quality of life was improving, with the towns throughout the county showing extensive new building and business expansion. During the decade leading to the years of the Great Depression, Cherokee County cities experienced good times and new leaders emerged. Building proceeded at a frenzied pace and as the 1920s drew to a close it seemed Cherokee County could not stop booming. The decade that came to be known throughout the country as the Roaring Twenties for its excess and wealth is remembered in Cherokee County for solidity and growth.

Those prosperous times would end more quickly than anyone could imagine and give way to the Great Depression of the 1930s. Even in 1929 as the building boom peaked and the finishing touches were still being put on the new marble courthouse in Canton, Cherokee County was beginning to feel the effects of the major economic downturn that started with the New York Stock Exchange crash in October 1929 and would affect the county and the nation for the next decade. The events of Black Thursday and the following days and weeks swept through the large cities and towns and eventually their impact began to be felt in smaller towns and rural areas. Cherokee County was not immune, but perhaps because of the conservative nature of the residents, and the fortitude that began with the early settlers and hardened during the war years, local residents came through the tough times better than most. Families struggled in those harsh years of the 1930s to put enough food on the table, but most did not go hungry as a barter system developed, and residents banded together to help each other make it through. For some a source of revenue flowed freely in the form of moonshine, as distribution of the homemade corn liquor expanded during the years of Prohibition. But the operations of stills also brought federal revenue agents into the hills of north Georgia.

Cherokee and its Cities Enjoy Heyday of Success

Canton, as the county seat, was the county's major center of commerce and business as well as

Canton Cotton Mill No. 2 was constructed in 1924 during a heyday of expansion in Canton.

government. In 1920 the town had a bustling population of about 2,679 people. In one 12-month period in the mid-1920s Canton saw 250 new homes constructed. But that was just the start of the major construction that fueled the town during much of the decade. The new First Methodist Church and the new First Baptist Church buildings in downtown Canton were constructed in the 1920s, with both facilities completed in 1925. The new Methodist church, which today is an arts center, was one of the few churches of its size which was paid for before it was dedicated by then Bishop Warren Chandler. In 1929 a new post office was built, a neo-classical building whose façade lent an impressive air to Main Street.

In 1929 the white marble courthouse was completed on the square in Canton, considered one of the most striking buildings at the time in any town in the state and region. The new courthouse was built after a fire on March 5, 1927, destroyed the circa 1874 courthouse. The old courthouse was already in some disrepair when it was destroyed, and the Cherokee County grand jury had previously recommended it be replaced. The gleaming new courthouse made of North Georgia marble seemed an appropriate icon of the halcyon days of the late 1920s, a time of great affluence for the city.

Canton Cotton Mills continued to grow with No. 2 Mill constructed around 1924 and the new North Canton Mill Village built in the 1920s to house the workers for the facility "across the river." The new mill was much larger than the original compound closer to town known as No. 1 Mill. The new mill contained state-of-the-art equipment and modern machinery including 750 looms and 23,000 spindles. It employed around 600 in its work force. To serve its employees, North Canton School was built and maintained by the Canton Cotton Mills for the convenience of the families in the mill village. In 1929 the mill office was built in the downtown Canton area, constructed of brick accented with marble. The new facility replaced the original frame office building and marked the continued success of the local mills.

The Bank of Canton was a strong bellwether of the state of affairs in the city. In the 1920s leading residents from across the county made up the bank's board, including R.T. Jones, Sam Tate, B.F. Crisler, P.W. Jones, J.E. Johnston, G.B. Johnston, E.A. McCanless, J.T. Moore, J.N. Simpson, H.C. McAfee and William Galt. In 1924 the Main Street bank building was given a major face-lift and expansion. The newly remodeled building was larger, featuring local Cherokee grey marble including two 17-foot columns on the front and marble fixtures throughout the interior. The new bank offices included a cashier's office, a room for ladies to conduct business, and a gallery overlooking the lobby, as well as a spectacular skylight with electric lights surrounding it.

A second major bank located in Canton in 1927, was the Etowah Bank. The first president of the new financial institute was Olin Fincher, and he remained a director and officer for 41 years. Others who were instrumental in the Etowah Bank's financial success included N.A. Thomason, one of the original employees of the bank, who was cashier when the bank opened and continued to serve in leadership roles for 52 years. N.E. Fackler was the assistant cashier and was associated with the bank for 45 years.

Other officers and directors included Henry Grady Vandiviere and J.H. Bagwell. The county was not without its bank failures however, as both the Bank of Cherokee and the Bank of Ball Ground shut their doors in the 1920s. The Farmers and Traders Bank which served Canton from 1910 to 1912 had also closed.

In 1926 a local Chamber of Commerce was initiated by a group of local businessmen, and in the next decade would lend support to commercial and business endeavors in the county. The new Chamber of Commerce met for the first time on November 4, 1926, with more than 150 people present, and 76 charter businesses and individuals signed up for membership. Early advertisements listed the new Chamber as an

Etowah Bank was chartered in 1927 and took the space of the failed Bank of Cherokee. Original employees included assistant cashier N.E. Fackler, left, and cashier N.A Thomason, left, here with another early employee, Miss Matthews.

agency for advertising this splendid section of Georgia to the homeseeker, and bringing to attention of the outsider the many advantages of this section.

The organization remained strong as the county moved into the years of the Great Depression, often dominating the front page of the newspaper with reports of its banquets and meetings. The organization met at the Hotel Canton. In an article in the *Cherokee Advance* in 1931, it was reported that the organization had its most successful banquet in its history. The organization pointed to high points from the year as sponsoring the Cherokee County Fair, helping to fund a new gymnasium for Reinhardt College, and efforts made by the Chamber to keep the passenger train service intact for the community. Earlier that year the Louisville and Nashville Railroad Company applied to the state Public Service Commission for permission to cut passenger service to Cherokee County in half, discontinuing two trains to the communities they served in the county. The Chamber of Commerce appointed P.W. Jones, W.S. Elliott, and Smith L. Johnston of Woodstock to a committee to formulate a plan to keep the train service intact.

The annual banquet was presided over by President E.A. McCanless and Vice President William Galt. W.S. Elliott, president of the Bank of Canton, was the toastmaster for the evening. R.B. "Dad" Sims provided the musical entertainment by the First Baptist Church choir.

Another effort of the organization included working to meet educational needs in the community and hosting a

The movie theatre in Canton opened in 1911 and by the 1930s was called the Haven Theatre. Here, a promotion for the movie *Tailspin* was under way in 1939.

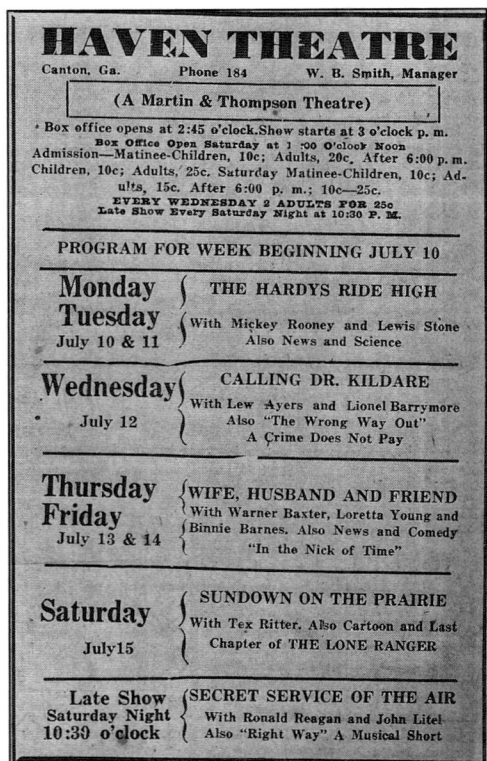

HAVEN THEATRE

Canton, Ga. Phone 184 W. B. Smith, Manager

(A Martin & Thompson Theatre)

Box office opens at 2:45 o'clock. Show starts at 3 o'clock p. m.
Box Office Open Saturday at 1 :00 O'clock Noon
Admission—Matinee-Children, 10c; Adults, 20c. After 6:00 p.m.
Children, 10c; Adults, 25c. Saturday Matinee-Children, 10c; Adults, 15c. After 6:00 p. m.; 10c—25c.
EVERY WEDNESDAY 2 ADULTS FOR 25c
Late Show Every Saturday Night at 10:30 P. M.

PROGRAM FOR WEEK BEGINNING JULY 10

Monday
Tuesday
July 10 & 11
{ THE HARDYS RIDE HIGH
With Mickey Rooney and Lewis Stone
Also News and Science

Wednesday
July 12
{ CALLING DR. KILDARE
With Lew Ayers and Lionel Barrymore
Also "The Wrong Way Out"
A Crime Does Not Pay

Thursday
Friday
July 13 & 14
{ WIFE, HUSBAND AND FRIEND
With Warner Baxter, Loretta Young and Binnie Barnes. Also News and Comedy
"In the Nick of Time"

Saturday
July15
{ SUNDOWN ON THE PRAIRIE
With Tex Ritter. Also Cartoon and Last Chapter of THE LONE RANGER

Late Show
Saturday Night
10:30 o'clock
{ SECRET SERVICE OF THE AIR
With Ronald Reagan and John Litel
Also "Right Way" A Musical Short

A playbill from the Canton Theatre when it was the Haven, 1939.

meeting of education leaders in the county, including Dr. N.J. Coker, president of the County Board of Education and Professor R.C. Sharp, county school superintendent.

Canton residents enjoyed such activities as the latest movies at the Canton theatre, which opened around 1911 with silent movies and magic lantern slide shows. By the 1920s the prominently located theatre on Main Street had new ownership and was called the Bonita and then later renamed the Haven. The popular entertainment location showed first run movies such as *Singing Fool*, the original talking picture that starred Al Jolson. By the 1930s, the movie house was elaborately remodeled in the Art Deco style of the day, with rich velvet hangings, the latest equipment and air conditioning to offer a cool respite during warm weather for movie watchers. Red and blue uniformed employees welcomed patrons and the Candy Bar concession stand beckoned with an array of tasty concoctions and popcorn. Neon lights inside and out showcased the popular offerings from Hollywood. Each week large advertisements in the local newspaper promised local residents a break from the monotony of the tough times of the Depression.

Woodstock was the center of some of the richest agricultural land in the county, which helped the south Cherokee city to grow and thrive during the early part of the twentieth century. With the train depot as the centerpiece of downtown, commerce was strong. Cotton warehouses lined the tracks, and farmers who produced major crops of cotton had access to gins and to procurers for their crops. Cotton suppliers with warehouses included J.H. Johnston, D.J. Haney, H.C. McAfee and O.D. Perkinson.

Woodstock did not claim to be a summer resort, but according to an article in the *Atlanta Constitution* in 1919, visitors viewed it as a beautiful summer spot providing a pleasant respite for those who spent time in the town. Woodstock was home to at least one hotel, the Dial, and according to the article, "it is not operated on such a plan as one would expect to find in any of the larger cities or towns, it is a comfortable house, where the best food that can be had, in a section where good food abounds, is always on the table, and where a man is made to feel that his host is genuinely glad to have him in his house."

Members of the Woodstock City Council at the time

Main Street in Woodstock was paved in 1929. The downtown, here circa 1935, was the commercial hub for the southern portion of Cherokee County and the farmers of the area.

Millicent Barnes Fox and her mother, Bertha McAfee Barnes, cross the railroad tracks at Main Street and Arnold Mill Road in downtown in Woodstock in 1940. Bank of Woodstock on the corner was founded in 1905.

were Paul Clark, W.P. Chandler, W.D. Bozeman, and J.W. Johnston. The mayor was H.C. McAfee. According to the *Atlanta Constitution*, "these gentlemen represent the substantial and yet the progressive business element of the community, and they are heartily in sympathy with every movement. That means a bigger and better Woodstock."

In 1929 Main Street in Woodstock was paved. The newly paved street was 18 feet wide at the time, enough for the automobiles of the day to get by. The first street lights were installed in Woodstock in 1925 by the Georgia Railway and Power Company. The street lights in the business district only consisted of four incandescent lights, but it was enough to illuminate the town for the residents and help usher in a new era. Woodstock also had a telephone system with as many as 150 subscribers to the exchange. Many of the farmers in the area had telephones in their homes, which were served by the Woodstock exchange.

One of the major farmers in the region was Henry Hubbard. Hubbard was one of the eight children of Newton Ervin Hubbard and Emily Lovinggood, descendants of early settlers of the Sweetwater area of the Etowah River, who married in 1861. The farm consisted of about 300 acres of land that produced cotton and other crops. Henry also operated the ferry near the farm.

Another family to contribute to the economy of south Cherokee was Samuel David McCleskey who married Mahalie Wheeler in 1901 and moved to Cherokee County from Cobb County. The couple purchased about 300 acres of land in the Trickum area off the Alabama Highway, which is now Highway 92. The couple raised cotton, corn and wheat, along with other crops. McCleskey also had a blacksmith shop and a store. The family members are buried at Little River United Methodist Church Cemetery.

The Bank of Woodstock, which had opened in 1905, was a major contributor to the success of the city. The bank was the second to be opened in Cherokee County and was the only bank within 10 miles of the city for the next 70 years. Original directors included J.H. Johnston, Robert F. Maddox, an Atlanta financier who helped start the bank, A.R. Fowler, W. Parks Dobbs, Wiley Dobbs and C.C. Dobbs. J.H. Johnston was the president and S.L. Johnston was vice president. W.L. Dupree was the cashier and the bank had a reputation of being one of the most solid and progressive banks of North Georgia.

In 1933 E.M. Barrett moved his mercantile business into the store on the corner of Palm and Hickory streets. Barrett, one of the city's leading citizens for decades, started his business in nearby Toonigh in 1907.

In Holly Springs, the city had lost population in the 1900s and in 1920 the marble quarry which employed a major portion of the town's population shut down leaving 70 men without jobs. Cotton prices also played a major part in the town's economy, as the years following the First World War saw cotton drop when the staple began to be imported. The agricultural land in the area was beginning to show signs of being overworked after decades of cotton production. Several of the large scale farms in the Holly Springs area were shut down and many tenant farmers who worked on them were displaced.

Nine large farms, however, continued to operate in the Holly Springs area, and in the city several stores, including a grocery and two mercantile stores, were in operation. Hardy DeLay was one of the merchants in the town who operated a store, but in 1925 the wooden building caught fire and burned to the ground. DeLay, who was also mayor of Holly Springs and the city judge at the time, rebuilt and restocked the store. But later that year, he sold the store to another proprietor, E.M. Barrett, who operated the store in the landmark building that stands at the corner of Hickory and Palm streets. As city judge DeLay was hearing cases involving public drunkenness, fighting and "jumping trains," which meant jumping aboard freight and passenger trains without paying, and sometimes riding the metal rods beneath the train cars.

In September 1925 the Holly Springs City Council voted to bring electricity to the rural town. Members of the council voting included George Kelly, R.L. Pool, Barrett and W.S. Elliot. The first lights installed in the city were six street lights. Residents who wanted the electric service paid a small fee to connect their wired homes to the power source. The town consisted of 34 homes, most of them in the Folk Victorian style, which was defined by porches with spindle-work detailing, L-shaped or gable fronts, simple details and asymmetrical floor plans. The late 19th century architecture was made possible when railroads expanded into small towns like Holly Springs and made mass-produced wooden trim features and ornament readily available.

Although Holly Springs had no theater, occasionally traveling projectionists would come through the town and go before the city council for permission to set up equipment and show movies. The city received a portion of the gate proceeds that was used to fund the Holly Springs School expenses. Baseball was also a recreational pastime in Holly Springs, and the city was home to the Wildcats team, a traveling club that played across north Georgia and built a

The Ball Ground post office was one of the busiest in the country during the city's heyday of marble finishing work.

reputation for the city. The Wildcats were financed by Barrett, who also served as mayor for a number of years from 1931 to 1939.

Ball Ground's most prosperous era was 1910 to 1930 when the town grew to more than 800 residents and was the second largest town in the county. In those prosperous decades Ball Ground boasted two hotels, a movie theater, three churches, a city school system, four doctors, a dentist, a swimming pool and other attractions for its residents and visitors. In 1915 the Nelson-Ball Ground Telephone Service offered residents the valuable service. The Roberts Marble Company during that time contributed to the prosperity of the town, helping to bring electricity in 1916 when the marble finishing company built a dam on Long Swamp Creek to furnish power for its mill. Soon the company was selling

The Stripling-Lovelady house is the largest and most elaborate Neoclassical Revival house in the county. D.C. Stripling, manager of the Bank of Ball Ground, built the residence in 1912. The original floor plan was a central hallway with three rooms on each side.

electricity to the city and Ball Ground became one of the first areas in the county to have power. The lake was also a popular recreational attraction until it was sold to Georgia Power Company in the 1930s. The utility company destroyed the dam following the purchase.

While the city was prosperous, there were also several tragedies and disasters. In 1915 a tornado hit, destroying the Baptist church, Methodist church and the school. All buildings were replaced. Both church congregations built brick places of worship, but the school was replaced with a wooden structure that burned in 1923. In 1927 the hotel on Gilmer Ferry Road next to the railroad was destroyed by fire, as well as the Lovelady Store next door. The entire business district was threatened by the blaze, but firemen set up a bucket brigade on the roofs of the nearby buildings and kept the fire from spreading

The city got its first bank in 1906. The Bank of Ball Ground was opened in a small building next to City Hall on Gilmer Ferry Road. In 1916 the bank declared bankruptcy after the manager, D.C. Stripling, allegedly embezzled money to build an impressive Neoclassical Revival Home on the highest hill in the city. The grand mansion with columns and inlaid floors later became known as the "house that broke the bank."

The financial facility quickly reopened with new management and a new name, Ball Ground Bank, but in the nationwide wave of bank closings in 1926 it shut its doors again. However, in October 1926 it once again reopened and this time with solid leadership the bank would last even during the rough years of the Depression. The Citizens Bank opened with Dr. M.G. Hendrix as president and Baker R. Jones as the cashier. Other founders of the Ball Ground Bank included A.P. Roberts, Judson Wheeler, C.W. Groover, L.R. Thomason and M.C. Roberts. Dr. Hendrix, a leading physician in the community, was one of four doctors to serve the community in the early 1900s. He also owned the pharmacy which featured a popular soda fountain for town residents.

In those days leading up to the Depression, Ball Ground sported a number of thriving businesses, including Roberts Marble Company, Standard Marble Company, Ball Ground Monument Company, and Consumers Monument Company. The Roberts Store, Hubbard's Store and Hardin's Store were among the commercial operations where shoppers could find what they needed. A Ford dealership selling Model-T's, a five-and-dime store and a barber shop were also located there. The town's streets were lined with trees. The largest hotel in town was owned by Jack Lovelady and the Cagles, but it burned in 1929. Another hotel was the Thomason Villa.

The Coca-Cola Bottling Company was owned by the Hendrix family and operated in the town from 1903 to 1933. The company was located in a two-story brick building at 255 Gilmer Ferry Road.

Trucks would drive through an entrance to pick up the bottles of the precious and popular commodity. John Wheeler founded a lumber yard in front of Roberts Marble Company, Wheeler Lumber Yard, which was a part of the thriving sawmilling industry of the town. The city had its own telephone company as well. But the Depression would make its mark on the community, perhaps harder than any other in the county.

The Thomason Villa, here circa 1940, was a hotel on the north side of Gilmer Ferry Road in Ball Ground. The structure was demolished in the 1960s. The site is now a park owned by the city of Ball Ground.

There were bright spots. The city enjoyed a good water supply from a deep well dug during a Public Works project to build a new public water system. Companies such as Harris Lumber began to thrive and bring new economic structure to the area.

Great Depression Hits the County

By 1929, much of the country was already mired in what would come to be known as the Great Depression, but in Cherokee County the state of affairs continued to be somewhat positive despite many adverse factors including the boll weevil, which during the 1920s had greatly reduced the cotton crop produced in Cherokee County. Cotton was the major crop and farming was still the main source of income for those living in Cherokee County. Many of those who did not farm worked in the cotton mill, another industry tied to cotton prices. The agricultural community also fueled the banks, the hardware stores, farm supply dealers and cotton merchants.

In his book of memoirs, *I Remember When,* Cherokee County native William G. Hasty, Sr. wrote of that time. "I remember when, in the early thirties, the depression was so severe that thousands of people returned to the farm. There was no work or food for them in the cities."

News reports of the day showed Cherokee County avoiding the worst of the Depression, although like most communities then, times were lean. The price of cotton was at an all-time low, but many farmers survived the Depression well in Cherokee County, and farming actually saw an increase during the Depression years. In 1930 there were about 2,450 farms in Cherokee County. Many farmers had to borrow money from the banks to keep their land, or even sell personal belongings and portions of their farms. Many went without except for the barest of necessities.

A letter submitted to the *Cherokee Advance* by a reader reflected the sentiment of many farmers. "Cotton, thou art my Shepherd and I am in want. Thou has caused me to feed in a dry pasture, thou has destroyed my land; thou has led me into the paths of poverty, lawsuits and near nakedness.

Farming kept food on the table and helped many weather the years of the Depression in Cherokee County. Two men work at Field's Plantation about 1932.

C.O. Chapman and his son, Charlie, reap wheat on their farm in Holly Springs, circa 1932-1933.

"Thou hast destroyed my soil and my happiness. Thou hast caused me to go to a banker with my hat under my arm and mortgage the muscle of my arm."

But despite the pain of many of the farmers in Cherokee County, most of the banks remained strong during the Great Depression, reflecting the county's state of economy. A news article about the Bank of Canton declaring its usual dividend in 1930 underscored the fact that Cherokee County residents were weathering the storm. "According to reports Canton and Cherokee County appear to be in better condition financially speaking than other parts of the country. Some authorities believe that the bottom of the depression has been reached and that soon business will start on the upgrade."

Cherokee County government remained strong also, despite the challenges of the Depression. The county in 1932 owned property, had money in the bank and had no debt. The officials even considered cutting taxes by 15 percent. Many of the county residents raised what they needed to subsist on their own land, using their cash crops to supplement and buy the supplies they could not produce on their own lands.

The editor of the *Atlanta Georgian*, James B. Nevin, wrote a column commending the community after he visited Canton.

"The smartest, livest(sic), and most aggressive little Georgia town I have visited in many a day is Canton, up in Cherokee County.... And did we find these Cantonites downhearted? Far from it. The farmers of Cherokee County grow good crops, sensible diversified, and Canton sees to it that they are satisfactorily marketed. Canton banks and businesses cooperate fully with the farmers. Many industries and varied are active in this little municipality, and for the most part they are owned locally.

"Canton has exceptionally fine schools and churches, too, the people there setting great store by education and spiritual things.

"This is a young man's town....You should drop off there some day and meet Banker Bill Elliott, Congressman John Wood and State Senator Henry Grady Vandiviere, all stalwart young men believing in their town and alert to its interests."

The newspapers of the day reported little negative about the economic times on

The Great Depression pushed the price of cotton down and the cost of most other products up, hurting many farmers in Cherokee County. Workers in Roberts field take a break from plowing.

Bernese Hawkins has his truck loaded with cotton bales. The Hawkins brothers hauled many loads of cotton and cloth to various locations during the 1930s through the 1950s.

the front pages. Articles told of plays and meetings of the Chamber of Commerce, glowing reports of sporting events and business meetings. Instead, readers had to view the advertisements and the editorials to get a different picture of the state of financial affairs. The newspaper made use of its ink to urge optimism during the bleak years.

A house advertisement printed in the *Cherokee Advance* in 1931 is entitled "We View with Alarm." "The world is full of them....those sincere visionless people who view with alarm every changing condition. We have them right here in Canton, even though they themselves may not be conscious of the fact that they are active members of a great army of obstructionists who are retarding the return of the march of normal business and even some prosperity.

"Every generation has had its 'viewers with alarm.' The strange part is that one generation will not learn from the experiences of others. Still more strange, when one considers that these cycles of bad times and good times have not been so widely separated by the years, that the middle-aged man and woman of today have been through several of them....And further that but a brief backward glance discloses the encouraging record of America never yet having failed to completely recover 100 percent and more or what have you."

The article goes on to say that soon people would once again begin to purchase homes, cars and goods. "Our only job here in Canton is to look after our own affairs. Other towns will attend theirs. No nation has ever known hard times while its cities and towns enjoyed good times. Canton was not built by pessimists, cynics, timid souls and 'viewers with alarm.' Canton is a heritage handed down to us to protect, to improve upon...to make it a better and better town in which to live.

"Let us all take off the smoked glasses of fear and pessimism. And let us forget to view with alarm. Let us remember that our forefathers rode through and over dark depressions in 1837, 1857, 1893, 1907 and 1914, some of them worse than any we have seen, the nation and our town coming through...not only unimpaired, but actually improved. Are we, the present citizens less courageous, less capable?

"The first step is to overcome fear; the second is to resume normal buying; the third loyalty to home industries and home merchants. The remaining steps will come naturally and immediately – namely normal employment and sane PROSPERITY."

Despite those sentiments expressed by the newspaper, as the year wound down a cartoon on the front page showed a Santa Claus with a wish list for "A JOB OR TWO which will enable the employed to pick his own Christmas." The newspaper also reported that the school children would not draw for names as usual, but give what they could to the more unfortunate.

As the New Year dawned in 1931, the economy continued to worsen. Merchants such as Crisler's Store urged people to spend and help the economy, saying "Here Goes Old Man Depression." The *Cherokee Advance* ran a front page plea for subscribers to pay their bills for their newspapers. "We have a number of subscribers whose subscriptions have expired. We offered to take eggs, sausage, quince preserves, some stove wood, potatoes, corn on account and have received quite a lot of this

The 1930s were hard times in Cherokee County. The Free Home Store, seen here in 1930, continued to do business. *Reprinted from Living, Laughing, Loving in Old Lathemtown.*

produce. But now we must insist on renewal of all expired subscriptions. We know money is scarce with us, and we suspect it is fairly scarce with our subscribers, but it would be foolish for us to pay cash for white newspaper and send it out in the form of a newspaper 52 issues for a dollar." The plea ends with regret that subscribers who did not pay would have their newspaper canceled.

For some the years presented a sort of opportunity. During the Great Depression peddlers and rolling stores on carts became a way for enterprising businessmen to eke a living while providing homemakers and families the means to purchase the necessities and sometimes even a little something extra. Bill Hasty wrote of rolling stores in his book, *I Remember When...* "During the darkest days of the terrible depression of the 1930s, a miracle happened in our community. A contraption called a rolling store suddenly appeared..." Hasty goes on to tell of how Buck Cline and Max Moore outfitted a truck with the help of Luther Cline to serve as a store to actually go to farmers in remote regions. Canned goods, sugar, coffee and other necessities were available for barter, and farmers would trade eggs, butter or use a little cash to purchase the needed supplies.

In November 1932 American voters elected a new president and in January 1933 Franklin Delano Roosevelt took office as the 32nd president of the United States. The new president immediately set out to create his New Deal legislation designed to generate government jobs for the unemployed, as well as regulate Wall Street and provide assistance and support for those facing financial distress.

Cherokee County writer Elree Worley writes in her book, *We Made It! On the Farm During the Depression*, about the changes that were wrought by the new administration.

"Times had rocked along slowly till things got worse than 'they could possibly be.' Everyone was at their wits end about a way to survive and pay their mounting debts at the local grocery and merchandise stores. Many businesses were bankrupt and banks were folding. These were indeed troublesome times, resulting in many suicides.

"As fates would have it, a presidential election that year was approaching and the candidate promising the most relief for the poverty stricken farmers and business world was naturally the forerunner. As soon as the elections were over we had a real progressive new president, whom the masses worshiped. He made long, personable speeches on the radio that seemed to address everyone's problems. At long last it looked like a new day was dawning."

Bill Hasty wrote of the Works Progress Administration program or WPA as it was called. The plan poured billions of dollars into building infrastructure and creating jobs in local communities. Hasty wrote that in Cherokee County WPA built auditoriums at Ball Ground and Woodstock schools and paved streets in Canton, including North Street, Archer, Academy, Elizabeth and Church streets. Sidewalks were also paved in several of the cities in the county.

Another project that benefited the economy was the payment to farmers to allow their lands to remain fallow as much of the soil was depleted causing poor crops. Mrs. Worley writes, "When planting time came in the spring, we went through the same rituals of planting the crops when a brand new program was implemented to aid the farmers. This required the farmers to plow up a certain portion of their cotton for a cash settlement. Who could resist that, with the threat of insects and inclement weather always a problem for crops? Everyone jumped at the chance to receive ready cash!"

Despite the new government's efforts, times remained lean in Cherokee County and surrounding areas for the rest of the 1930s. In the mid-1930s Canton Cotton Mills was often on a week-on/week-off schedule at its two mills, but the almost 1,200 employees did have a steady income on which to depend. The mill villages also provided a place to live and education for the children and other opportunities during those lean years.

By early 1933 another problem was presenting itself, as people all across the country began to worry about the money they had in their bank and whether it was safe. As more and more people pulled their savings and deposits out of the banks, a crisis began to develop. President Roosevelt ordered all banks to

The Work Progress Administration helped create local jobs by improving infrastructure. West Main Street and the Mill Village in Canton were paved in the 1930s through the WPA.

close for three days on March 6 of that year. The Bank Holiday, which also closed the stock exchange, was ultimately extended on March 9, and banks were not allowed to reopen until March 13. The banks in Cherokee County complied. Many banks across the United States failed to open their doors following the forced holiday, but many others saw depositors return their money to the banks with renewed confidence. All banks in Cherokee County including Bank of Woodstock, Bank of Canton, Citizens Bank in Ball Ground and Etowah Bank reopened. While times remained hard throughout the 1930s and the standard of living was meager for most people in Cherokee County up until the end of World War II in the 1940s, the greatest banking crisis was over for the country and for Cherokee County. Now it would be a matter of hanging on until happy days were here again. That would take a war being fought and won and the troops returning home before the transition to a stronger economic time would be complete.

Local Newspapers Deliver

Cherokee County residents have always loved their news, from the days of the county's founding to the Civil War into the new millennium, and over the decades a number of newspapers have supplied the information those living in the community needed to stay informed. The first known newspaper in Cherokee County was the *Cherokee Intelligencer*, which started publication when the town later named Canton was called Cherokee Courthouse. The first issue was published February 16, 1833. Howell Cobb, a local attorney, was the editor. The newspaper continued publication in 1834 with the town name listed as Edahwah on the banner. The newspaper appears to have discontinued publication at the end of 1834 as no known issues exist after that time. The population of the community was small at that time, and the residents who could read and write even smaller.

The next attempt at a newspaper was launched in 1861 by W.J. Sloan and called the *Cherokee Mountaineer*, but it lasted only a year. Its demise was hastened by the difficulty of getting ink and paper during the tough years of the Civil War. Almost 15 years would go by before another attempt was made at a local newspaper when Judge James O. Dowda began publication of the *Cherokee Georgian* in 1875 with the help of Col. John J.A. Sharp and P.H. Brewster. About four years later the fledging publication was merged into a religious newspaper, the *Cherokee Advocate*, which was published in Cherokee County for about a year before being located to Atlanta by then owner W.T. Laine.

The early attempts at a publication to serve Cherokee County paved the way for the first newspaper that truly identified with and reflected the community. The *Cherokee Advance* was begun in 1880 as a weekly publication by Benjamin Franklin Perry, Sr., when the Marietta native was only 20 years old. Perry went on to have a stellar career in banking

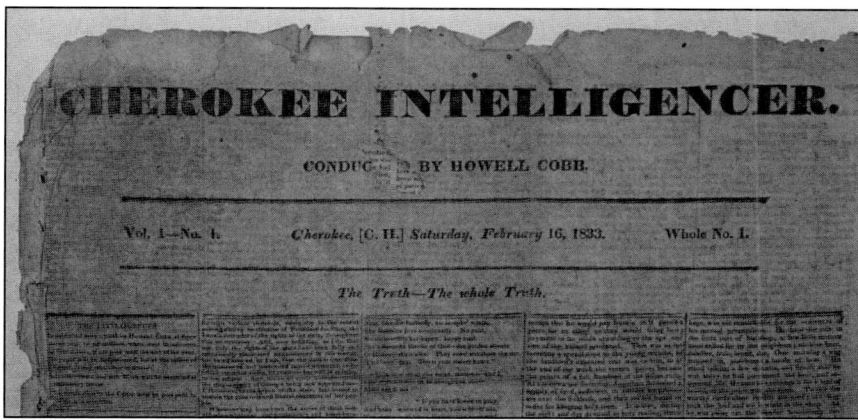

The *Intelligencer* published in 1833 and 1834 is the oldest known newspaper in Cherokee County. *Magruder Newspaper Collection at the Atlanta History Center.*

and commerce in Cherokee County and to be a leader in journalism throughout the state of Georgia. He helped organize the Bank of Canton, and was later cashier. He served as postmaster of Canton and in 1908 became the assistant state treasurer in Atlanta. He was a state bank examiner later in his career and helped form the Realty Trust Company. Under his leadership, the *Cherokee Advance* became one of the leading weeklies in the state. The newspaper was published in a four-page, five-column format and published continuously from 1880 to 1937 under the leadership of different owners and editors.

Perry, with little formal education or training, established the newspaper as one of the best in Georgia, installed new presses in the late 1880s and moved the newspaper into a brick building on Main Street. In 1885 a tornado struck the northern part of Cherokee County and Perry held the newspaper while he went to the area to survey the damage and file a story which appeared the next day in the *Advance*, scooping the state newspapers and helping rush relief to the victims. In 1888, he persuaded the Georgia Press Association to hold its annual meeting in Canton, a major coup of the day. Perry's son, Ben Perry, Jr. later was the editor of the newspaper for a number of years.

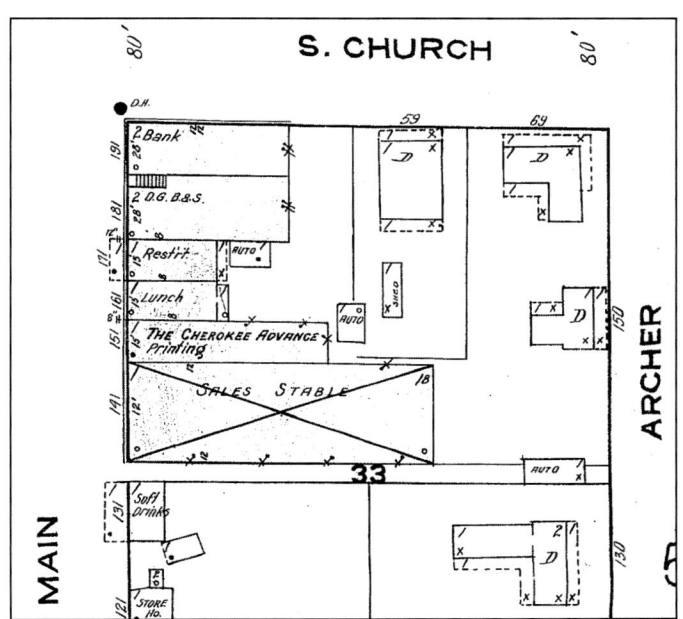

A 1921 Sanborn Fire Insurance map shows the *Cherokee Advance* office on Main Street in Canton. Ben Perry started the newspaper in 1880 when he was 20 years old.

In 1921 Johnnie P. Rudasill and his brother E.M. Rudasill purchased the *Cherokee Advance* from Perry. J.P. Rudasill would be at its helm for almost the next 20 years. In 1929 the newspaper offices were moved to Academy Street to the Rudasill Building.

As the Jones family became more prominent and the Cotton Mill more dominant in the Canton marketplace, the business leaders in the family decided to start their own newspaper in 1934. The new publication was titled the *North Georgia Tribune* and would publish as a weekly newspaper for the next decade, first under the editorship of Tom Arnold and then with Mrs. Blanche Jones Lewis, granddaughter of Ben Perry, at the helm of the editorial staff.

In 1944 Ralph Owen and his brother C.E. "Buster" Owen purchased the *North Georgia Tribune* from the Jones family and later consolidated it with the *Cherokee Advance*. Ralph Owen was married to the former Frances Rudasill, whose family owned the older publication. For the next several decades the *North Georgia Tribune* served the community with news and information. In the fire of 1955 in downtown Canton the *Tribune* office was destroyed, but the newspaper was printed in Dalton that week and did not miss an issue. The offices were rebuilt and continued to serve the newspaper until 1973, when it enjoyed a circulation of almost 6,500.

On September 1, 1973, the Owens brothers sold the newspaper to the *Marietta Daily Journal* organization owned by Otis Brumby. The name of the newspaper was changed to the *Cherokee Tribune*, and continued to serve the community as the legal organ and twice-weekly newspaper. The newspaper would later evolve to a daily format published five days a week by the Cobb County owners. The *Cherokee Tribune* won numerous state and national awards for its level of excellence. Over the years other newspapers attempted to gain a foothold in the Cherokee market, including the *North Georgia Press* and the *Cherokee Citizen*, both of which subsequently went out of business.

In the south end of Cherokee County the *Woodstock News* first went to press in 1962, but did not last long before closing its doors. In 1963 Otis Brumby established the *Woodstock Star* to serve the area. The weekly newspaper was consolidated and changed to the *Woodstock Neighbor* in the 1970s when

Ralph Owen and C.E. Owen purchased the North Georgia Tribune in 1944 and published the newspaper for almost 30 years. Here Ralph Owen attaches mailing labels to newspapers in preparation for mailing.

Brumby purchased the *Tribune*. The *News Shopper* was also published in Woodstock for a number of years.

On May 1, 1995, Woodstock and the south Cherokee area saw the *Lakeside Ledger* established as a free weekly. Started by Dave and Sherry Caughman in their basement, the newspaper's first issue was mailed to 30,000 households. The couple produced the south end newspaper for three months out of their house before moving into an office in downtown Woodstock. In January 1996 they moved into the Smith Johnston building and within 18 months had purchased the Dean House and moved the newspaper to its present location. In 2000 they changed the name of the newspaper to *The Cherokee Ledger-News* to reflect its plan to serve all of Cherokee County with news and information. The newspaper continues to be published by the Caughmans and has won numerous state and national awards in the newspaper industry. The owners estimate the publication produces 42,000 issues each week, with about 90 percent of those mailed to homes and businesses and the rest distributed on news stands. The newspaper is also mailed by subscription to military personnel overseas and to people with ties to Cherokee County across the country.

Moonshine Strong Brew in These Hills

The history of making corn whiskey in Cherokee County is as long as that of the county, and just as rich. But it was in 1919 that Prohibition made the cottage industry that had long been a part of life in the hills of north Georgia into a lucrative business. Cherokee County was home to one of the most successful and largest producers and distributors of moonshine in the entire state of Georgia during those years. Even after the repeal of the law making it illegal to drink and to sell liquor in 1933, Cherokee County continued to be a dry county for several decades, a condition that spurred the distribution and manufacturing of illegal whiskey and spirits. The rich bottom lands along the Etowah River, the easy hiding places in hills and valleys in the north part of the county, the streams and creeks needed to run a still and the fierce independent nature of the people all contributed to making Cherokee County a haven for moonshiners.

Much that is known about the making of corn liquor and other alcoholic spirits prior to World War I is through oral history, tales handed down among families of stills built and recipes perfected. Settlers coming into the region, especially those of Scotch-Irish descent, brought their love of grain whiskey with them when they immigrated to America, and soon they were setting up copper kettles and perfecting ways to make liquor with the ingredients at hand. Corn was the preferred ingredient in the new world, where it grew well. Many farmers measured their production of corn by the barrel, not by the bushel. The word moonshine was also imported from Great Britain, where it was long used as a term for those who produced and distributed illegal spirits by the light of the moon, so that they would go undetected.

In the north Georgia region in the years leading up to the Civil War, many farmers supplemented their meager incomes by producing corn whiskey to sell to their neighbors and to those living in the towns. Fiercely independent, these early farmers did not consider it the government's business what they did on their own land.

Following the Civil War, and because the federal government in 1862 had begun to impose licensing taxes on whiskey, the business of moonshine became one of almost a perverse pride with many of the farmers and landowners returning from the war. Then in the 1870s, the revenue agents for the federal government who were charged with enforcement of the tax began to be paid on a fee basis for the number of arrests made and stills seized. That system kicked off the famous North Georgia Moonshine War of 1876 when the president of the United States at the time, Ulysses Grant, ordered the U.S. Army be used for protection of the agents. In Cherokee County, there were still those who had sided with the North during the war, and now they began to report their neighbors who were making moonshine. In 1879 Congress ordered the use of troops ceased, and the moonshine war wore down.

After that and for the next 40 years the making of moonshine began to take on a new aura of acceptance, and many of the key moonshiners were highly respected members of the community, businessmen, farmers and leaders in their churches and communities. Many of them did not drink themselves, but looked at making moonshine as an economic opportunity. Their operations helped improve local economies and make many of them rich

John Henry Hardin earned the title of the Moonshine King for having the largest corn liquor operation in the state. His stills, such as this one, were located in Cherokee County near the Etowah River in Sutallee. Because the illegal whiskey was produced clandestinely, the liquor could be extremely strong and even toxic.

men. None was more well-known or notorious than Cherokee County's John Henry Hardin. Born in the Ophir community of north Cherokee County in 1865, by the 1920s John Henry Hardin was known as the Moonshine King. His empire was a series of farms he owned and leased along the Etowah River in the Laughingal section of Sutallee in Cherokee County, which was believed to be named for a Cherokee princess. Canton native Frances Rudasill Owen, who was a Civil Works Administration caseworker in the 1930s and through her work for the government knew Hardin personally, wrote of Hardin in *Cherokee Glimpses*, a publication of the Cherokee County Historical Society in 1981. "Those were the perilous days of the deep depression years when there were no jobs or money but most of the men in the Laughingal community had work and means for life's necessities. Mr. Hardin made a lot of money and at one period of his career was worth perhaps a half a million dollars. This was more money than a dozen mountain farmers ever dreamed of holding even in unison and tells something of the scope of his enterprise. However, through the years, John Henry suffered many losses and served several penitentiary sentences. He died a pauper and a broken man."

Career federal revenue agent Duff Floyd is quoted as saying of Hardin, "The man who stood out over all the rest was a tall, quiet stoop-shouldered old Cherokee County man known as the Moonshine King of Georgia. He was one of the state's biggest farmers, yet aside from his illicit liquor transgressions, was a man of great nobility, integrity and honor."

In 1906, Hardin purchased a large tract of land on the bank of the Etowah River and built a home, farm buildings, a general store and a dining hall. According to Mrs. Owen's account, he also had his own gristmill and grew corn in the bottom lands and

For years federal revenue agents such as Duff Floyd battled with John Henry Hardin, who operated as many as 20 stills, including this one during the years of the Depression. This photograph was submitted as evidence at one of Hardin's many trials. He died a broken man.

cotton on the higher ground of his farm. He was a steward at his church, Sixes Methodist Church, where he also served as Sunday school superintendent and teacher, and led the singing. Just before World War I, Hardin's bottom lands flooded during a time of unusual rainfall, and his corn crop soured. The loss of his crop meant he could not repay loans he owed, and Hardin faced financial ruin. One of his workers suggested he grind the soured corn and use it for mash for whiskey. Soon he was operating as many as 20 stills using as many as 100 workers. Hardin was producing thousands of gallons of untaxed and illegal whiskey each year. He was also subcontracting moonshine from many of his neighbors, whom he paid $2 per gallon for their whiskey. He then sold it to the bootleggers from the area and to haulers for $4 per gallon.

Hardin dealt only in cash, and was known as a man who was rich but did not flaunt his wealth. He and his wife, Mary Hardin, lived a simple life and were known for their plain manners. The couple had ten children, and all the family's sons and sons-in-law were involved in the family business. Hardin, in addition to farming and moonshine production, bought and sold farm land and real estate, and made loans to his neighbors.

By the late 1920s as Prohibition took hold of the nation, Hardin was believed to be the single largest producer and distributor of corn whiskey in the state. His operation and his farm were producing a large annual income. Some of his more law-abiding neighbors did not look favorably on the operation.

One of Hardin's sons, Paul Hardin, married Lesa Woodall in 1925, and the two became well-known in the community as a handsome couple with a fine home, clothes, jewelry and all the finer things money could buy. The couple had an open touring car and Paul Hardin even taught his wife to drive. Over the next few years the couple became parents to four young children.

Then in 1932 the younger Hardin was arrested when one of his father's stills was raided. He was out on bond awaiting trial in October when tragedy struck. An article in the *Georgia Backroads* magazine of August 2010 tells of the horrific deaths of the couple and their children. Newspaper accounts of the day also report what was believed by the authorities to be suicide-murder.

John Henry Hardin was one of many men who made their money by making illegal whiskey, or moonshine, in the backwoods of Cherokee County. This still is one of many that Hardin and his men operated.

On June 20, 1932, a relative went to Paul Hardin's home early in the morning. After knocking on the door and getting no answer, the relative looked in a window and saw a horrible sight. Lesa Hardin's body was on one bed with two of her children, and Paul Hardin's body was on the other bed with another child. The baby lay dead in his crib. Cherokee County Sheriff J.O. McCollum and Coroner Claude Peacock arrived on the scene after the relative drove to a nearby house and telephoned to report the crime. The investigators determined that Hardin shot himself after killing his family. There had been reports of Hardin being depressed about his arrest and that he had been drinking heavily.

Headlines in the newspapers read, "Son of John Hardin, Moonshine King, Slays Wife, Four Children and Self." The next day a group funeral was held and the family was buried at Stamp Creek cemetery. Speculation was that Paul Hardin did not kill himself or his family, but that they were all murdered by their enemies. The investigation found no merit to those rumors.

The elder Hardin continued his whiskey operation, and some reports say he was arrested as many as 19 times. Each time he was convicted, he was assessed fines, and eventually lost most of his land and money. He died in 1943.

Mrs. Owen wrote, "Today, when I ride through Sutallee District on a good paved road and see beautiful Allatoona Lake covering the fertile corn fields of Mr. Hardin's former 'moonshine empire,' I sometimes recall the past. It is as though I had dreamed of another world, but my memories of Mr.

Hardin are very real and clear. Now and then I have thoughts of man-made barriers and restrictions men set up against each other. I wonder who is right and who is wrong and perhaps there is no issue pure black or pure white, but I have one deep abiding conviction about it all. I believe Mr. Hardin suffered enough for his sins while living here on earth, and that his moonshining transgressions will be dealt with kindly by our Great Judge on that final day of reckoning."

The moonshine industry continued in Cherokee County long after Hardin died. Joe Dabney writes in his book *Mountain Spirits* that in the 1960s and early 1970s there were many moonshiners still in operation in Georgia. The federal government put estimates of taxes owed by illegal whiskey operators as high as $97 million annually. Cherokee County continued to be a dry county for the most part for many decades.

Sheriffs Walk Tall in Cherokee County

The early 1900s were years of great highs and lows for county residents. Prohibition was just one source of trouble. As times grew tougher economically, the need for strong law enforcement was on the rise. Racial unrest, suicides because of finances and a slew of other problems plagued communities. In

Cherokee County a series of sheriffs rode the county's back roads, enforcing the laws and keeping the peace. One such man was Joshua P. Spears. Spears was first elected sheriff in 1881 when he served two years. Then in 1895 he was chosen as high sheriff once again and served two two-year terms. Enoch Gramling, William Kitchens and Augustus Coggins all served terms in the interim years. The voters once again chose Joshua Spears in 1910 and he would stay in office another ten years. When he died at age 78 an article on the front page of the *Cherokee Advance* praised him for his 32 years of service as sheriff of the county. "His entire life has been as an up-right honorable citizen," the obituary read. "No citizen of Cherokee County was better or more favorably known than Josh Spears, for more than 30 years sheriff of Cherokee county and identified with the progress and upbuilding of this section for more than half a century."

Spears was born and raised at the family homeplace three miles east of Ball Ground. He was a member of the Baptist church at Hopewell and a member of the Masonic fraternity. He was married to his wife for 57 years and they had three children.

Joshua Spears, above, was sheriff for Cherokee County for many years and one of the most respected men in the community. His son, Lee Spears, right, went on to be sheriff also and to have a long and illustrious career as the county's top law enforcement officer.

His son, Lee Spears, went on to be sheriff himself for one of the longest terms in office in the county history. Lee Spears served in the job from 1924 to 1930 and then again from 1933 to 1940. J.O. McCollum served one term in office during that time.

Residents Join Up in Clubs and Organizations

Because Cherokee County was such a civic minded community, it is impossible to list every club and organization that was formed within the county. Cherokee County residents love to serve and to work for the betterment of their community, and a number of organizations including garden clubs, civic clubs and business organizations were initiated. These groups made a lasting contribution to life in Cherokee County. Following are just a few of the many groups that serve for the greater good in Cherokee County.

Cherokee County's oldest service organization was the Canton Woman's Club, begun on October 12, 1921, when some ladies gathered together to talk about the need for a community club. Organizational meetings were held by Mrs. Bessie Johnston and Mrs. Maria Rudasill, with the ladies feasting on chicken salad, homemade biscuits and iced tea. Before the year of 1921 was out the club had bylaws and officers, including Mrs. Johnston as president, Mrs. Jesse McClain as vice president, Mrs. George C. Brooke as secretary and Mrs. Carl Edge as treasurer. Mrs. James Garrison served as corresponding secretary.

The club stated its mission, "To bring the women of Canton together for mutual council and helpfulness, and to unite their influence and service to promote the educational, civic and moral advancement of the town." Within a few months, in February 1922, local business leader B.F. Coggins donated a tract of land and $500 to build a clubhouse to house the new organization. The clubhouse near the Coker Hospital and the First Baptist Church was completed and the ladies began meeting there in December of 1925.

Soon the organization was making its mark. A night school was organized in 1923 for the benefit of workers in the cotton mill who were illiterate. The club made a substantial contribution to the monument in Brown Park and sponsored the first ever county fair. To raise money in the 1930s the club operated a tea room in the Galt Building in Canton and sold sandwiches, cakes and tea. The club used its funds to make one of the first donations to having a public library in Cherokee County.

In later years the Woman's Club, in partnership with the town of Canton, was given funds by the Harmon Foundation to purchase the land that was later used for Harmon Field at a cost of $2,000. The organization sponsored a journalism award

The Canton Glee Club, pictured here in Atlanta in 1924, was under the direction of Martha Galt. Members included, first row from left, Rochelle McClure Daisye Crisler, Nevada Garrison, Director Martha Galt, Irene P. Rudasill, Lucille Coker, Amanda Perry, Clera Rudasill, Martha Delay, Pearl Sandow, Frances Galt. Second Row from left, Ida Christy, Nelle Michael Chamlee, Nettie Groover, Orleans Humphries, Estelle Greene, Mary Bates, Nina Thompson, Racheal Keith, Mrs. George G. Doss, Mildred Martyn, Margret Martyn, Berta McCox. Third Row from left, Malinda Galt, Mary Jones, Mrs. Charles Goodman, Ruth Pund McCanless, Viola Tooler, Ernet Hogan Conn, Erlyn Cobb, Jessie Deadwyler Winn, and Mellie Harpe Moody.

at the high school and published a cookbook entitled *The Art of Cooking in Cherokee County.*

Another organization, the Service League of Canton, which later became the Service League of Cherokee County, formed on March 28, 1935, to assist needy children and conduct charity work in the community. Officers were President Mrs. R. Tyre Jones; Vice President Mrs. H.G. Vandiviere, Recording Secretary Mrs. J.E. Darnell, Corresponding Secretary Mrs. Ed Garlington, Treasurer Miss Mary Lee Johnston and Ways and Means, Mrs. Rube Jones, Mrs. A.V. Jones Jr., Mrs. John S. Wood and Miss

Blanche Jones. To raise funds in the early days the organization held a bridge and Rook tournament at the Hotel Canton. Later they held several fundraisers including plays to raise money for milk at the public school for underprivileged children. In 1949 the organization started the Milk Fund Ball at the Canton Golf Club to raise money to help in the need. Admission was $1.50 per couple.

The Rotary Club of Canton began forming on May 7, 1937, when a group of prominent Cherokee County businessmen met for lunch at the hotel on the square in downtown Canton. The speaker for the inaugural

The Service League of Canton, which later became the Service League of Cherokee County, was started in 1935 to help children in need in the community. Here, Andy Roach, Louise Roach, Dr. Carl and Ann Edge and Bill and Hazel Hasty enjoy the Service League ball, an annual affair for years to raise funds for the community.

event was Thomas C. Law of the Atlanta Rotary Club, along with a representative from Rotary International. The group assembled voted unanimously to form the club with the Marietta Rotary Club as the sponsor.

The first officers were President W.S. Elliott, Vice President A.V. Jones, Secretary R. Tyre Jones, Jr., Treasurer Dr. T.G. Fowler and Sergeant at Arms Dr. John T. Petitt. Other directors included Smith L. Johnston, The Reverend O.M. Seigler and Dr. M.G. Hendrix. Other charter members were Ed Barrett, Dr. Walter Bratton, Dr. William Fincher, Dr. Tommy Fowler, Ed Garlington, Bill Greene, Dr. Arthur M. Hendrix, Sr., Jim Holcombe, Joe Johnston, Paul W. Jones, Sr., Jasper Keith, Gene McCanless, O.C. Omer, Claude Peacock, Stratford Pressley, Luther Westbrook, Joe Wheeler, John Wood and Melvin Young.

The club met for 23 years at the Canton Hotel. As the threat of war grew, the club became active in relief efforts and played a basketball game with the Canton Lions for Finnish Relief. Tom Jones was the first Rotarian to enter the armed services in 1941. In October 1941 the Rotary Club of Canton led efforts to organize a Home Defense Corps with the National Guard.

The Rotary Club of Canton was formed in 1937 and held its first meeting May 23 at the Hotel Canton. Here, the inaugural membership poses on the steps of the hotel.

In the 1950s members participated in the first Little League organizational meeting in the state of Georgia and helped bring Little League baseball to Canton. Little League rules did not allow a club to sponsor the formation of the activity in a community, but the Rotary helped get several interested groups together to organize Canton Little League and the club sponsored a team for many years.

Canton also boasted the Canton Lion's Club, founded in 1932, and the Kiwanis Club for local businessmen to participate in and give back to the community. Both of these organizations had a lasting impact on the community through their projects and their members.

In Woodstock, one of the earliest organizations was the Woodstock Garden Club, which was begun in 1940 to beautify the community. Charter members were Mrs. J.A. Abercrombie, Mrs. H.A. Bennett,

Boy Scouts were active in Cherokee County in the 1930s. The Nelson Boy Scout Troop 257 included Jimmy Bishop, William Kimberly, Ted Klein, Charles Hammontree, Donald Bishop, Jimmy Hamby, Jimmy Goss, Lamar Cantrell, Frank Kimberly, and Benny Harbin.

Several clubs and organizations in Cherokee County helped get the Little League Baseball program started in the community. Two young players in 1952 are Arlen Peanut Smith, left, and Jerry Weaver.

Mrs. E.T. Booth, Mrs. W.D. Bozeman, Mrs. S.R. Dawson, Mrs. L.A. Dean, Mrs. H.L. Delay, Mrs. Clyde Dobbs, Miss Iris Dobbs, Mrs. W.L. Dupree, Mrs. A.D. Echols, Mrs. L.M. Hames, Mrs. L.E. Howell, Mrs. H.L. Johnston, Mrs. S.L. Johnston, Mrs. P.S. Kemp, Sr., Mrs. V.T. Ingram, Mrs. Will Lovingood, Mrs. W.R. Lunsford, Mrs. H.C. McAfee, Mrs. Laura Mobley, Mrs. Belle Pace, Mrs. A.F. Poor, Mrs. W.D. Power, Mrs. Gid Reeves, Mrs. J.M. Rickman, Mrs. Jessie Robertson, Mrs. E.L. Rusk, Mrs. C.E. Tarpley, Mrs. T.J. Vansant and Mrs. C.C. Wheeler. To fund special projects, the group held dinner parties and Rook tournaments. One of the major undertakings of the organization was to build the Woodstock Community House, which was built on land donated by Joe Johnston and Smith Johnston in 1944. The building was in the south Main Street area. In 1950 famed Woodstock architect Miller Barnes sketched plans for a new community building, and that center was completed in 1961.

The Woodstock Junior Woman's Club was organized in 1963 and helped to get a public library in the south Cherokee community. The club organized

the effort to open a public library in Woodstock and the Woodstock City Council voted to help fund the effort to the tune of $25 per month. The library was opened in 1964 with 2,000 books on its shelves. The library was housed in a room in the building owned by Smith Johnston, who donated the space. Sara Poor was the first librarian at the new public facility. The new library was adopted as a part of the Sequoyah Regional Library System.

The Woodstock Lions Club was one of the premier civic organizations in Woodstock's growth. The club was chartered on October 24, 1961, and had 50 charter members. The club was sponsored by the Canton Lions Club. In the 1960s, the city of Woodstock was focusing on being a great community in which to live, work and play, and the new organization helped residents realize that goal. Charter member Bill Drinkard was mayor of Woodstock at the time of the club being chartered. The club raised

The Woodstock Lions Club, here at a meeting in 1961, has a long history of community service. Members at the time included, back row from left, Hugh Lee Dobbs, George Young, Glenn Hubbard, Don Keenum, Alton Edwards, Douglas Chandler, Calvin Parker and Miller Barnes. Front row from left are visitor Byron Vann, regional head of Boy Scouts, speaker Dr. Glenn Reed, visitor Don Busby of Bell Telephone, J.D. Ragsdale and W.B. Drinkard.

The Cherokee Shrine Club was a familiar part of parades and celebrations in Cherokee County. Here Billy Jackson, far left, and Gene Holcomb, one of the bailiffs, fourth from the left, along with other members turn out to entertain young people at an event.

funds for needy families, and assisted underprivileged residents in attaining eye glasses and eye care.

Ball Ground had its share of clubs and organizations as well. The Ball Ground Lions Club was one of the earliest organizations formed in the city. Land for the Lions Club ballpark was donated by C.W. Groover, and the Lions Club built and maintained it to serve the community. The Anetsa-Ga-Da Garden Club, federated in 1951, and the Community Club both contributed to the community. The city also had a Masonic Lodge.

Poultry production was big business throughout Cherokee County in the 1950s and 1960s and the community was proud to be considered the Poultry Capital of the World. The poultry industry was one of the leading employers of Cherokee County during those days and many residents made fortunes in the business. Canton's Fourth of July and Poultry Celebration drew large crowds of residents to downtown for the festivity.

Chapter Six

Meeting Challenge of World War and Aftermath

The long shadow of the war in Europe was already casting its pall over the country as Cherokee County celebrated the beginning of the new decade of the 1940s. With memories of the Great Depression still fresh in their minds, those living in Cherokee County joined the rest of the nation in hoping that America would stay out of the global conflict as the New Year began. It would be many months before America officially joined the fray, but in the meantime Cherokee County joined with the rest of the country in preparing for the threat. World War II struck to the heart of the nation when Pearl Harbor was bombed on December 7, 1941. President Franklin D. Roosevelt's speech declaring America's entrance into the war was heard in living rooms across Cherokee County. Already Cherokee County's young men and women were enlisting to be part of the war effort at home and abroad, but with the infamy of the Pearl Harbor attack the rosters swelled. For those who signed up and shipped out, it would be months or even years before they would return to their homes and families in the community. Many never made it back. As many as 2,000 Cherokee County residents served in World War II, a tenth of the county's population at the time. At least 43 of those serving their country were killed in the line of duty.

For those left to keep the home fires burning, it was a time of food and gasoline rationing, victory gardens and conservation of supplies, of air drills and somber news from those away fighting. The years of the war were also a time of virtually no growth in the community. Few people wanted to take out loans or build new houses or businesses. Every available resource was poured into the war effort. Jobs were still available, though, as local industries began producing goods for the war effort. Canton Cotton Mills turned to manufacturing a fabric known as osnaburg which was used in the production of tents and sand bags for the war effort. The United States Government also purchased denim from the local cotton mills for uniforms. However, with a diminished work force Canton Cotton Mills was only able to operate two shifts a day, often turning toward women workers to fill what jobs they could. In Woodstock, the Rope Mills churned out cotton rope for tents and other uses in the war effort.

By the late 1940s and the 1950s, with the help of GI loans and a growing poultry industry, Cherokee County was going great guns again. But for those who graduated from Canton High School those first few years of the 1940s, a different future awaited as America entered the war. Those years were times of mostly stagnant growth for the county. Cherokee County had a population of 20,126 in 1940 and by 1950 that number would climb only to 20,750. During the 1950s, more people began to move in and the county would experience a population growth of more than 2,000 new residents during that decade. During the 1950s, residents would begin to build new houses, open businesses, and purchase cars and modern conveniences such as the latest kitchen appliances and televisions. A new lake was on the horizon for Cherokee County, sure to bring more visitors to the county and to give those who lived there enhanced recreational opportunities. Finally, in the mid 1940s and 1950s, better days arrived.

Responding to the War Effort.

In the autumn of 1941 the war in Europe still seemed far away to those living in Cherokee County. Finally there was something to be thankful for that Thanksgiving as the financial struggles that had marked the previous decade were beginning to fade. Families were looking forward to Christmas, shopping at Jones Mercantile Company and other local retailers, and enjoying the beginning of the holiday season. The *North Georgia Tribune* reported in its December 5 issue that Christmas shopping was off to a bang. A free movie was planned at the Canton Theatre for December 11 sponsored by the local merchants and the Junior Chamber of Commerce. The movie theater was showing *A Yank in the R.A.F.* The Canton High School Band was kicking off its concert season with a benefit for the newly organized Home Defense Corps. Clubs and organizations were busy, with the Etowah Garden Club planning to donate $25 for those less fortunate and the Service League and the Junior Woman's Club set to meet in the coming week. There was a little talk of the war with the United States Navy announcing plans for its recruiting office in Canton to be open the following Monday looking for enlistees.

James Cannon of Canton served as a Marine in World War II. He was one of about 2,000 Cherokee residents who served their country during the war. He was later mayor of Canton.

But within days all that changed. On that Sunday, December 7, 1941, the world as people knew it would be transformed forever.

The December 12, 1941, issue of the *North Georgia Tribune* was full of war news.

The Japanese made their first attack on Pearl Harbor at 7:55 A.M. Hawaiian time that Sunday morning. In the deadly sneak attack more than 100 Japanese aircraft attacked the Naval Base and Army Air Force Base on the island of Oahu. Five American battleships were sunk and three others were damaged. Three destroyers, a mine layer and a tanker vessel were also destroyed. More than 2,340 servicemen were killed in the attack with another 1,200 wounded and almost 1,000 missing.

Cherokee County families were stunned by the news. For many, fear for family members already stationed around the world in danger zones was gripping and real. Ensign Seth Howard

Soldiers shipping out overseas could send their personal items by train using War Won't Wait shipping tags such as these used for A.F. Jones.

was aboard the aircraft carrier Saratoga, Thomas Harold Ponder was with the Asiatic Fleet somewhere in the Pacific, Wesley Thomas was stationed in the Philippines, Johnny Ralph Crane was at Schofield Barracks in Honolulu and Ralph Whelchel was stationed in Hawaii. John Townsend, Truman Wright and C.W. Wright Jr. were also at Honolulu at the time of the attack. T.P. Whitfield was a Marine who had stopped there on his way to Wake Island. Fred Boling was in the Panama Canal Zone. Othie L. Bailey was with the coastal artillery unit in Panama. James Garrison was on board a transport ship that had just left Pearl Harbor days before the attack. His ship was ordered immediately to return to Honolulu following the attack.

Local writer Bill Hasty, like everyone who was old enough to remember that fateful day, would recall exactly where he was when he heard the news. He wrote in his column for the newspaper 50 years later what happened to him that Sunday. "There are certain events that happen in everyone's life that will forever be frozen in their memory. Pearl Harbor was certainly one of those occasions. My brother, Alex, and I, along with some friends, had been riding around Canton when we popped into the old Green Rail restaurant for a hot dog. To our surprise we saw two or three servicemen running out of the Green Rail to their cars and speeding away. It was just after two o'clock Eastern Standard Time. The Japanese had made their first attack on Pearl Harbor... The servicemen were ordered to return to their posts immediately. That order was given by the military leaders and announced by radio throughout America. We were no longer surprised when we saw service men speeding away."

In the next edition of the *North Georgia Tribune* following the attack at Pearl Harbor, it was reported, "Thus on December 11, 23 years and one month to the day after the Hun shouted, 'Kamerad' to end World War I, the United States has again drawn the sword to defend herself and civilization against enslavement by power mad dictators of the Axis." War once again had engulfed Cherokee County and the nation.

The community quickly responded. Air warning stations, of which Cherokee County had six, were placed on

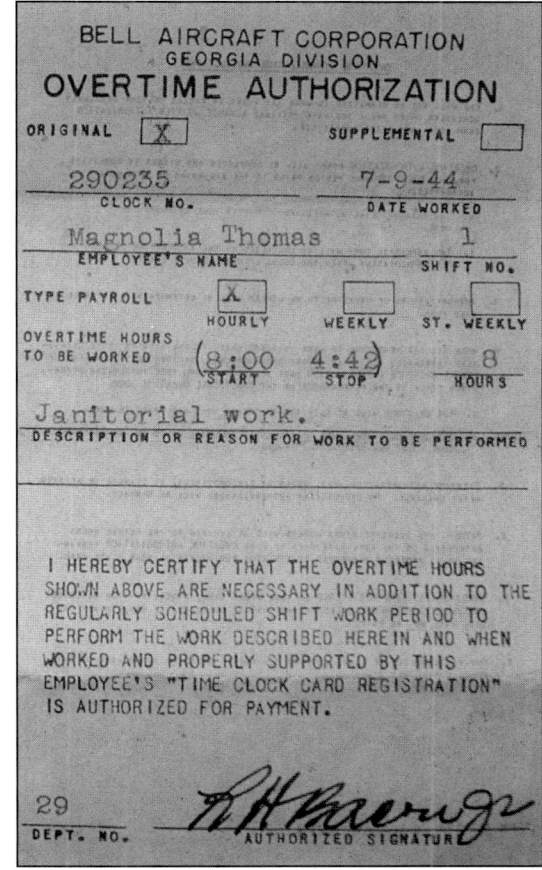

Many women helped the war effort by taking on men's jobs. Magnolia Thomas of Woodstock was authorized for overtime at the Bell Aircraft Plant which later became Lockheed.

active duty, their locations cloaked in mystery. Georgia Governor Eugene Talmadge set up a defense fund and pledged the resources of the state to the effort. Seventh-grade student Carl Edge, Jr. announced that he was helping to form a Junior Defense Corps to do odd jobs and errands for pay, which would be used to buy defense stamps. An editorial in the local newspaper talked about Cherokee residents raising food for the war. Other news topics included the Red Cross, civilian defense, rationing, potential consumer shortages, the need for skilled workers, movement of military convoys on highways and military casualties. Farmers were busy repairing their farm tools to keep replacements low so supplies could be used for the war effort.

Norman Sosebee was drafted into the United States Army after he graduated from Canton High School in 1944. Sosebee would go on to fight in the Battle of the Bulge, a major engagement that claimed the lives of thousands, including about 19,000 Americans. Sosebee, whose family for generations

Sesabo Harbor in Nagasaki, Japan, above, was damaged by the atomic bombing of 1945. Canton resident J.T. Holbrook, right, took the photograph of the harbor from the deck of the ship on which he was serving. Radiation was too high for him to be allowed on shore.

operated Sosebee Funeral Home, later set up a war memorial at his business which features the stories of many of those who fought in the war. Among those is Floyd Land of Hickory Flat, who fought in the conflict in Italy, was captured by the Nazis and held as a prisoner of war for almost a year. On the other side of the world, fellow Hickory Flat resident Jake McGarity served in the war in Burma and India, helping to construct a fuel supply line for the Allied forces. Woodstock resident Claude Barnes was one of the men from Cherokee County who stormed the beaches at Normandy. Military pilot J.O. Garrett flew dangerous military missions over enemy territory in Europe.

Canton resident Marion Pope, who later became a Georgia Court of Appeals judge, was a teenager working at the Canton Theater and serving as a member of the local home guard during the early years of the war. When he turned 18, Pope joined the Navy and served in the Pacific during the final days of the war. Pope was just one of hundreds of his fellow residents to see duty during World War II.

Often several members of the same family served. Woodstock resident Smith Johnston, Jr. served as an officer in the Army in New Guinea and the Philippines, while his brother, Army Lt. Richard Johnston, was in England fighting the war on that front. The two were sons of Mr. and Mrs. Smith L. Johnston and the grandsons of J.H. Johnston and Avis Johnston.

The women of Cherokee County made their own sacrifices during the war. Some women served at home in various capacities, some served overseas, and many who remained behind had to pick up a

Irene Howell served in the Women's Army Corps in World War II. She and her family owned Howell's Restaurant and Howell's Drive-In, a popular spot in Canton.

man's tools and go to work to keep the community moving. Elizabeth Wheeler of Canton, a registered nurse who had worked at Coker Hospital, joined the U.S. Army where she became a lieutenant. Miss Wheeler served in North Africa and was among the first women to land with Patton's troops in the D-Day invasion of Italy. Irene Howell of Canton, whose family owned the Howell Drive-In and Howell Restaurant, joined the Women's Army Auxiliary Corps, which later became the Women's Army Corps, and was attached to the Fifth Service Command based in Ohio. Members of the WAAC were the first women other than nurses to serve with the Army.

In 1945 Cherokee County residents watched with the rest of the world as in early August the final act of World War II occurred with the bombings of Hiroshima and Nagasaki. The long and costly war was at last at an end. People in Canton began celebrating on August 14, 1945, as the church bells rang throughout the town and residents ran up and down Main Street hugging each other. At the Canton Cotton Mills the whistles blew to signal the news. Within days, gas rationing was suspended, local baseball teams began playing again and a renewed spirit and optimism began to spread, ushering in better days in the last half of the decade.

By 1949 Canton Cotton Mills was celebrating its golden anniversary of 50 years in business. The company celebrated with newspaper advertisements and the publishing of the book, *A Man, A Town, and A Mill*. At the time of the anniversary the mills were enjoying an era of prosperity and success. Other advertisements in the local newspaper read, "Hot Dog! The GREEN RAIL is Open Again." The popular short order restaurant promised hot dogs, hamburgers and home cooked meals. "The Remodeled Green Rail is the Cheerfulest Place In Town," the promotion promised. The Etowah Restaurant was also offering up some good cooking, including hickory barbecue chicken, pork and beef. Frank Palmer's Garage, and Holbrook and Lindsey Motor Company were doing business in Canton. The newspaper also featured news stories and advertisements about various poultry equipment and processing companies. But before long, another story would dominate the front page, as fire swept through downtown Canton and in a cruel trick of fate struck at the very heart of the city just as it was prospering.

In Woodstock city residents were also enjoying improved times. The city residents got their first water system in 1952. Smith L. Johnston was

Walter Foster of Cherokee County was one of several local African-Americans who served in World War II. Here he and his detachment make it into Paris for Peace Day celebrations on the Champs-Elysees in front of the Arc de Triomphe. Foster served in a medical detachment mobile unit truck company.

mayor of the city during the early 1950s followed by Arthur Poor, and later Frank Ward who served late in the decade as mayor of Woodstock. In 1959 acclaimed architect Miller Barnes was elected to the job at city hall. The town got its first dial telephone system and several new businesses during those days of the 1950s. In 1940 Woodstock had 389 residents and by 1950 that number had grown to a population of 545. Another decade would bring the number to 726.

Holly Springs seemed to slow down in the 1940s with the effects of the war, the loss of the marble quarry and agriculture declining in the area. The passenger rail service was also on the decline in the years following World War II and by the 1950s the Holly Springs Depot that stood as the center of town was no longer in use. In the late 1950s the rail company donated the depot to the city and it would soon begin a new life as City Hall.

The decline of Ball Ground's downtown area began in the 1930s during the Depression. However, the town did receive a water system as part of the Public Works Administration Project of the thirties, which would provide residents with some of the purest and best tasting water in the region. But the relocation of Highway 5 in 1947 diverted traffic from the downtown area, and caused growth to occur outside the city limits, reducing business in the downtown area and spurring a decline in population within the actual town itself.

Allatoona Lake Reshapes Community

A project that would change the landscape of Cherokee County forever began with the Flood Control Acts of August 18, 1941, and December 21, 1944. As the federal government initiated a plan to build lakes for flood control and recreation, the first site chosen in the Southeast was centered in Cherokee County. So began the Allatoona project which culminated with the construction of the lake by the

Following construction of Allatoona Dam, the newly formed lake, seen here near Kellogg Creek in 1958, reshaped Cherokee County, covering small communities, farmland and homes. Galt's Ferry was located in the upper right corner of this aerial view.

Families such as the Field family, who owned 3,000 acres and sold 2,000 of those to the U.S. Army Corps of Engineers for Allatoona Lake, saw their holdings substantially reduced. This land was part of the 1,000 acres not used for the lake and the family later developed into Copper Hill Subdivision. Here the property is graded for Highway 20.

same name. With the completion of the project and dam in 1950, one of the most popular lakes in the state was created where once there were only forests and farmland. By its completion, Allatoona Lake covered 12,000 acres with the majority located in Cherokee County, a portion in Bartow and a small portion in Cobb County near Acworth. The lake encompasses 270 miles of shoreline. The federal government authorized the lake for flood control, hydroelectric power generation, water supply and water quality, as well as recreation and fish and wildlife management. Today around six million people visit the lake annually.

Built on the Etowah River and Little River, with a 1,110 square-mile drainage basin, the lake depends on rainfall for additional water. Other major tributaries include Allatoona Creek, Rose Creek, and Kellogg Creek. The *Cherokee Advance* reported that the average flow of the Etowah River was 2,210 cubic feet per second in an article about the completion of the lake. The total cost of the project including purchase of the land, clearing, construction and relocation of buildings and families supplanted by the project was $31.5 million.

The lake covered over the site of the town of Allatoona, which was on a creek that fed into the Etowah River. Many large farms and plantations were also covered by the lake, following condemnation of the property for the project by the U.S. Army Corps of Engineers. One of the most significant was the Field property, a plantation known as Etowah Vale. Settled by Jeremiah Field, the farm covered a large swath of land along the banks of the Etowah in the Sutallee community. The farm was at Field's Crossing or Downing Ferry, as it was formerly known. In the 1850 census Jeremiah Field's worth was put at $50,000, one of the largest and richest landowners in Cherokee County. He owned 39 slaves in the 1850 Census of Georgia Slave Owners. Etowah Vale operated from the time it was settled in the early 1800s until 1949 when it was covered with the waters of Allatoona Lake. The plantation produced cotton, corn, cattle and hogs, along with other crops. Jeremiah Field did not move to Cherokee County until he was over 50 years old and had four children

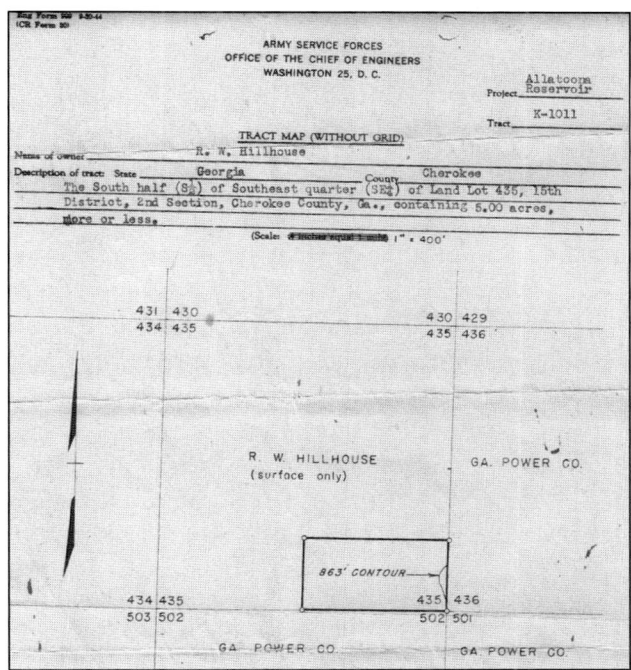

Local residents such as R.W. Hillhouse were paid only $10 an acre for the land taken by the U.S. Army Corps of Engineers for Allatoona Lake. This tract map is for the five acres of land belonging to Hillhouse.

Swimming is a fun pastime at Kellogg Creek Beach on Lake Allatoona for youngsters such as Keegan Treadaway and Ashley Clay.

by his first wife who was deceased. His second wife, Anna Murphy, gave him four additional children, including daughter Malinda Ann Field who married one of Canton's first settlers, Joseph Donaldson. Donaldson joined with his father-in-law in a number of land deals. The three sons by the second marriage were James Madison Field, who settled in Gordon County and twins Elijah Murphy and Elias Earl Field. Elijah moved to Bartow County and Elias stayed with his father in Cherokee County where he went on to be a merchant in Canton and farm the family plantation. Elias Field also served as a Cherokee County Superior Court judge, and was a member of the Constitutional Convention in 1877. Members of the Field family continued to farm Etowah Vale well into the 20th century. The Field property is remembered in the name of one of the lake's recreational areas, "Field's Landing."

The development of Cherokee Mills on Little River was also covered over by the new lake. Cherokee Mills was an early community with a post office, a store, and grist mills and sawmills operated by the flow of Little River. Former Georgia Governor Joseph M. Brown, the son of Governor Joseph E. Brown, bought the property at Cherokee Mills in 1915 and later sold it to Georgia Power Company in anticipation of the construction of the lake. Many other properties in Cherokee County were also bought up by Georgia Power Co. over the years to make way for the new source of power.

An article in the *Cherokee Advance* in 1949 told of the new lake calling it a "Big Attraction, A Future Paradise for Fishermen and Pleasure Seekers."

"Things are different – much different- down on the river where the back waters of the Allatoona Dam are gradually creeping higher and higher. A two-inch rise today, another two inches tomorrow; a rock near the present shore line in plain view last Sunday has slid into obscurity this Sunday. Another swimming hole, where boys of both Indian and white parentage for hundreds of years scampered and played, bids farewell to the sound of voices and slapped wet thighs. Another 15 feet higher and the lake will have reached its normal summer height (power pool height.)

"In a country scant of population – its narrow, twisting roads unchanged in numerous decades, - a bustling activity of travel suddenly becomes evident. A country cross roads, silent for all these years but for the rare movement of some passing vehicle, beast or human being, suddenly is in need of a traffic light. A throng of curious spectators each Sunday stampede the place while still the lake is less than half full of water. What will it be like with numerous cities within less than 50 miles away?

"People from far and near are making inquiries about summer camps, commercial boating areas, fishing camps and the like. Supply stores for the fisherman, the boating man, the hunter, the pleasure seekers are beginning to spring up. And the Canton area, which forms the headwaters, will be looked upon as the angler's paradise, for the headwaters provide the best fishing.

"Not since the day of the creation has the geography of Cherokee County undergone such a sudden alteration. As the lake waters grow bigger, our county map grows more and more out-of-date. With all the water producing a year-round playground where once lay wilderness we can look to some change in the economic and social life of our county. We didn't exactly ask for it, but we got it. Let's make an asset by developing its potentialities and making it worthwhile to us and the millions that will visit annually."

Those words were certainly prophetic.

Soon, many visitors were enjoying the lake each year. Recreational facilities boomed and many Atlanta businesses and organizations, including C&S Bank and Delta Airlines built recreational camps for their employees on the shoreline of the lake.

The new lake offered plenty of recreational opportunities for local residents, such as this Boy Scout Troop camping at Allatoona Boy Scout Camp.

Today, the lake is one of the most frequently visited Corps of Engineer lakes in the United States. It is believed to contribute around $250 million annually to the economy of the counties it touches. There are 688 campsites around the lake, along with 453 picnic sites. The lake has nine city and county parks, one state park and eight commercial marinas. The Corps collects more than $1 million in camping and day use fees per year.

Since 1950 more than 290 drowning deaths have occurred. The presence of the dam is believed to have prevented more than $80 million in flood damage since it was constructed.

Poultry Industry Hatches New Money

The poultry industry in Cherokee County arose out of the humble beginnings of necessity during the early years of the twentieth century and grew into one of the most important segments of the county's economy at its peak. By the 1950s Cherokee County was claiming the title of "The Poultry Capital of the World." Every major road into Cherokee County boasted a large sign with a big white chicken on it announcing "World's Largest Broiler Producing County." At the time there were 227 independent growers doing business in Cherokee County, according to research conducted by Karen Smithwick of Canton. Early pioneers in the poultry industry in Cherokee County included J.L. (Lint) Lawson, W.L. (Lloyd) Lawson, T.B. Bradshaw, John Brown, Arthur Gray, Ed Long, Leland Bagwell and many more.

One of the first families to scratch out an existence by selling chickens was R.O. Anderson and his grandson W.B. Anderson of Woodstock. They, and inventive men like them, would take chickens and other tasty produce grown on the rural farms in Cherokee County south to larger communities such as Marietta and even Atlanta to sell to the households that could still afford a nice Sunday dinner during the days of the Great Depression.

As the county left the Depression behind and prosperity slowly returned to the land, the business of raising chickens became an important segment of the agricultural community in Cherokee County. When President Herbert Hoover promised a chicken in every pot, the farmers in Cherokee County

1949 trucks carrying chickens such as this Canton Poultry vehicle were becoming familiar sights in Cherokee County as the community was on the way to earning the title of Poultry Capital of the World.

toiled to deliver those fowls. With cotton no longer king and prices on the once profitable commodity low, farmers and businesses looked to poultry as a way to turn their fortunes. The first broiler houses began to appear next to homes and in pastures in rural areas, built cheaply and quickly. In the early days of poultry farming, farmers would order their chickens from suppliers in states such as Missouri and Arkansas and the chickens in turn were shipped south by railroad or sent through the postal service. Farmers could order 100 chickens to as many as 1,000, depending on their need.

Brothers Lint Lawson and Lloyd Lawson realized the need and opportunity to get the chickens from the farmers to a processing plant, and they purchased trucks for the task. Soon the growers were contracting with the brothers for their trucks to come directly to the chicken houses and pick up the chickens for transport. The chickens would then be hauled to Atlanta, or sometimes to Miami in the early days for processing, according to research by Mrs. Smithwick. For a trip to Miami the Lawsons would load the chickens into large coops and then onto the trucks. Feed would also be loaded on so that the driver could stop along the way and feed the chickens. Some of the chickens were also sold on the streets of the cities directly to consumers.

In Holly Springs one of the first people to become heavily involved in the poultry business was E.M. Barrett. While poultry sales on a small scale had been successful, Barrett realized that refrigeration would make it possible to process and store poultry on a larger level. Barrett established a small, successful processing plant in the 1930s in Holly Springs.

The broiler business experienced great growth and expansion in the 1940s before and during World War II. In 1940 Arthur Gray moved to Cherokee County and built the first broiler hatchery in the state of Georgia. Live chickens hatched in Cherokee County were hauled all over north Georgia and even further to broiler operations by such industry pioneers as Leland Bagwell. Gray joined with W.L. Lawson and Ed Long of Gainesville in 1945 to build the first broiler processing plant in Cherokee County and soon local producers were providing chickens to the highly profitable northeast United States markets such as New York and Pennsylvania. Ed Long was the manager of the new plant known as Canton Poultry. It was later sold to Gold Kist.

In 1944 another important milestone for the poultry industry occurred when

The Fred Haley Farms, here in 1961, were one of the most successful operations in Cherokee County and owner Fred Haley attained a national reputation as a leader in the world of agriculture.

successful Atlanta poultry producer T.B. Bradshaw decided to locate a portion of his operations to Cherokee County. Before long his business was mainly in Cherokee County. Bradshaw hired John Brown to be the manager of his new hatchery, Cherokee Hatchery, which was on North Street in Canton in the top floor of a mule barn. Bradshaw soon expanded his operation and along with

W.L. Lawson, owner of W.L. Lawson & Son, along with men such as Leland Bagwell, Ed Long and Arthur Gray, was one of the pioneers in the poultry business in Cherokee County.

Lint Lawson opened B & L Feed Store. Clyde Manous was the manager of the feed store. The hatchery was then moved to the top floor of the feed store.

Bradshaw was a colorful figure around town, towering over most men at six feet, five inches tall, and remembered for always driving a new Cadillac and smoking a cigar. Bradshaw was born in Norwood, Georgia, and left school and moved to Atlanta to seek a living when his father died. Working by delivering groceries, he saw the need for fresh produce in the city. He opened Piedmont Poultry Company in 1939 and was soon providing poultry to major grocery A & P Tea Company in Atlanta. Several of Bradshaw's early farmers to provide the chickens were Grady Stancil, Broughton Stancil, Aubrey Chadwick and W.L. Lawson, all of Cherokee County. By 1941 Bradshaw was buying farms in Cherokee County and converting them to poultry operations to meet the growing demands. Over the years his land holdings increased and he was one of the largest land owners in Cherokee County with more than 3,000 acres of farm land. Bradshaw was the first chairman of the Cherokee Water and Sewerage Authority, helping to expand the county's water supply to serve the growing needs.

In 1953 Bradshaw moved his entire operation to Holly Springs and later located his Cherokee Poultry Company to a site on Univeter Road. His was the first, and for many years the largest, integrated poultry operation in Cherokee County. Along with the feed mill and hatchery, Bradshaw was the second largest employer in Cherokee County. In 1963 Bradshaw sold the operations to Central Soya Corporation, which later became Seaboard Farms and eventually was sold to Pilgrim's Pride Corp. which later became known as Pilgrim's, one of the world's largest poultry producers. Throughout its history, the processing plant remained at Bradshaw's location on Univeter Road. When Bradshaw got out of the poultry business, he turned his eye to his 1,500-acre farm in Hickory Flat and his Angus beef operation. In the 1990s his farm was developed

T.B. Bradshaw, here with his wife Kate Bradshaw, was one of the most successful men in the poultry industry in Cherokee County and owned vast expanses of land in the community.

into a golf course community named Bradshaw Farms on East Cherokee Drive.

In the 1950s during the most profitable years of the poultry industry, it was said that more Cadillacs and Lincolns were purchased per capita in north Georgia, including Canton and Cherokee County, than even in Texas where the oil industry was booming. Out of the scratching of chickens around the farmhouse door an industry had grown that proved highly

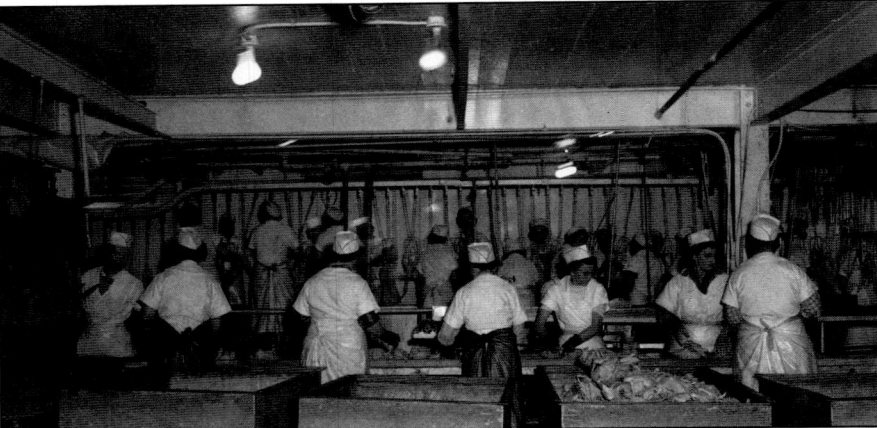

Gold Kist Poultry was one of the county's larger employers, shown here in 1955. In 1970 the poultry processing plant employed 500 workers.

profitable for the growers, as well as those who provided the feed, processed the chickens and sold them to the retail market. Georgia was the number one broiler producing region in the nation, and Canton and Cherokee County were often touted as the top county in the state for poultry production. The farmers who wanted to stay on their land benefited, and the businessmen, many of whom were pioneers in the industry became some of the wealthiest people in north Georgia. Many of them, such as Fred Haley, Veachel Gray, and S.L. Johnston, became nationally known leaders in their industry. Leland Bagwell was president of the Southeastern Poultry and Egg Association.

During the years of poultry production advances were also made in how poultry was processed, thanks in part to those in Cherokee County. Carl Hill, born in Cherokee County the son of a sharecropper, returned from serving in World War II to join the fledgling poultry industry. Hill invented and developed the first successful gizzard processing system. From 1957 to 1967 he owned, and operated General Research, Inc., a company dedicated to the development of automated equipment for the processing industry. Hill & Sons, Inc. was founded in 1969 and located in Ball Ground. Following Hill's death, his son Billy Hill led the company to further success.

By the 1960s the glory get-rich days of the poultry industry were beginning to fade, although Cherokee County continued to be a center for both broiler production and poultry processing, and poultry production continued to have a significant impact on Cherokee County's economy into the new millennium.

Disastrous Fire Blazes in Downtown Canton

The morning of June 29, 1955, started like any other in downtown Canton, but at 9:00 on that early summer morning a disaster struck that would change the face of the city forever. A fire broke out at Cantex Manufacturing Company that Wednesday morning, shooting flames high into the air and starting a blaze that would destroy or damage several key buildings along Main Street and threaten the entire business district before it could be brought under control. The fire started when a newly-installed boiler booster pump malfunctioned and caused the boiler to explode. Within minutes the fire had spread throughout the four-and-a-half story building and turned the manufacturing plant into an inferno. Several of those working in the boiler room were injured as they escaped and one man was presumed dead. At the time of the blaze there were 115 workers on site, most of whom were able to escape the blaze without injury. Those injured included Ralph Harrison of Ball Ground, James T. White of Canton and Hubert Tillery of Waleska. They were taken to area hospitals for treatment. Jonah Chadwick, age 44, a boiler room employee, was presumed killed in the fire.

The fire quickly spread along Main Street from building to building, even as firefighters began to arrive on the scene. Soon the Vaughn Building, a large two-story brick building that housed Grist-Landers Drug Store and numerous offices upstairs, was ablaze. The fire quickly spread to Yarbrough Brothers Grocery Store, the Main Street Garage and the *North Georgia Tribune* printing facilities, eventually destroying those buildings. Other buildings that received damage included Hotel Canton, Smith

There were 115 workers inside Cantex Manufacturing Company when fire broke out on June 29, 1955, but most escaped unharmed. This photograph was taken earlier in the company's history.

Grocery, and Poole Furniture. Firefighters on the roof of Poole Furniture were able to stop the fire's destructive path. Two residences in the area, including that of Miss Cleva Rudasill on School Street, were spared.

Fire units from throughout North Georgia were dispatched to help the Canton Fire Department work to try to save the city business district and keep it from being completely destroyed, including fire engines and crews from Gainesville, Atlanta, Cumming, Roswell, Marietta and the Lockheed plant in Cobb County. Atlanta sent a river pump that began pumping water from the Etowah River. Meantime, the water pressure had dropped as the firefighters worked to pump water onto the blaze. A relay was set up from the river to try to build water pressure.

Volunteer firefighters from across the region began pouring into the city, and several of their automobiles were burned on Main Street in front of the hotel where they parked to help with the fire, including those belonging to James Yancey, Billy Cleghorn and the Reverend Harry Wood. Several volunteers received injuries and had to be taken to the hospital. State Trooper Jack Denney was also injured in the fire.

Many of the spectators stood crying in the street and several fainted as the fire spread out of control and shot flames high into the air. The fire was called the worst disaster that had

The Cantex fire in 1955 destroyed the manufacturing plant and threatened much of downtown Canton before the blaze was brought under control. One man died in the fire and several others were injured.

ever struck Canton. The *North Georgia Tribune* managed to publish a newspaper the next day by carrying everything to a printing company in Dalton owned by publishers C.E. Owen and Ralph Owen's uncles. Eventually most of the businesses would be restored or replaced in the downtown area. But the Cantex site would stay vacant for the next 54 years before a new office building was constructed on the lot where the blaze occurred, a grim reminder for many decades of the day Canton almost burned a second time.

Cherokee High School Expands Education

A new era of education in Cherokee County was ushered in with the opening of Cherokee High School in 1956. That year an act by the Georgia Legislature merged the Canton Independent School System with the Cherokee County School System, leading to the consolidation of two of the county's three high schools, Canton High and Reinhardt Institute. The third high school, Ralph Bunche High serving the African-American community, was later merged with Cherokee High School in 1967 during the state's federally ordered integration of schools.

The new high school, the first of its kind for Cherokee County, was designed by the architectural firm of Finch, Alexander, Barnes, Rothschild and Paschal, of which Woodstock resident and native Miller Barnes was a partner. Constructed on the banks of the Etowah River, the modern buildings were a marvel to the first academic class of 1956-57. Classrooms and offices opened that year, but students continued to make use of the old auditorium and gymnasium at Canton High in the downtown area until the rest of the educational complex was completed in 1958. The new football field was opened that year and named in memory of a student, Tommy Baker, who had died the year before of polio.

The first principal was Hal W. Clements. He headed up the staff for two years, then in 1958 Jim Jordan became the second principal, and he remained in that role until 1966. Dr. Edwin Casey took over as principal following Jordan, a post he would hold for the next two decades. The school excelled in

Cherokee High School, above, opened in the fall of 1956 and the gymnasium and auditorium were completed in 1958, shown here.

Students from throughout the county attended Cherokee High School. After it opened in 1956 it was the only high school in the county except for the Ralph Bunche School which was attended by the African-American students until integration in the 1960s.

academics and in athletics and a tradition of achievement and school spirit was established. In 1963 "Squat," the school mascot, appeared in the pages of the school newspaper, *The Chieftain*, as a cartoon character. That same year the totem pole was erected in front of the school, a proud reminder of the county's Native American heritage. The school's first yearbook, "The Sequoyah," was produced in 1957. An annual tradition was the Sequoyah Pageant and dance.

In those early years, the school had about 35 teachers and 800 students. There were no middle schools in the county, and the elementary schools went from first to eighth grade. Students came to Cherokee High School from every area of the county. Elementary schools that fed into the high school included Avery, Ball Ground, Buffington, Canton, Clayton, Free Home, Hickory Flat, Holly Springs, R.M. Moore, North Canton, Oak Grove, Union Hill and Woodstock.

In 1967 Ralph Bunche School upper grades were consolidated with Cherokee High School and in August of that year they entered the county high school. The total integration of Cherokee County schools was completed with few reported problems.

By 1975, Cherokee High School had 2,300 students and the need for a new high school in the rapidly growing south end of the county was pressing. In 1976 the county's second high school, Etowah High, opened its doors. The student population of Cherokee High was reduced to 1,560 students and a new era for county schools began.

Reinhardt College Faces Hard Times

In 1940 one of the largest classes, 51 students, graduated from Reinhardt College in Waleska. But as World War II touched the county, by 1943 only 15 students were enrolled and nine expected for the following school year. The current president of the college was ready to retire and the college's trustees were on the lookout for a replacement. That man came in the form of Dr. Rowland Burgess, school superintendent from Baxley, Georgia. Dr. Burgess would lead the college for the next 30 years, bringing a patient and kind determination to make Reinhardt all it could be. Those first years were a slow go, as he drove across north Georgia personally recruiting students for the college. In 1944 the school had about 16 college students and 50 high school attendees. Seven of

Vice President Alben Barkley speaks to the crowed during Conservation Field Day.

those Burgess recruited in Cherokee County, and none of them paid the full tuition of $270. Not only was the student population low, but buildings were in disrepair, teacher morale was low and the future looked dismal.

Burgess's hard work eventually paid off and after the war the school began to see an increase in enrollment. However, debt continued to pile up and create problems for the school and administration.

In May 1949 Reinhardt College held Conservation Day that drew 50,000 people to the campus in Waleska and included a visit by the Vice President of the United States.

Burgess later wrote of those times, "If the student had heard of the college, he knew conditions were so bad as to seem hopeless. If a student had not heard of the college, he wondered why and had to be convinced that it was worth attending." Slowly enrollment did increase as the war ended and the college worked to improve conditions.

By the late 1940s Reinhardt was finally beginning to be back on the map. In May 1949 the college planned a major publicity stunt that included a visit by the Vice President of the United States to attract attention to the school. The college's farm was rebuilt in a day using a thousand volunteers and over 100 machines. The event, called Conservation Field Day, saw 50 acres cleared, four buildings erected and a 10-acre athletic field completed. United States Vice President Alben Barkley spoke at the event which drew more than 50,000 people to the college campus.

Dr. Burgess is also remembered for the legacy of horticulture he left the college, choosing many of the landscaping trees and shrubs and overseeing the grounds even after he retired as president.

In 1973 a long-time friend of the college, Dr. Allen O. Jernigan, became president. The retired missionary to China and college minister agreed to take the role on as an interim position, but was soon committed to the role full-time. Jernigan first visited Reinhardt in 1950 when he returned from mainland China. He spoke at the graduation ceremony that year. When Jernigan came on board the school was still heavily in debt. The year he assumed the reins, Reinhardt had 204 students. Jernigan also hired University of Georgia professor Floyd Falany that first year. Falany's service to the college would be great, first as dean of students and later as college president himself. At the time Falany joined the college, none of the teachers there had doctorates, all students enrolled took the same courses, and the Methodist Church was considering closing the college. Through the years of dedicated leadership by Burgess and his successors, the college eventually succeeded in becoming one of the most treasured resources of Cherokee County.

Gospel Singer County's Legendary Star

Lee Roy Abernathy had already made a name in music and cut an album with Columbia Records when at age 14 he and his family moved to Cherokee County so that his father could find work at the Canton Cotton Mills. His father, Dee Abernathy, was a gospel songwriter who along with his wife Clara sang gospel music in the early 1900s in rural north Georgia. Soon at age five little Lee Roy was singing tenor for the Atco Quartet and at age 10 cut his first album. The future Gospel Hall of Fame member at age 12 was forced to quit singing because of tonsil problems, but soon was playing the piano for the Abernathy Quartet at local funerals and singings. When Lee Roy was 15 he accompanied his father and his quartet when they recorded "I'm Redeemed" and "Don't Forget to Pray" at RCA Victor. In 1928,

Abernathy also started his own quartet, the Modern Mountaineers, which played theaters, churches and banquets.

Also that year, Abernathy was invited to play for a quartet in Atlanta, but discovered that he could not read the popular music that the group performed. He made a vow to himself that he would learn to read music and started a philosophy he called Positive Mental Attitude, or PMA, which he would eventually teach to others. Abernathy enrolled in the Atlanta Conservatory in Atlanta and would walk the 49 miles each way to and from Canton for the next three years. To pay for his studies, he began to go door-to-door offering music lessons for 25 cents each. When Abernathy was 19 he married Louise Ammons, who would be his life partner and was the daughter of his supervisor at the Canton Cotton Mills. The couple settled into a life in the mill village, with the first piece of furniture they bought a piano.

Gospel songwriter and singer Lee Roy Abernathy had a long and illustrious career and was a national celebrity.

During the 1930s Abernathy experienced several milestones. He began writing his own piano course of study and he and his father wrote several songs together including "Won't We Have A Good Time" and "My Labor Will Be O'er." Abernathy also began making movies of talent shows and gospel singings and was one of the first people to use recording and public address equipment at gospel singings. In 1936 he wrote a campaign song for FDR entitled "Good Times are Coming Soon," and also wrote a song for Eugene Talmadge's run for governor of Georgia called '$3-Dollar Tag Song," which was extremely popular.

In 1942 Abernathy introduced the first piano arrangement of gospel music and in 1943 published the sheet music for "I'll Thank My Savior For It All." He toured with the USO during World War II and later joined a group to reform the Swanee River Boys in Atlanta. He narrowly missed being burned in the famous Winecoff Hotel fire in 1946 and wrote an award-winning song, "The Burning of the Winecoff," to commemorate the disaster. Also that year he introduced the "Battle of Songs" in Atlanta. He joined the Homeland Harmony group who later recorded his hit song, "Everybody's Gonna Have a Wonderful Time Up There." The song swept the country under the name "Gospel Boogie" and sold more than 5 million copies. It was also recorded by popular stars of the day, Johnny Mathis, Pat Boone and Johnny Cash. Abernathy by 1947 was attracting national attention and appearing on television in Atlanta.

Abernathy and long-time collaborator Shorty Bradford joined forces as the Happy Two in 1949 and for seven years they did a top-rated national television show from WAGA in Atlanta. He wrote a number of commercials, including "You'd Better Get Wild Root Cream Oil, Charlie," which is considered the first singing commercial in the country. During the 1950s he toured some 5 million miles for concerts and formed other quartets including the Lee Roy Abernathy Quartet.

In 1958 Abernathy took a run at the position of governor of the state of Georgia. He did not win, but achieved further notoriety. He also studied for his doctorate in music. As the years went by he began to teach more and more students, and during the 1960s was teaching as many as 60 per week. In 1973 he was inducted into the Gospel Music Hall of Fame.

In later years Abernathy constructed his Music Hall of Fame School of Music across from his home in Canton. The bottom floor contained a concert room and the upper floors housed a museum of the history of gospel music and of Abernathy's career. His achievements over his lifetime make him one of the most nationally known citizens of Cherokee County.

On the Air with WCHK

WCHK radio station was started by radio pioneer Charles McClure in 1957. Here at the station's twenty-fifth anniversary, Bob Peterson, from left, Laura McGhee, Byron Dobbs, Mike McDougald, and Jim Axel were among the original employees.

In April 1957 WCHK Radio Station was licensed by the Federal Communications Commission to Cherokee Broadcasting Company with owner Charles McClure, a Canton native. The local radio station had 1,000 watts of power and was embraced by the community as a new way to stay informed. Known for years as Georgia's Good Neighbor, the station continued to be housed in its original office on Marietta Highway in South Canton for almost 50 years. During that time it was owned continuously by the McClure family. Charles or "Chuck" McClure, Sr. was a

radio pioneer inducted into the Georgia Association of Broadcasters Hall of Fame. McClure was born in Canton in 1923, attended school there and later served with distinction in World War II in the United States Air Force as a member of the 409th Bomb Squadron. He participated in 49 combat missions and was awarded the Flying Cross and U.S. Air Force Air Medal with Cluster.

Under McClure's leadership WCHK eventually went to 5,000 watts of power and a 50,000 watt FM station, WCHK 105.7, was licensed to Canton. Long-time local broadcaster Byron Dobbs was one of those working at WCHK when it went on the air in 1957 and later served as popular general manager and vice president of the company for many years. Several

Mike McDougald goes on the first remote broadcast for WCHK radio station in 1957.

of those involved in the start-up of the local station went on to rise in broadcasting, including Jim Axel, who later worked at WAGA TV in Atlanta. Other original broadcasters were Mike McDougald and Bob Peterson, who were co-managers of the station when it went on the air in 1957. Laura McGee and Dobbs worked in the office at the time the station went on the air.

That first broadcast on April 11, 1957, opened with the "Star Spangled Banner," then Bob Peterson giving the station identification. The first news story was about the passage of a $640,000 bond referendum for the Cherokee High School gymnasium and auditorium.

Cherokee County native and U.S. Secretary of State Dean Rusk speaks at Reinhardt's homecoming celebration in 1961. Secretary of State Rusk had 13 relatives who graduated from Reinhardt College. On the
grandstand seated in the front row with Secretary of State Rusk are: Ninth District U.S. Congressman Phil
Landrum; Ed Bridges, press secretary for the governor of Georgia; Reinhardt College President Dr. James
R. Burgess; Georgia Governor Ernest Vandiver Jr.; First Lady Betty Vandiver; Grady Vandiviere, Canton
attorney; and Mrs. Phil Landrum.

Chapter 7

Coming of Age in Changing Times

When 1960 began, a plethora of issues including Civil Rights, unions, the rise of a youthful counterculture, and social revolution were beginning to be felt, even in smaller communities like Cherokee County. Along with the rest of the world, Cherokee County residents would watch as the Vietnam War unfolded on their television sets, as a man walked on the moon, and as men and women marched, fought and sometimes died for a new equality. The Sixties began a time of radical change that would be felt for decades to come. Despite the unrest and turbulence of the times, Cherokee County residents continued to attend church faithfully, turn out at football and basketball games throughout the county, work hard to provide a living and enjoy time with families. The 1970s saw the end of the war that had brought so much protest and upheaval. In Cherokee County world events such as the oil crisis and Watergate had their impact. Women were increasingly entering the workplace, demanding equal pay for equal work. Soon a new president, this time from Georgia, was stepping forward to lead. The times were a dichotomy of the complex and simple.

In the fall of 1960 local residents turned out at the polls in record numbers to help elect a new president. In the heaviest general election voter turnout in county history, more than 8,000 people cast their ballot in Cherokee County that fall, helping to select the first Roman Catholic elected to the White House, Senator John F. Kennedy, and his running mate Senator Lyndon Baines Johnson from Texas. The election ushered in the Camelot years and would also bring about the prestigious appointment of a Cherokee County native to one of the highest positions in the country. Interest was high locally for the election as well, with contested races such as that of incumbent Sheriff Dan Stringer drawing significant attention. Eight thousand ballots were printed in Cherokee County, but the 16 precincts were so inundated with voters that, according to the *North Georgia Tribune*, they ran out of the ballots and county Ordinary Walter Owen had to have more printed in the final minutes of the election. When the polls officially closed at 7:00 that evening, the Cherokee County courthouse was still filled with long lines of people waiting to cast their votes in the historic election that many saw as a turning point for the country.

As Cherokee County moved firmly into the second half of the 20th century, the community had 23,001 people residing within its boundaries. Roads Commissioner Trammell Carmichael was lobbying for new and better highways to tie Cherokee County to metro Atlanta. Ways to improve local highways and streets would be the topic of many headlines over the next few years. Despite significant population growth in the Sixties, by 1970 Cherokee County was still a relatively small community with about 31,059 residents. Through the years of agriculture and farming, poultry, cotton production, and industry such as the cotton and marble mills, Cherokee County and its five cities and numerous small communities remained insular, complete unto themselves, removed from the Atlanta area. That would begin to change in the coming decades, as the county moved from a rural environment to a more suburban setting. In the 1970s the county began to develop more rapidly, but that was just a foreshadowing of the population explosion that would follow. Despite what the future held, in the 1960s and 1970s the feel of a small community where everyone knew everyone else still existed.

Cherokee Native Son Plays Role on National Scene

In early December 1960 newly-elected President John F. Kennedy appointed Cherokee County native Dean Rusk as Secretary of State, the highest post in the new president's Cabinet. Rusk was sworn in to the post in January 1961 and went on to be the second longest serving Secretary of State, serving under both Kennedy and President Lyndon Johnson until 1969. The local newspaper reported that in making the appointment to Rusk, the President also "at the same time imparted a great feeling of honor and gratitude to those of his (Rusk's) native sod."

David Dean Rusk was born on February 9, 1909, on his family farm about six miles east of Woodstock on Arnold Mill Road in the Lickskillet Community. His parents were Frances Clotfelter Rusk, a local schoolteacher, and Robert H. Rusk, a former minister turned farmer. The family lived in Cherokee County until Dean Rusk was five years old, at which time they moved to Atlanta so Robert Rusk could accept a job with the postal service. Later in life Rusk's father became a schoolmaster at Little River Academy in Woodstock. As the son of two school teachers, Rusk's tale has been hailed as the quintessential story of the American dream where humble beginnings lead to great places. As an adult, Rusk often pointed to his modest beginnings as inspiration for his many successes.

Dean Rusk attended public schools in Atlanta before going to Davidson College in North Carolina. He was awarded a Rhodes scholarship to Oxford University in England where he specialized in international relations and in 1934 earned a master's degree. After teaching at the college level and serving in World War II where he reached the rank of colonel, Rusk served a short term at the

Secretary of State Dean Rusk returned to his native Cherokee County shortly after his appointment by President John F. Kennedy to the position of secretary of state. His speech at Reinhardt College drew a record crowd.

State Department, worked at the War Department, and then returned to the State Department as an undersecretary, quickly moving up through the ranks over the next five years to hold several powerful posts. In 1952 he assumed a new role outside government, as president of the Rockefeller Foundation. From there he went on to take President Kennedy's appointment. In assuming the role of Secretary of State, Rusk beat out such worthy candidates as Sen. Adlai Stevenson, unsuccessful Democratic presidential candidate in 1952 and 1956, and Sen. J.W. Fulbright of Texas.

Rusk felt a strong tie to Cherokee County, the community where he was born, and it was not long after he assumed the job of Secretary of State that he visited his home county. Reinhardt College President Dr. Row-

Reinhardt College homecoming 1961 took place right after the Bay of Pigs incident and thousands showed up to hear native son and Secretary of State Dean Rusk speak about that and other issues.

land Burgess invited Rusk to speak at the college's homecoming in April of the following year. Rusk addressed the crowd of more than 4,000 with information about the Cuban missile crisis, one of the biggest news stories of the times. The visit to his home county made the front page of the *Atlanta Constitution*, the *North Georgia Tribune* and other newspapers around the state that day. Rusk told the crowd that he was pleased to be back in his home county where he could draw strength from his own people and his own soil. "When I see the transformation that has occurred in my home county of Cherokee, I know rapid improvement can occur in a democracy," Rusk said in his speech. He urged the students of Reinhardt to take advantage of the many opportunities for service their generation would have. The invasion of the Bay of Pigs happened only days before Rusk's visit to Cherokee County. The invasion of Cuba is often called the biggest embarrassment of President Kennedy's administration. It occurred on April 17, 1961, only days before Secretary Rusk spoke at Reinhardt College.

Rusk is also remembered for supporting America's involvement in the Vietnam War and was often the target of war protests. He is remembered as an intellectual, and was viewed by his peers as professional and courteous. Rusk was highly respected by President Johnson, who relied heavily on his expertise in foreign affairs. After leaving Washington in 1969, Rusk taught international law at the University of Georgia School of Law in Athens from 1970 to 1984. He died in 1994 and is buried in Athens. Dean Rusk Middle School in the Hickory Flat Community was named in his honor as was the Dean Rusk Hall at the University of Georgia.

Hard Times Hit When Union Strikes at Mills

The fall of 1963 was a time of trouble and unhappiness for many Cherokee County residents as the Canton Cotton Mills closed when the Textile Workers Union and management of the county's primary employer failed to reach an agreement on several labor issues. Just as tensions escalated to a peak a tragic event galvanized every man, woman and child in the nation. President John F. Kennedy was assassinated on November 22, 1963, and Cherokee County joined the rest of the world in mourning his untimely death. As the holidays came that year there was little good news to cheer the community.

Problems began to develop when Canton Cotton Mills implemented a series of changes in the workplace. The Textile Workers Union began meeting with employees urging them to organize, join the Union and fight the changes. Mill President L.L. Jones Sr. addressed the issues in a letter dated September 20, 1963, and printed in the *North Georgia Tribune* on September 26. Jones wrote the letter to all employees of the mills. In running the letter in its entirety on a full page in the newspaper, the editorial staff stated that it was important to the entire community as well. In the letter, Jones

Picketers during the strike at Canton Cotton Mills were under a court order not to block the entrance to the mill. Despite the cold that winter, Union workers out on strike showed up faithfully to fight for better conditions and wages.

pointed to the 64 years the mills had been in business and provided jobs for the community. He said that the company had a history of operating with an eye to the future so that it could continue to offer the workers steady employment and job security. "During these years of service we have passed through many crises, wars, depressions and other difficulties. As friends we have weathered these storms."

Jones explained that due to factors that had occurred since World War II, such as a two-price cotton system, increased competition from abroad and a difficult tariff situation, many mills had been put out of business. He said the local company was facing difficulties and must make changes. He urged the workers to give the changes a chance before considering such measures as bringing in the Union.

"Just at the time when we had completed the job and were beginning to make it work, a group of outsiders, the Textile Workers Union, came along and criticized us. It is easy for them to stand on the outside and criticize and find fault with whatever we do because they have no obligation or responsibility to you or this community."

Jones went on to say that the Union maintained that the new work loads put in by management were too high and that they were unnecessary. Jones said he was addressing the situation in a letter because he had been ill and could not come into the mills in person. He said that the changes were necessary and that they were made with his full knowledge and approval. Jones closed the letter with the following. "I have complete faith in your good judgment and am sure you will make the proper decision."

The majority of the employees of the mills did not agree, and within days they ratified a proposal to join the Textile Workers of America.

Within a month, on a Sunday afternoon in the Avery community, by a vote of 364 to 138, the new Union voted to strike. The strike was not an economic strike asking for increase in pay, but rather for improved working conditions and standards, Union officials said.

The next day, Monday morning, large numbers of picketers with placards congregated at the entrances to Mill No. 1 and Mill No. 2. As the week went on, the mill management announced the mills would continue to operate on one shift, and about 40 workers, many of them management themselves, crossed the line to work.

Twenty-five State Troopers were sent in to Canton to keep the peace in the community and at the picket lines. A court order was issued by Cherokee County Superior Court Judge Sam Burtz ordering those picketing not to block the entrances of the mills and prohibiting any mass picketing. The order also stated that the picketers could not attempt to prevent Canton Cotton Mills from operating or receiving deliveries of materials and supplies.

On November 7, 1963, bold headlines in the *North Georgia Tribune* read "Canton Mills Closed Indefinitely." The article reported that despite the court order, several acts of violence and vandalism had occurred against those who had still attempted to work. A number of the employees' homes were rocked with considerable damage done to doors and windows. Dillard Smith of Macedonia reported that his home was fired into several times by a .22 rifle from an automobile. Three bullets went into his living room and two into a bedroom where a child was sleeping. At the picket lines, a police officer was beaten. The article went on to report that the Union battle was centered on four painters who worked at the mill and were ordered to climb a stack and paint it in what they asserted were unsafe conditions using inadequate equipment. The men filed a complaint with the State Department of Labor.

Even after meetings between the two sides during the next weeks, no agreement could be reached, and the mills were closed when picketing continued. The winter was a harsh one and, as the strike continued, fresh loads of firewood were delivered to the picket lines to keep fires burning. The strike would eventually result in more than one million dollars in lost wages for the employees of the mill.

On November 22 another event took attention away from the strike as all Americans were stunned with the news that President John F. Kennedy was shot. Schools in Cherokee County were closed for the days of mourning. In the *North Georgia Tribune* the news took the headlines, with a black bordered picture of the popular leader headlined "President Kennedy – Summoned Across Death's Frontier." Special services were held in Cherokee County on the following Monday, the day of the President's funeral in Washington, D.C. Large crowds packed the services at Reinhardt College where President J.R. Burgess spoke and in Canton at the First Baptist Church where a joint service was held with the Methodist Church and the Reverend Fred Shelnutt preached.

By the next issue of the newspaper, the strike was back in the headlines, but the report indicated that little progress had been made, and that despite rumors and hopes that an agreement would soon be reached, no such end was in sight. The community went into the holiday season with little to celebrate and many people struggling to continue to put food on their tables.

The New Year brought a fresh start. Finally, on January 24, 1964, the Union members met at the National Guard Armory in Canton and voted

The strike at Canton Cotton Mills was ignited when four workers were ordered to paint a smokestack in what they contended were unsafe conditions. Here, the smokestack is being painted by Blake Young.

555 to 27 to accept the terms finally hammered out by the two sides. By early February the mills were back in operation, but the strike was costly for both sides and the price high for the workers, the community and the company.

Civil Rights and the Struggle for Racial Equality

Official reports of integration and desegregation of schools in Cherokee County are almost diametrically opposite firsthand accounts of the escalating tensions that sometimes erupted into violence and often in racial slurs and ugliness during the mid-1960s. The brave African-Americans in Cherokee County who were willing to be the first to cross the deeply entrenched line of segregation in the South remember their acts of courage more as instances of necessity and obligation than as the valorous deeds they actually were. For Samuel Pitts and Edward McMickens, two of the four African-American men who integrated the Canton Theatre in the summer of 1964, they were only doing what needed to be done to help advance the cause of equality for all Americans. The events of that tense and potentially violent night when they put their lives and safety on the line in the struggle for Civil Rights were significant in their far-reaching effect, but for Pitts and

Signs such as this one at a bus station in Rome, Georgia, in 1943, indicated separate facilities for African-Americans. Segregation of blacks and whites became a common occurrence in the South with the rise of Jim Crow laws in the 1890s. *Courtesy of Library of Congress Prints and Photographs Division*

McMickens they were just doing the right thing. Cynthia Durham and Priscilla Strickland Moody, the first two African-Americans to attend Cherokee High School, crossed the line because they wanted equal opportunity and a better education for themselves and others in their community. The high school juniors were greeted with hate and bigotry, but instead of being bitter about the treatment, they say their experiences helped them to grow up faster and to accomplish more with their life than they would have if they had not stood up for racial equality.

In the 1960s, Cherokee County had a black population of less than 10 percent, unlike many of the counties in the southern part of the state and the Atlanta area where the percentage was greater. In the northern counties, the number was less, with some neighboring counties having no African-Americans. While firsthand accounts and oral histories indicate the Ku Klux Klan was active in Cherokee County as it was in neighboring counties such as Forsyth, there are no public records of the local organization. Very little is mentioned in local newspapers about the changes that took place in Cherokee County as a result of the Civil Rights movement. The racial violence that rocked the community

The Reverend Ralph Freeman, left, was a leader in the struggle for freedom for African-Americans in Cherokee County during the Civil Rights movement. Reverend Freeman, here with Mary Crawford, center, and his wife, Emma Jean Freeman, was pastor of the Hickory Log Baptist Church.

in the summer of 1964 was not reported in the local newspaper. One of the few mentions of any racial tensions was an advertisement headlined "What About the Civil Rights Bill!!!" sponsored by the Cherokee County Young Democrats. The ad pointed out that presidential candidate Barry Goldwater voted for the bill "everytime but once." The ad went on to point out, "Goldwater gave his views clearly in the Congressional Record June 18, 1964. 'I am unalterably opposed to discrimination on the basis of race, color or creed.' So he would have signed the bill, too! At least he would have for the Northern part of America. He probably would have vetoed it for the South."

President Johnson went on to win the election, but did not carry the Deep South, including the state of Georgia. Analysis of the results of the election said that the South harbored resentment because Johnson signed the Civil Rights Act of 1964. In Cherokee County Goldwater took 3,396 votes to Johnson's 3,189, a turnaround for the traditionally Democrat majority county.

The summer of 1964 the Reverend Ralph Freeman, pastor at Hickory Log Baptist Church, worked to propel the civil

Senior year photo of Samuel Pitts at Ralph Bunche School.

rights movement forward in Cherokee County by organizing young people in the Freedom League, according to an interview with Pitts and McMickens. All across the South that summer efforts were under way to break down the barriers of repression used for decades to isolate the African-American population. In Cherokee County, as in many parts of the South, the old Jim Crow laws were still adhered to. African-Americans were required to use separate water fountains in Canton, were prohibited the use of public restrooms, could not eat in local restaurants and had to sit in the balcony of the movie theater if they were allowed in at all. African-Americans were expected to walk on the other side of the street if meeting white people in passing.

Reverend Freeman and his members were ready to challenge the oppression and began meeting to decide where each member would go to take a stand. Edward McMickens agreed to go to the lunch counter at Grist Landers drugstore in Canton on a Saturday that summer with a group of men and eat lunch. On the designated weekend they went, sat down and ate lunch without incident. Other groups of freedom members took a similar stance at the Green Rail Restaurant, Pine Crest Inn and other local dining establishments.

On Monday night the group of African-Americans planned on attending the Canton Theatre and sitting in the downstairs where they were prohibited. Samuel Pitts and Edward McMickens, along with the Reverend Freeman's son Ralph Freeman and Joe McMickens, purchased their tickets at the ticket booth on Main Street without incident and walked in. Once they were seated in the main section of the

---

Jones Park Opening

(A COLORED RECREATIONAL CENTER)

Canton, Ga. Saturday, June 17

Hrs. 2 to 5 P. M.

Program

Song

Invocation _____ Rev. P. R. Geer

Song

Object of Meeting Stated

Talk: What the Park Will Mean to the Colored People _____ Rev. E. P. Yorpp

Song _____ Quartet

Talk: Extending Thanks for the Gift in Behalf of Colored

    Citizens _____ H. W. Ware

Talks by the following white friends:

    (a) Mr. P. W. Jones, Donor

    (b) Dr. J. T. Pettit, Mayor

    (c) Mr. E. A. McCanless

    (d) Col. A. J. Henderson

Acceptance of Park _____ W. A. Thompson

Song

Benediction _____ Rev. P. R. Geer

The entire colored population is expected and urged to be present, and our many white friends are cordially invited.

REFRESHMENTS FREE FOR ALL

Park Committee

Recreational facilities in Cherokee County were segregated prior to the Civil Rights Act of 1964 which ended unequal application of voter registration requirements and racial segregation in schools, the workplace and facilities that served the general public. Jones Park was one such facility and was located behind the two churches, Zion Baptist and St. Paul AME, on Crisler Street in Canton. The property was deeded to both churches. This program likely dates to the 1920s.

theater. Some of the other patrons began throwing ice at
them. The four decided to leave
the theater early.

"When we walked out
the town was full. We had to go
across the street where we were
parked. We had guns in our car
and we were trying to make it
over there. They were calling us
names. The police were there
but they were clearly on the
other side of the situation. A
pickup truck was there and the
men had rocks. One man who
we knew was a member of the
Ku Klux Klan pulled out a gun
and another man put a gun to
the head of one of the men.
Suddenly it came up a big

Four young men integrated the Canton Theatre in the summer of 1964. Their attendance at the movie sparked a tense confrontation in the streets that night which ended
without bloodshed.

shower of rain. It was raining so hard we had to step back up against the theater. Just then Ozella Tanner
pulled up in her car and we got in and left town," Pitts said.

The men had to abandon the car in town. It was subsequently turned over that night by those attempting to thwart integration of the theater. They then destroyed the car. That was just the beginning of
the violence that rocked the town during those hot days of Freedom Summer.

According to the interviews, later that same night men in pickup trucks drove through the African
-American communities throwing rocks and bottles and sometimes shooting at some of the houses. But
the men in Stumptown, Nineteen and Pea Ridge communities were ready and would not back down. The
violence continued to escalate over the next few days and on the second night and third night they came

African-Americans in Cherokee County formed the Freedom
League in the mid-1960s to challenge segregation at restaurants such
as the Pine Crest Inn and other establishments in the community.

back through and there was a lot of shooting.
But some of those white people, who planned
on inflicting fear and terrorizing the residents,
instead got a touch of buckshot themselves.

In the next few days, the Federal Bureau of Investigation was called in to probe the
escalating incidents in the community. According to the two men, the "fanfare" went on for
about a week. Then, when it became apparent
that African-Americans were not going to back
down, the tensions died down, at least for the
moment.

For Cynthia Durham and Priscilla
Strickland Moody the decision to be the first
African- American students to attend Cherokee
High School in the fall of 1965 marked the be-
ginning of two tense years of almost unrelent-
ing ostracism.

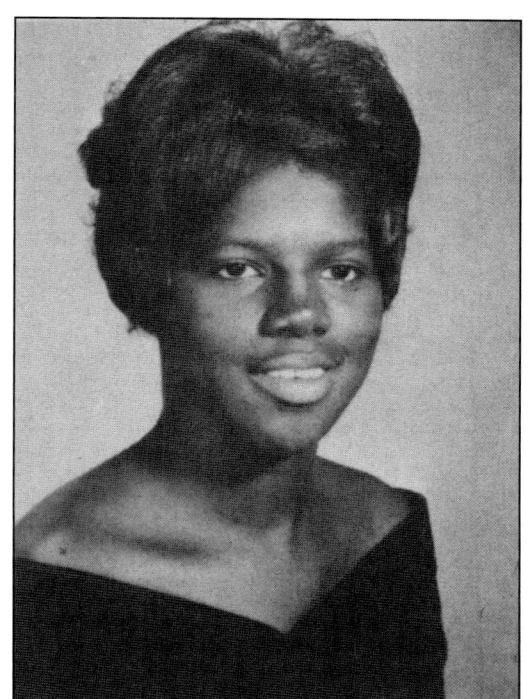

Senior year photo of Priscilla Strickland at Cherokee High School.

When Ms. Durham participated in a program at Knoxville College through the United Negro College fund the summer before her junior year in high school, she realized many of the people she met had a broader educational experience. She had seen a notice at Ralph Bunche School promoting freedom of choice and she decided she wanted to attend Cherokee High School, despite the obstacles.

"Priscilla and I were writing and I suggested we go to CHS. We talked to our parents and they said okay. We had a couple of meetings with the principal and their message of the school was that the other students were not going to be nice to us and that they didn't want us running and telling them everything. They said if you are not hurt, we do not want to hear from you. My mother made it clear that she expected us to be treated like every other student," Cynthia Durham said in an interview. The two young girls quickly learned that there were many ways to be hurt.

Each of the women remembers the first day of school as extremely painful from the moment they walked through the door. There was a large crowd of people around the school that day and Cynthia remembers some police presence, but they were not provided protection as they entered the school. Instead, many of those in the crowd were calling them names and saying cruel racial slurs. Both adults and young people were throwing things at them.

Priscilla Strickland Moody recalled the events of that morning. "I remember us coming in one of the back halls and coming down the hall. It was as if everyone in the school had converged there and as we walked down the hall they backed out of the way. They were very antagonistic. I do believe that there were good people at the school, but they were not in the front of the line that day. Some of them were throwing things at us and as we walked by, I could hear them muttering and calling us ugly names."

"It was just the two of us and we did not stop as we walked down the hall. Both of us believed in a nonviolent stance but I had to exert more temperance than Cynthia. I never imagined how inhumane man could be to man. That night when I got home I cried because I could not believe that one person could treat another person that way."

Cynthia recalls thinking that morning, "Okay we don't talk, and we don't react." For Priscilla what had started as support for her friend quickly hardened into resolve.

"The day I walked in and heard someone say go home, nigger, I knew the cause was much bigger than me. I buckled down and resolved to stay the course. Perhaps that was the purpose for which we were born. I thought, you have been called by God to do this. If I perish, let me perish, but I'm going to finish Cherokee High School."

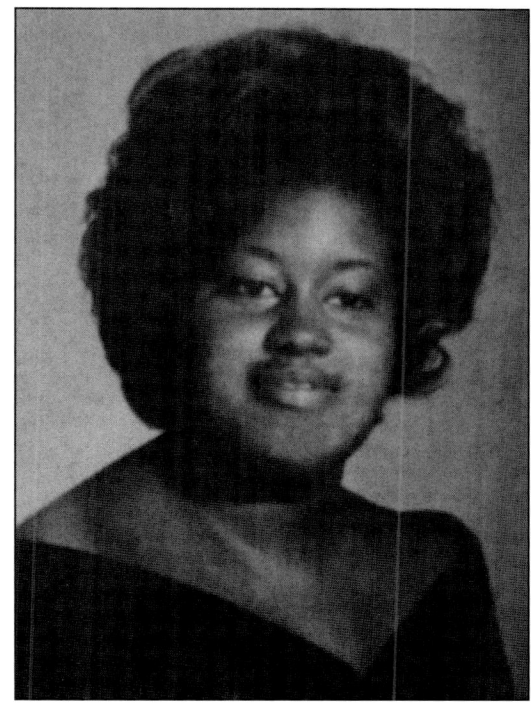

Senior year photo of Cynthia Durham at Cherokee High School.

When they went into the auditorium for the official opening gathering, no one would sit next to them. Priscilla remembers that the school superintendent who spoke that morning urged all students to treat others as they themselves would want to be treated, advice that was all too often not followed by students and teachers alike.

The two girls were separated in different classes and did not have lunch together. Cynthia recalls that on the first day when she sat down to eat the meal she had brought from home every person at the table she chose stood up and moved, leaving her completely isolated. Cynthia said that was okay, but she just ate her lunch and left. Often, as the young ladies would leave the lunchroom students would throw pennies at them. That behavior would continue for months.

In November, Cynthia's mother, Ida Pearl Durham, died. At that time Cynthia says she began to feel some compassion and tolerance from the teachers. Some of the teachers accepted the students from the beginning and showed them kindness. Cynthia particularly remembers Doris Yarborough, her home economics teacher, as well as Mr. Bill Teasley and Mrs. Sarah Donley as being supportive throughout her time at the school.

For Priscilla, Ms. Helen Mauldin was a lifeline. "Ms. Mauldin was a seasoned teacher and at her stage in life, one might have expected her to be prejudiced. But I do not believe there was a prejudiced bone in her body. She always let me know that she cared about me as a person and academically."

Priscilla remembers one especially painful episode in American government when a mock campaign debate was held featuring gubernatorial candidate Lester Maddox. The student who played Maddox took the opportunity to denigrate African-Americans in horrific terms, Priscilla said, weeping as she recalled the painful episode.

After the diatribe had gone on for about thirty minutes, another student, a young white woman, stood up with tears streaming down her face and said "Stop it," Priscilla recalls. "The girl said, 'Y'all are being rude and you don't have to treat Priscilla that way, I want you to stop.' She was almost screaming at that time. The teacher never did anything to stop the boy."

There would be many other instances of discrimination and cruelty during the girls' two-year tenure at Cherokee High School, but at the end they graduated and both went on to college. During those years, the young girls often walked with sharpened pencils in their hands in case they were attacked and they were often

African-American students in the county attended Cherokee High in the years following its desegregation. Teacher Doris Yarborough, left, is remembered for treating students equally and with respect regardless of their race. She taught home economics to students such as Sue Ann Chastain, Judy Jordan, Sandra Johnson, and Tamara Teague Owen, here in 1969.

Canton Public School offered black students an education in Cherokee County in the late 1800s and early 1900s. The one-room school was originally located in what became Zion Baptist Church and later met at Hickory Log Baptist Church. Here, students and Professor J.A. Burge, along with other teachers at the school.

pushed by other students. But by the beginning of the second year they did begin to make some new friends and be included in some activities, including extracurricular activities, such as the school play. By then a few other African-American students, including Carolyn Durham had joined them at Cherokee High School.

Neither of the women regrets the sacrifices they made and the abuse they endured to be the first students to integrate the high school in Cherokee County.

Despite all that she went through Cynthia Durham remembers her time at Cherokee High School kindly. "It was a benefit to me. It caused me to mature a little faster and it gave me more opportunities in my education. Was it pleasant? No, but there were some high points," Cynthia said.

For Priscilla Strickland Moody there are no regrets. Mrs. Moody said that her mother was employed as a domestic worker and that she wanted to show her that all of the things her mother endured so that her daughter could have a better life were not in vain.

"I would do it all again. It is a cause I embrace. It grew me and made me appreciate who I am, and in that growth process helped me be where I am today," Mrs. Moody said.

Mrs. Moody feared for her life and for the lives of her family members during those bitter times. She can remember many nights when she and her family sat in the dark, amid rumors of possible retaliation, waiting for a possible attack. But for her it was worth the pain.

"We have a saying that we uphold our race. We were carrying our people on our shoulders. It was about the African-American community in Canton. And in those moments history was made and that is what made us."

According to the book *Public Education in Cherokee County*, published in 1982 by the school system, during the first years of integration in the county students were free to attend any school in the Cherokee County school system "regardless of race, national origin or color." In addition to the students who elected to attend Cherokee High School, four African-American students were in attendance at Canton Elementary. In the fall of 1967 Ralph Bunche School was closed as a regular school and students consolidated into the Cherokee County Schools including Cherokee High School, which became the only high school in the county. "This total integration of students and faculty was accomplished with a minimum number of problems," a history of the school in the book stated.

Ralph Bunche School, originally called the Cherokee County Training School, was built in the 1950s as an elementary and high school to consolidate all African-American students in Cherokee County. Some consolidation took place among African-American schools in Cherokee County in 1947 when the state Board of Education urged the concept statewide and funded bus service Then in 1956 following a statewide survey, further consolidation was urged leading to one school being constructed.

Magnolia Thomas was a well-known and respected teacher in Woodstock.

Until the consolidation, African-American students attended community schools, many of which were started immediately after the Civil War. Others were organized in the early 1900s. The Canton School was founded in 1902 on property adjacent to the new public schools in downtown Canton. The new public school was built on property donated by the Brown family and at that time was adjacent to the St. Paul African Methodist Episcopal Church. On that site, with help from the local residents and city government a Canton Public School was erected for the African-American population, or as they were designated at the time, the "children of color."

In Woodstock, the elementary school on Arnold Mill Road was started in a two-story structure in the early 1900s for the African-American children. That structure was later replaced with a one-story building. Two teachers usually taught at the school. Parents were responsible for their children's books and supplies and helped pay the teachers. Among the teachers there was Magnolia Thomas, a well-known and respected teacher who had graduated from Spelman College in Atlanta. Born in Canton in 1890, Miss Thomas lived in Woodstock with her mother in a lovely home built for Miss Magnolia, as she was known, and her mother by her brother Robert Thomas. Miss Magnolia also taught at the African-American school in Hickory Flat. Another community school was the Olive Vine School off Highway 140 near Reinhardt Chapel in Waleska. Olive Vine School was started in 1914 and was a one-story building with outdoor toilets.

With the opening of the new school, Cherokee Training School, on the site of Hickory Log School, students came from Woodstock, Nelson, Waleska, Pea Ridge, South Canton and Nineteen communities to attend. Those students who lived within a mile and a half of the school walked to school, other students were transported from throughout the county by bus. The school was located between Canton and Waleska off Highway 140. The school was constructed as a part of the same bond referendum that financed the new Cherokee High School on Marietta Highway. The county school superinten-

dent at the time, Bill Hasty, initiated the plan to build the two new high schools in the county. The school opened for students in the fall of 1956. The new school had about 162 students.

Gertrude Herbert was the first principal of the new Cherokee Training School, but left for a position in Atlanta after a year and at that time H.A. Bell became principal. According to a history of the school by teacher Willie Benning, Principal Bell had a remarkable ability to extract the best efforts from his teachers for the students of the school, despite a lack of many resources. Bell also worked hard and was successful in getting

Ralph Bunche School was originally known as the Cherokee County Training School and was where African-American students attended public school prior to integration in the 1960s.

the community involved in the school, which helped to have the grounds landscaped, provide playground equipment for the elementary students and to outfit a school band. Bell also helped students to acquire scholarships to colleges, enabling many of the students at the school to continue their education despite financial challenges. In 1961 the name Cherokee County Training Center was changed to Ralph J. Bunche School to honor Dr. Ralph Bunche, the first African-American to receive the Nobel Peace Prize in 1950. The school was also accredited by the Southern Association of Colleges and Secondary Schools under Bell's leadership and attained several other honors.

R.T. Jones Memorial Hospital Opens

Health care in Cherokee County got a shot in the arm in August 1960 when a contract was signed for construction of a new public hospital to serve Cherokee County under the federal government's Hill-Burton Hospital Act. The new hospital in Canton was to be funded with local, state and federal funds and cost $1.5 million. Congress passed the Hill-Burton Act in the mid-1940s to help provide funding for hospitals as the Great Depression and World War II had taken a

R.T. Jones Memorial Hospital was the first public hospital in Cherokee County and opened in 1962 as a modern medical facility with 66 patient beds.

toll on the fiscal health of many small medical facilities, causing them to close. Canton did have a private hospital, Coker Hospital, in operation through the 1950s. The new public hospital would provide free care to those patients who could not afford it, under the terms of the federal funding.

In 1956 a Cherokee County Hospital Authority was formed with Chairman Carl Barrett of Holly Springs, Dr. Jack Jones of Atlanta as vice chairman, N.A. Thomason of Canton as treasurer and members Roy Reynolds Sr. of Canton, Smith Johnston of Woodstock, Hamrick Smith of Lathemtown and Max Stancil of Ball Ground. Dr. Jones died before the new hospital could be built and L.L. Jones, Sr. was appointed in his place.

The Hill-Burton Act mandated that to receive federal funds, a portion of the money needed by a community had to come from local and other funding. The Cherokee County government provided $100,000 of the needed $1.5 million and the R.T. Jones Memorial Community Foundation provided $500,000. At the time, L.L. Jones, Sr., who was chairman of the foundation, said it was a pleasure to have the opportunity to give to such an honorable and beneficial institution. The state and federal government

Community leaders and residents attended the grand opening of R.T. Jones Memorial Hospital in 1962.

made up the remainder. Dr. William Nichols was also instrumental in starting the new hospital, as were a number of members of the medical community at the time.

The hospital offered the latest advancements at the time of its construction, and was even to be fully air conditioned. The 66-bed hospital provided state-of the art medical expertise along with high-quality patient care in a local setting.

By the 1970s, the local hospital was busy expanding its services and keeping up with the demand for patient care. Physicians who practiced at the hospital during the 1960s and 1970s included Dr. William Cutts, Jr., Dr. L. Austin Flint, Dr. Carlton Hudson, Dr. John Cauble, Dr. David Fields, Dr. H.L. Gold, Dr. Harry Davis, Dr. Arthur Hendrix, Dr. B.K. Looper, Dr. Harry B. Johnston, Jr., Dr. William H. Nichols, Jr., Dr. Charles R. Andrews, and Dr. Grady Coker.

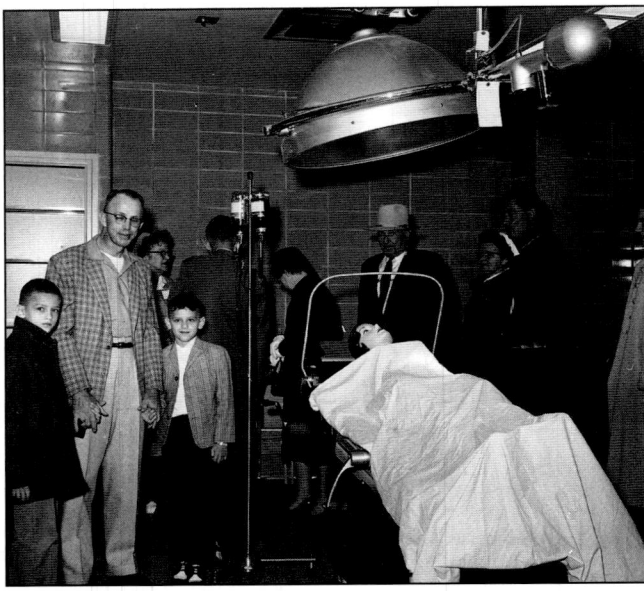

The new hospital in Canton featured a state-of-the-art operating room when it opened in 1962. Here, visitors tour the facility at the grand opening.

In 1978 the hospital employed 192 health-care workers and support service employees. The surgical facilities at R.T. Jones Memorial Hospital were considered first-rate with two operating rooms, which handled close to 100 surgeries a month. New equipment had been purchased for the operating room, which allowed doctors to perform many sensitive surgeries. The hospital also had added new x-ray facilities and was handling around 12,000 x-rays per year. The hospital had its own food production center and a completely stocked pharmacy staffed by two full-time pharmacists who dispensed more than 12,000 doses of medication per month. The pharmacy was open 24 hours a day and pharmacists Billy Whitmire and Deborah Fincher reported a tremendous increase in work as the number of patients increased at the hospital. The emergency room was experiencing a tremendous demand as well.

In the 1990s, the local hospital was taken over for operations by Northside Hospital and eventually renamed Northside Hospital Cherokee. By 2004 the hospital had 40,000 patients in in-patient and out-patient care and in 2009 that number had multiplied to 100,000 patients seen at the local hospital. The hospital underwent several major expansions and renovations, including the emergency room. In 2010 a new facility was planned at Exit 19 of Interstate 575 on 140 acres that Northside Hospital purchased for the new hospital.

South Cherokee County Moves Ahead

The south end of Cherokee County had experienced substantial growth following World War II. Woodstock was still a small town in the 1960s, but had many businesses and commerce for the residents. After getting its first water system in 1952 which serviced about 125 customers, in the 1960s the city began to purchase water from neighboring Cobb County, allowing for more expansion. In 1961 several new businesses opened, including Morgan Ace Hardware which opened on the northwest corner of Main Street and Church Street, which is now Towne Lake Parkway. Keenum's Drug Store opened its doors and Southern Bell in 1962 announced that it would add Woodstock to the Atlanta calling area. Many of the stores along Main Street participated in a plan to update the facades along the business portion of town. A street directory compiled by Miller Barnes of Woodstock in 1962 showed 28 businesses and five churches in the city limits. The town had a population of 775. In 1963 South Cherokee Recreation Association was

The Woodstock Atomedic Hospital opened in July 1969 on the day that man walked on the moon.

organized by some local residents to serve the recreational needs of the area's children. Also in 1963 the Woodstock Business Association was formed. The city was also given the Postal Zip Code of 30188.

In June 1962 ground was broken for a new medical center in Woodstock. The shovel at the ceremony was held by Mayor W.B. Drinkard and Dr. Tom J. VanSant, who for 50 years had served Woodstock as a doctor, and for many of those as the only doctor. Building committee chairman Miller Barnes pointed to the long line of doctors who had served the community, including Dr. W.H. Dean, Dr. Will Dean, Dr. Jim Boring, Dr. W.H. Perkinson. He praised Dr. Tom VanSant for his years of service "through depressions, two wars and prosperous times." Ninth District Congressman Phil Landrum also spoke at the ground breaking ceremony. The new clinic was to be constructed for $40,000 and located between the Dean home and the McAfee home on East Main Street.

Dr. VanSant, who at the time was treating patients although he was blind, had retired at the age of 85 and the town was left without a doctor. Community leaders and city officials began a search that resulted in Dr. Evan Boddy locating to the south Cherokee city where he would make a substantial contribution to the health of the community for the next several decades. Dr. Boddy began his practice at the new Woodstock Medical Center in August 1962. The new brick building had waiting areas, examination rooms, an x-ray room and other facilities. Dr. Boddy said at the time of the ground-breaking that he hoped the medical center would "not only help to heal the sick, but also help to keep us well."

In 1969 Dr. Boddy helped bring the first hospital to Woodstock, and for many people the new Cherokee Atomedic Hospital on Arnold Mill Road seemed out of this world. The new building looked something like a space ship and had been on exhibit at the New York World's Fair in 1964 where space age wonders were the order of the day. Purchasing the facility cost $180,000. The hospital had closed circuit television and a computer used for tracking and dispensing medicine to the patients and managing resources such as linens and medical supplies. The building, which some people said resembled a flying saucer, had four examination rooms and an intensive care unit as well as 22 patient rooms which could hold a maximum of 40 patients. The hospital was funded by the non-profit organization that was headed by seven local trustees. Two other doctors along with Boddy, Dr. J. Thomas Cooper and Dr. Robert Townsend, were on staff at the Woodstock hospital.

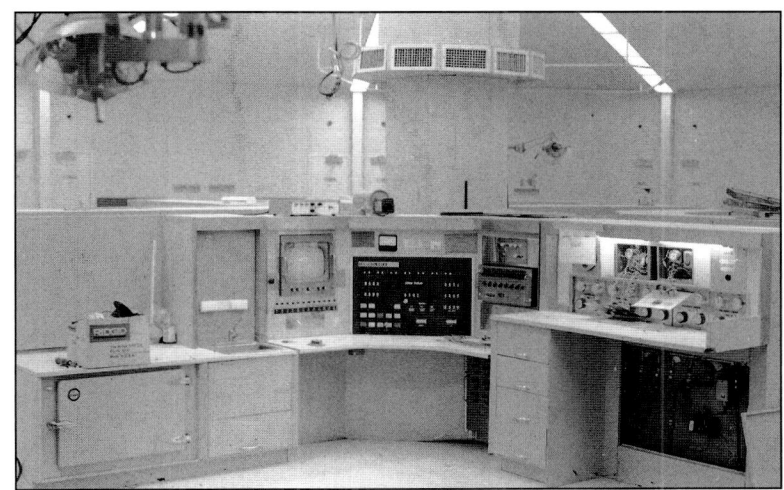

The Woodstock Atomedic Hospital offered residents in the south Cherokee community the latest in medical advancements.

In the next two decades as the south end of Cherokee County grew in population, the Woodstock hospital was almost always operated at capacity. Julia Ellis was hospital administrator in the 1980s. In 1988 the hospital underwent a half-million-dollar renovation. The Cherokee County Hospital Authority purchased the hospital from Dr. Boddy, and in 1994, made the decision to close the facility.

Opening a Fresh Page on Public Libraries

In 1968 Cherokee County got a new public library in downtown Canton, the first facility in the county built specifically for a library. Public libraries were not a new idea to the county and its residents. In the early 1930s members of the Canton Woman's Club helped establish the county's first public lending library in some rent-free space behind Higgins Jewelry Store in downtown Canton on Main Street next to Canton Drug Company. Miss Melinda Roberts volunteered two days a week as the librarian. Later Irene Stovall and Mrs. Rhodes McClure served as librarians. As demands for the library grew, Mrs. P.W. Jones, also known as Miss Mary, donated funds to purchase an old building which had at one time been the Presbyterian Church in Canton. In 1947 that building

The McAfee house in downtown Canton was purchased by the R.T. Jones Foundation in 1957 for use as a public library. The house was later torn down to make way for a new library building.

was sold and the library moved into a room above the Canton City Hall provided by the city. The city, county and board of education each began paying $25 per month to fund a staff member for the library.

In 1956 the county, city and school board appointed the first library board to oversee libraries in the county. Members included Mrs. P.W. Jones, Mrs. Jack Jones, Mrs. C.K. Cobb, Mrs. E.M. McCanless, Mrs. Odie Galt, Mrs. Nina Jones, L.L. Jones Jr., W.L. Blackwell, E.W. Owen and Bill Hasty, who was school superintendent at the time.

In 1957 the R.T. Jones Foundation purchased the old McAfee home on Main Street to house the library and also gave funding to remodel the house for its new use. In 1958 the local library joined with Pickens and Gilmer counties to form the Sequoyah Regional Library System with the new R.T. Jones Memorial Library serving as the headquarters. The library system was also now eligible for state funding. Cal Hendrix served as the first professional library director for the system. The library began to expand and bought its first bookmobile.

In 1968 the library board decided a new modern library was needed and the decision was made to raise funds to replace the McAfee House with a new library. Local businesses and residents helped put together the money to fund the new library building. Mrs. S.E. Hyatt headed the capital campaign for the new library.

The R.T. Jones Memorial Library was built in Canton in 1968 and later converted to the Cherokee County Elections and Registration Office.

In 1963 the Woodstock Public Library was formed with support from the Woodstock Junior Woman's Club and Mrs. Smith L. Johnston of Woodstock. At first the library in the south end city was housed in a rent-free store in the city, but soon moved into the old Woodstock Bank building which it owned through the efforts of the local residents. Sara Poor was the librarian. Juanita Hughes later joined the staff.

In the early 1990s the need was there once again for a new building. The new R.T. Jones Memorial Library on Brown Industrial Parkway in Canton was opened on May 1, 1991. Library branches at Rose Creek near Woodstock, Hickory Flat and Ball Ground were also opened.

Dixie Speedway Laps County

In the late 1960s Cherokee County saw the opening of a new type of spectator sport for the community. Some might say it was born out of the days of driving carloads of moonshine over the dirt roads in the rural areas of north Georgia. Speed was needed to make sure that the revenuers and the police didn't catch up. But soon Saturday night dirt tracks were as much a part of the times as country churches, state parks and mom-and-pop stores.

Dixie Speedway in Woodstock opened in 1969 as a dirt track by racing legend Bud Lunsford and Cherokee County businessman Max Simpson. But for the major part of the next 40 years, Dixie Speedway was operated by the Mickey Swims family. "I heard Dixie was for sale, and I went down there on a Friday afternoon to see about it," Mickey Swims said. "I asked if it was for sale. They said it wasn't for sale to just anybody, but they'd sell it to me because they knew I would carry it on." Swims and his wife Martha, the long-time owners, were later helped by their children, Mike and Mia, at the track.

Bill Elliot, here in 1974 at Dixie, won his first race ever at Dixie Speedway in Woodstock and went on to become a NASCAR legend.

Dixie Speedway is a racing institution and has welcomed generations of fans to its track in south Cherokee County. The VIP Suites, above, replaced the former tower at the dirt track.

Over the years, some of the most talented drivers have raced at Dixie. Perhaps the most famous is NASCAR champion Bill Elliott. "Dixie is where it all started for me," Elliott said. "I ran Dixie when it was dirt in '73, and then they paved it between '73 and '74 and that's when I won my first race. I beat [asphalt racing legend] Ronnie Sanders."

Elliott was not the only famous driver to race at Dixie. Elliott faced Dale Earnhardt on the dirt at Dixie. Mickey Swims said of the event, "That's the biggest crowd we ever had at Dixie. Both of them came to win. I told them that both cars were pretty well equal. Dale wanted to know which one was

Dixie Speedway is a family-owned business run by parents Mickey and Martha Swims, seated, and their children, the late Mike Swims, center back row, and Mia Swims Green. In this picture taken before his death Mike Swims is shown with wife Debra and children Chase and Breanna, and Mia is pictured with husband Marshall Green and Marla and Macy.

higher in points. It was a good race. Dale won. When he got killed at Daytona, it really upset me because he was a really good guy."

Richard Petty also raced at Dixie. "He raced here before I had the track, and they tell me that Jody Ridley and his Falcon almost lapped him. When he came here for us, he signed autographs as long as there were people in line. He didn't cut it short. He's the kind that will sit there until the cows come home. A lot of the young drivers in NASCAR today could learn from him," Swims said.

Every Saturday night during the racing season, drivers from across the area showed up with their cars washed, polished and tuned to perfection, in search of the often-elusive checkered flag.

Atlanta Motor Speedway president Ed Clark was quoted in a release by the family about Dixie and the Swims family. "If you mention their names anywhere in racing, people totally respect them for what they've done and for their character," Clark said, adding that it's exceptional for any family business to be successful as long as the Swims have been and even more unusual for it to come in the challenging field of racing promotion. He said the Swims' secret is in their passion for what they do. "They're a family that loves doing what they do."

There were several other race tracks in Cherokee County, including a popular venue in the Sutallee community where races were held for several years.

Chamber of Commerce Networks in Community

In 1970, a group of local leaders was ready to get down to business concerning the Cherokee County Chamber of Commerce. A number of past attempts were made to organize a local chamber, but each time interest waned and the organization eventually failed. This time, leaders determined, would be different.

In the 1940s a group of businessmen formed a Chamber of Commerce and incorporated under the name Cherokee County Chamber of Commerce and Agriculture Inc. At that time, E.A. McCanless, a leader in the marble industry, invited 35 other citizens to have dinner with him at the Hotel Canton to discuss plans to start a Chamber of Commerce. McCanless became chairman of the group and other business leaders

Members of the Cherokee County Chamber of Commerce visit the state Capitol.

involved included J.D. Foster, N.A. Thomason, E.O. McFather, Grady Vandiviere, W.W. Fincher, Max McCanless, Dr. Grady Coker, L.L. Jones, Sr., D.R. Jones of Ball Ground and Joe Johnston of Woodstock. Some of the other leading directors who were soon involved included S.E. Hyatt, D.S. Pressley, J.H. Bagwell, Bob Lathem, Dr. Carl Edge, Sr., E.M. Barrett and C.E. Owen.

On April 7, 1945, The Cherokee County Chamber of Commerce and Agriculture, Inc. was incorporated by the Secretary of State. The group went on to meet for a number of years and organized a selection of committees,

Governor Joe Frank Harris, front row left, state Representative Bill Hasty, second from left, and state Representative Wendall Anderson, front right, welcome a group of community leaders and Chamber of Commerce members to the state Capitol.

including Mines and Minerals, Health and Sanitation, National Affairs, Public Roads and Highways, Wholesale and Retail Merchants, Transportation, Forest Fire Protection, Public Morals, Aviation, and Rural Urban Affairs. However, chamber records indicate that in the early 1950s membership fell off, interest waned and the organization became dormant.

In 1964 another attempt was made to form a Cherokee County Chamber of Commerce. The group met on July 1 to select a president and chose prominent Canton businessman James Cannon, according to an article in the *North Georgia Tribune*. Other officers included Carl Barrett of Holly Springs as the vice president, Bob Peterson of WCHK as secretary, and Clyde Worley as treasurer. Other directors who soon joined the roster included Norman Sosebee, Dr. Bill Nichols, Trammell Carmichael, Marion Pope, and Judge Sam Burtz. At the time, the organization had already reached 45 members and the club was soliciting for additional membership. There are few records of what happened following the initial organization. However, within a few years a new group formed and this time the organization would be permanent.

Cherokee County Chamber member Nathan Brandon, right, chaired the Beautify for Better Business committee that recognized businesses for their efforts.

The meeting took place on Monday, May 25, 1970, at the Lakeland Restaurant to begin the task of reforming the organization. Those in attendance that day were Wally Poss, Roy Roberts, A.B. Chandler, Arthur Poor, Johnny Tatum, Trammell Carmichael, Don Snell, Elliott Baker, Byron Dobbs, Hollis Lathem, Lamar Harris and Fred Haley. Roy Roberts reported that Leland Bagwell had offered to donate office space in the former Etowah Bank building until such time as the organization could afford to pay rent. The board voted to accept the offer. Wally Poss was nominated as president, and Roy Roberts as vice president. The board also discussed hiring a temporary executive and Byron Dobbs was

the acting secretary. Those appointments are part of the first recorded minutes of the revived organization. The organizers reactivated the name Cherokee County Chamber of Commerce and Agriculture, Incorporated, the official name to this day.

The group eventually hired George Hames to work for them, and in 1971 an economic development profile was done for the county by the Georgia Department of Industry and Trade. At the time Cherokee County had a population of just over 31,000 and Canton showed a population of 3,654 people. Major employers included Canton Textile Mills with a workforce of 1,200 and Gold Kist Poultry processing plant, which employed 500. Other major manufacturers doing business in the county included Bramco Products, Central Soya, J.P. Hames Lumber Company, and McKinney Wood Products Company. In all, 2,574 people were employed by local manufacturers.

The chamber had an initial membership of 184 members. The new organization quickly helped form the Cherokee County Industrial Development Authority. That year the board of commissioners recognized Cherokee County Commissioner Trammell Carmichael for his service in the development of the County and his involvement in providing good road and recreational facilities, as well as promoting industrial development. The chamber was meeting at the Pine Crest Inn.

The Chamber moved into their new building on Marietta Highway in July 1993.

The Cherokee County Chamber of Commerce began awarding its prestigious First Citizen designation in 1971. The award was designed to honor a community leader who had made a significant lifetime achievement in service and in business. In 1987 Leadership Cherokee was initiated to promote emerging leaders and to help them prepare for their roles in the community.

The chamber was active in the Clean Commission, which came out of the Chamber of Commerce committee. Partners in Education, which encourages community involvement with the school system, got underway in 1991. Other programs of the organization include Drugs Don't Work, Teen Leadership, and Existing Industry Initiative in which the chamber partnered with the Cherokee Office of Economic Development to support industries located in the community.

President and CEO Pam Carnes joined the organization initially in 1991 and then in February 1996, took the reins of the organization. In 2011, she continued to lead the organization and its staff. The chamber had grown to more than 1,000 in membership.

The Development Authority of Cherokee County was created in 1981 under state development authority law. The Development Authority also has a second entity, a county constitutional authority, and the two authorities work in partnership with the county commission and local cities to support quality industry and business development in the community. In 1996, the Development Authority split into a separate entity with its own staff and leadership. The organization later changed its name to the Cherokee Office of Economic Development.

New Airport Takes off

In October of 1964 a short article on the front page of the *North Georgia Tribune,* reported that Cherokee County had been allotted $61,000 for a new airport. In a letter signed by U.S. Senators Herman Talmadge and Richard Russell, county leaders were informed that the funds would be available in 1965, to acquire land, construct a runway 3,414 feet long and 50 feet wide, to install a wind cone and other equipment, and build an access road. Local funds were required to match the federal funds on a 50-50 basis.

The allocation of funds was the result of a study begun by Cherokee County Commissioner Trammell Carmichael back in 1963. Carmichael appointed an airport committee including Lee Wynn, Jr.,

Cherokee County Airport is a county-owned public airport and opened in 1966 on 152 acres between Canton and Ball Ground.

Grady Bobo, Marion C. Pope, Jr., J.C. Jones, Dr. W.H. Nichols, Lamar Lawson and J.D. Moore. The project was sponsored locally by the Canton Junior Chamber of Commerce which later became the Canton Jaycees. Three sites were under consideration for the airport, one on Pole Cat Mountain, one at Cushing Memorial Park and a place near Keithburg, according to an article in the *North Georgia Tribune*.

Eventually the site near Keithburg was chosen and the airport was constructed on 152 acres on the ridge behind the home of Fred Wilbanks. On October 1, 1966, the new airport was dedicated. At the dedication the Canton Jaycees was credited with being the originator of the new airport project. Speeches were given by local dignitaries and U.S. Congressman Phil Landrum of Jasper. Flyovers by a C-130 and a C-97 were planned as well as skydivers and a square dance held in the evening. The new airport was hailed as a major advancement for Cherokee County.

In the 1970s a new hangar and office building were built at the airport. An industrial park was being developed by the county Industrial Authority chaired by N.J. Wilbanks. The 70-acre park was expected to bring significant new jobs to the county. Change was on the horizon and it would not be long before growth took off. Commissioner Trammell Carmichael summed it up when he told the *Cherokee Tribune*, "Growth is wonderful. We welcome new citizens and new business to our community. But, then you hate to see the small-town life style change, too."

Canton Textile Mills closed its doors in 1981 after 82 years in business in Cherokee County. At the time 825 workers depended on the textile mill for their livelihood and it appeared that the closing would negatively impact the community's economy. Instead, the opening of Interstate 575 helped open up Cherokee County for more development and made commuting to the metro area easier. Soon the majority of the county's workforce was driving south each day. *Photo courtesy of Jack Tuszynski.*

Chapter Eight

Door Wide Open for Growth

In the 1980s and 1990s Cherokee County saw rapid changes and meteoric growth as it almost tripled in population from 51,699 residents in 1980 to 141,903 people choosing to call it home by the year 2000. With a 67.3 percent population increase from 1980 to 1990 when the county topped 90,000 people, the United States Census Bureau put Cherokee County as the fifth fastest growing county in the state of Georgia for the decade. Farmlands and forests were giving way to subdivisions as more and more people crowded into the county. Agriculture was still strong as an industry, with Cherokee County ranked in the top ten counties in the state in agricultural income by the year 1990. However, major change was on the way. With the closing of an industry that had fueled the county for almost a century and the completion of a new highway that opened Cherokee County to easy access to the metro Atlanta area, a new era began in the county's history. Just as transportation throughout the county's history was a key to Cherokee's prosperity, Interstate 575 paved the way for a new wave of growth and development that saw the county listed in the top fastest-growing communities in the nation. Cherokee County's median household income also saw a significant rise, jumping 66 percent from $48,492 in 1980 to $30,486 in 2000, according to census figures.

A new sheriff assumed the duties of the county's top law enforcement officer in 1980. Bo Ballard won the Democratic primary to start what was hailed in the newspaper as a new era in the Cherokee County Sheriff's office. Ballard moved the sheriff's office out of the white marble courthouse into a former home behind the courthouse that had once been used as the sheriff's residence. But the jail was still housed on the top floor of the Cherokee County Courthouse, a controversial situation that was receiving much attention in 1980 after 26 inmates escaped the facility in various breakouts in the previous year alone. At least five of the inmates had escaped through holes they tore in the ceiling of the historic building. They then made their way to freedom by crawling over the prison and down the stairs from the fourth floor of the building. The county began contemplating construction of a new jail, and it would not be many years before a new court facility was also needed. That would be just the first of many changes for the county law enforcement over the next two decades.

In 1981 a bank robbery by two former law enforcement officers rocked the community. Headlines in the *Cherokee Tribune* reported that a former bank security guard and Cherokee County deputy and a former deputy and Acworth Police Officer attempted to rob the Etowah Bank in Woodstock with a sawed-off shotgun and a 12-gauge shotgun. During the attempt, the two men took five bank employees and the

Woodstock Police Chief Joe Hames hostage. It seemed that major crime was beginning to plague the community.

Cherokee County also got a new Superior Court judge. Frank C. Mills III was appointed by Governor George Busbee to fill the spot left when Judge Marion Pope was appointed to the Georgia Court of Appeals, one of the highest courts in the state. Judge Mills had served as district attorney since 1978 and chief assistant district attorney from 1974 to 1978. He was elected in 1978 and re-elected in 1980 to that post before being appointed as judge.

In Holly Springs leaders began work on a proposed waste water treatment system to help bring growth to the area, but area residents opposed the idea. The city also signed up for cable television and made improvements to its police department, hoping to attract a greater portion of the new residents locating in Cherokee County with its expanded services.

While Holly Springs city leaders tried to court new growth, Cherokee County Commissioner Trammel Carmichael worried that the county could not keep up with the demands for services brought on by growing population figures. He pointed to the growth from 1970 when Cherokee County had 31,059 residents to 1980 when it had expanded to 51,699 as putting a burden on government. "We'll see a real problem in meeting the demand for services," Carmichael was quoted as saying in the *Cherokee Tribune*. Carmichael adopted an almost $4 million budget for 1981, which reduced spending on roads and other projects because of decreasing revenues. Financing the solutions for county problems "has always been difficult," the commissioner told the newspaper, "but now that the county has reached 50,000 in population, state officials are giving more attention to Cherokee County." Commissioner Carmichael said, "I can remember when we were 20,000 and didn't get any attention at all."

But long-time sole Commissioner Carmichael did not stay in office much longer. In 1983 the county's tax commissioner, Gene Hobgood, defeated Carmichael to take office and lead the county for the rest of the decade. Hobgood would be the last sole commissioner for the county and would lead through years of rapid growth. By 1990 when he left office the county had burgeoned to 90,204 people living within its boundaries. By then the door was wide open and would not close again as Cherokee County became one of the fastest-growing areas in the nation.

Era Ends as Canton Textile Mills Close Doors

The faces of the employees and the community showed the shock as the news spread. Canton Textile Mills was closing its doors forever. The mill was the economic engine of Cherokee County, employing 825 people in early 1981 with an annual payroll of $10 million. As word trickled out that the mill was about to be shut down, reports indicated that the company, with annual sales of $30 to $40 million, had lost $10 million in the four years leading up to the closure. After 82 years in operation as the county's top employer, indeed as the defining industry of Canton and Cherokee County, life without the presence of the mills was almost unimaginable. The decision came suddenly and unexpectedly for most people in the community.

On March 14, 1981, the mill's management issued a prepared statement that the company was exploring options on how to keep the

Charles Cash, mill supervisor, on the last day the mill in Canton was in operation. Canton Cotton Mill opened in 1899 and the company closed its doors 82 years later in 1981.

plants running "in view of current operating circumstances." Options included sale of the company to another organization, reducing operations to half-strength, continuing operations or shutting down. With

some 800 of the company's workers members of the Textile Union Workers, union representatives began a series of hurried meetings with mill management in an attempt to keep the mills operational. Company officials at one point said that it might be possible to keep the mills going if the Union workers would make some concessions, including an immediate 20 percent pay cut.

On that Sunday afternoon almost 500 Union workers met at the Local 1604 Union Hall on Highway 5 and voted overwhelmingly to accept the pay cut. But it was too late. Before they could even meet, the decision by mill management had already been made. The mill and offices would shut their doors immediately.

The next day, Monday, March 16, 1981, Louis Lindley Jones, Jr., grandson of the man who founded the mills, R.T. Jones, and the present chairman of the board, issued another statement.

Leona Sims in the spinning room of Canton Textile Mills. Many of the employees of the local cotton mill worked their entire careers at the facility. The mill announced it would cease operations on March 16, 1981.

"In light of current operations and market conditions, it is in the best interest of the stockholders to enter a plan of orderly closing of the Mill." A four- to six-week timetable was given for completion of the shutdown to allow orders for cloth already on the books to be manufactured. Members of the Board of Directors at Canton Textile Mills at the time of its closing were Jones, Cranston Gray, Frank Jones, P.W. Jones, Jr., Clayton Reid, Louis Jones III, Ralph Williams and Turner B. Smith.

Stunned workers were suddenly facing an unknown future, many who had worked their whole lives in the mill and whose parents had worked there uncertain of what was ahead for the first time ever. Workers were told they would be eligible for unemployment insurance from the State of Georgia Department of Labor in the sum of $27 to $90 per week, and Union workers were also exploring the possibility of federal funds to be used to relocate workers since one of the reasons for the plant's closing and loss of jobs was the effect of foreign imports on the market. The future did not look bright.

In an article in the *Cherokee Tribune* only weeks before the closing, company president Cranston Gray talked of the general state of recession for the nation's economy and the weak market. He said the company had a difficult year because of a bad cotton crop that brought down production and because of excessive absenteeism in the mills' workforce. But he said in February just days before the mill's announcement that he still remained optimistic. That optimism proved to be unfounded.

Only a few short weeks after the initial announcement, the mill shut its door forever. The looms were silenced for good, the haze of cotton lint

Carol Chastain was one of more than 1,200 workers at the Canton Textile Mills in the 1970s. By the time the mill closed in 1981 that number was down to 825.

that drifted through the air of the card room and clung to the clothes and hair of the workers was gone, and the lines of people pouring out through the gates at shift changing time ended forever. With the closing of the Canton Textile Mills, an era in Cherokee County history ended.

Mill Number One had already closed in the late 1960s, but Mill Number Two was running on two shifts a day, producing pure cotton denim as well as stretch denim, which it began making in 1979. A tough fabric, according to Gray, stretch denim was made from a texturized nylon, polyester or spandex. Canton Textile Mills had also purchased two additional mills in Alabama in the early 1970s, W.A. Handley Manufacturing Co. in Roanoke, Alabama., and Siluria Mill in Shelby County, Alabama, but they were both shut down in the late 1970s. Canton Textile Mill in early 1980 continued to try to keep up with the times, and made improvements for better quality control with more than $2 million in new equipment. But again, the efforts did not prove to be enough. Dwindling export markets in Europe, cheaper foreign imports and an economic crisis in the United States were all factors that played into the closing of one of the county's top employers.

A blue-ribbon committee of local business and Cherokee County Chamber of Com-

Canton Cotton Mill No. 2 sat vacant for much of the 1990s before being converted to loft apartments. The second mill was built in the early 1920s and for many of the years following operated around the clock on three shifts per day. In the early 1960s the mills were unionized. For many families the cotton mills were a way of life.

merce leaders was formed to try to help find potential buyers for the mills, but the market was not robust and despite their efforts no purchaser was found for the properties. The company ultimately did not find a buyer, despite numerous efforts. Canton Textile Mills went into Chapter 11 bankruptcy protection and began to sell off equipment, timber from lands the company owned and other holdings. The liquidated assets were used to pay off creditors and to pay taxes on the land still owned. For the next 15 years the mills sat mostly vacant, but Mill Number Two was finally sold in 1996 to Aderhold Properties who converted it into loft apartments, Canton Mill Lofts. The company maintained the historic façade of the old mill, effectively keeping the legacy of the days of the Cotton Mill alive in residents' memories.

But for those who worked in the mills in 1981, whose families were employed there, sometimes for generations, who had depended on the management to chart the course for the community, a chapter ended. As those who were left without jobs began to cast around for employment, opportunity was on the horizon. A new highway was about to open and bring change forever to Cherokee County.

Interstate 575 Paves the Way for Growth

While the news of the closing of the mill stunned Canton and the surrounding community, another news story was grabbing headlines, and once more transportation opportunities for Cherokee

County were charting a new course of growth and prosperity for the community. For years Cherokee County business and community leaders had lobbied for a better route to the metro Atlanta area than State Route Highway 5, a two-lane strip of asphalt that made traveling south for work or play difficult and slow at best, dangerous and treacherous at worst. But just as the mill shut down, a new route was opening up linking Cherokee County with the metro area, and the dream was finally about to become a reality. The timing could not have been better. The new developmental highway was

In the 1980s many changes came to Canton and Cherokee County. With the advent of new and better transportation available, travel by train was now obsolete and the Canton Depot, which was no longer in use, was eventually torn down.

designed to spur growth and expansion in what was viewed as an underdeveloped community, not to relieve traffic congestion. The new highway did such a good job of the former, that it would not be many years before traffic congestion followed, becoming an issue for those who traveled the highway each day. What the railroad did for Cherokee County and its cities in the 1880s, Interstate 575 would do 100 years later.

The new Interstate 575 from Interstate 75 in Cobb County to Highway 92 in Woodstock opened for traffic October 16, 1980. The first phase helped open up the south end of Cherokee County for growth, but the second phase was even more urgently needed following the mill closing so that the unemployed work force could commute south each day to where jobs were more readily available. Jerry Stargell with the State Department of Transportation told the Canton Optimists in November 1980 that work was expected to go more slowly north of Woodstock to Holly Springs and ultimately to Canton. He said the DOT was reworking the Mill Street interchange, which later was named the Towne Lake interchange, and that could take two more years to complete. Meantime two more lanes were being added to the Canton by-pass and they were expected to also be completed by 1982. Stargell told local residents the current by-pass would then provide "full access in both directions" at Highways 140 and 20. It was in March 1985 that Interstate 575 opened to Canton. The section of Interstate 575 north

The Holly Springs interchange being constructed on Interstate 575 in 1981. The new highway opened Cherokee County to growth and development. The new interstate opened just at the time the Canton Textile Mills shut down and once more available transportation helped spur economic prosperity.

of Canton from the Cherokee County Airport to Nelson was to be contracted and begun sometime in 1982 and was completed in 1986. In Nelson, Interstate 575 would then merge with the proposed Appalachian Development Highway to parallel Highway 5 as it made its way north.

The new interstate roadway ran west of Highway 5 to Holly Springs, where it would cross over and then go between Cherokee Memorial Park and Central Soya before tying in to the by-pass. I-575 would then cross the Etowah River at a massive new interchange. In 1980 alone the state DOT poured $89 million into new and improved roads for Cherokee County. The newspaper reported, "Construction of Interstate-575 is continuing at a brisk pace, as evidenced by the massive interchange going up just north of Canton. Looking northward from the bluff above the Etowah River, massive concrete pylons are being set to handle the weight of the four 700-foot-long bridges crossing the river."

The new interstate covered 31 miles in Cherokee County, but its impact was greater than perhaps any other factor in accelerating the growth in the county and making it one of the fastest growing communities in the nation for parts of the 1980s and 1990s. In fact, I-575 exceeded the state DOT's predictions for traffic and just 20 years after it opened was already handling as much traffic as the state thought it would experience after 40 years.

Law and Order Makes Its Mark

As Cherokee County grew in population in the last decades of the twentieth century, crime was also on the rise. Distribution of illegal drugs and narcotics violations became more commonplace and the days of bootleg whiskey arrests began to fade. With more homes in the county, burglaries were on the increase, a number of banks were the target of robberies and violent crimes such as murder, rape and assault also topped the local headlines. The Cherokee County Sheriff's Office remained the chief law agency in the county, despite occasional efforts to start a county police force. Four of the county's five cities maintained police departments of their own, and when needed state and federal agencies were brought into the county to assist in investigations. But despite the increase in crime, Cherokee County remained for the most part a safe community in which to live.

Several high profile murders were never solved and at least one that captured attention ended in an arrest but no conviction. A murder in the early hours of New Year's Day 1985 stunned Cherokee County when a man and his wife were shot multiple times and killed during a robbery of their convenience store. The murders happened around 1:30A.M. at Danny's Mini Market on Highway 140 three miles east of Canton. The murder victims were the store owner, Lawton Flournoy, age 62, who was shot twice in the chest and once in the head, and his wife, Elizabeth Flournoy, 56 years

Roger Garrison speaks with a deputy in front of the jail in the mid 1990s. Garrison served one of the longest terms in office of any sheriff in the county's history.

of age, who was shot twice in the head. Investigators believed a .22 caliber gun was used in the shootings. Mr. Flournoy's wallet and Mrs. Flournoy's purse were both taken, as well as money from the cash register. Another $2,500 was found in the store, and Sheriff Bo Ballard theorized that customers coming into the store around 1:00A.M. may have surprised the robbers while the murders were in progress. Two weeks later Jerry Alton Jones, age 30, of Tunnel Hill, Georgia, was arrested and charged in the case. After a high profile trial with Barry Bishop of Canton as his defense attorney, Jones was found innocent of the crime.

Later that same year, a string of murders occurred across North Georgia, including Cherokee County, which was never solved. The series of shootings became known as the .22 caliber killings because of the type of gun used. The first took place on October 11, 1985, when Billy Ray Keith was shot and killed as he drove a logging truck in a wooded area in Bartow County near the Cherokee County line. A total of $1,000 was taken from Keith who operated a sawmill on Highway 20 near Cherokee County. Then on October 28 of that same year Herbert Scott was shot and killed while he was inside his travel trailer. He was shot initially through the glass sliding door of the trailer. Scott lived in the trailer behind his hardware store on Highway 92 near Interstate 75 in Cherokee County. Scott was known to carry large amounts of cash.

The next in the string of killings occurred on December 3, 1985, when a 74-year-old barber was shot and killed at his home on Putnam Ford Drive in Cherokee County as he stepped from his car. The victim was Robert Webb and more than $1,000 was taken from the man, who ran a barber shop in Kennesaw. The last killing occurred in neighboring Cobb County on January 12, 1986, when George Jackson, age 34, was shot and killed while he sat in his MG sports car along I-75 at Wade Green Road in Cobb County. An unknown amount of cash was taken from Jackson. Jackson was initially shot through the rear window of his car and then shot again at close range. According to the Cherokee County Sheriff's Office, which investigated the shootings, the same .22 rifle was used in the first three murders. A different .22 caliber rifle was used in the murder of Jackson.

In 1988 residents elected a new sheriff when John Seay defeated two-term incumbent Sheriff Bo Ballard. Ballard, a Cherokee County native, had promised change eight years earlier. Now, residents wanted a new direction in law enforcement. Seay, a Cobb County police officer and Woodstock resident, promised a more professional department. But before long Seay was involved in a number of controversies including budget overruns and accusations of a hit list of local residents and leaders he targeted for subversive investigation. Seay also battled an overcrowded jail situation during his years in office.

Four years later, Cherokee County elected a sheriff who would carry them forward for a number of years. Sheriff Roger Garrison took office on January 1, 1993, at age 31. He went on to serve one of the longest terms in office of any sheriff in the county's history. Sheriff Garrison was elected with plans to be recognized as one of the most progressive and professional law enforcement agencies in the state and to rebuild relationships with other public safety agencies in Cherokee County. In 1996 the Cherokee County Sheriff's Office became the first nationally accredited sheriff's department in Georgia. Garrison created the Cherokee Multi-Agency Narcotics Squad which united the drug fighting efforts of all law enforcement agencies in the county as well as the district attorney's office. Under his leadership progressive educational career paths for his command staff were emphasized and master's degrees were obtained by all senior staff. Garrison's department led the largest manhunt in Georgia history for a cop killer who was later convicted and is on the state's death row. Over 500 law enforcement officers participated in the operation. During Garrison's tenure a new adult detention facility was built to house the county's growing jail overcrowding.

New Multi-Member Commission Shapes Future

In 1989 a push to change the county's way of governing from a single commission chair to a multi-member commission gathered momentum, causing the county's legislators to change the local law to allow for a five-member board. The plan also called for a county manager to run the day-to-day operations of Cherokee County, a first for the community. Then sole County Commissioner Gene Hobgood said that while he favored a multi-member commission, he felt the chairman should be full-time. Other residents spoke in favor of a county manager at a series of standing-room-only public hearings around the county. Evelyn Chambers, who was mayor of Woodstock at the time, summed up the feelings of many in saying, "By having a county manager to run the daily operations of the county, we can safely remove politics from the day-to-day affairs of the county." A similar plan for a three-member commission with a full-time chairman had failed to be passed by voters in 1986.

State Representatives Bill Hasty, Democrat, and Steve Stancil, Republican, introduced the new legislation to allow the

A new historical marker was erected outside the white marble Cherokee County Courthouse in 1989 commemorating the community's days as a gold mining area. At the dedication were, from left, Albert Cagle, Mary Free, Coy Free, Mrs. Jeff Stancil, Mark Hitt, Margaret Hitt, Jeff Stancil, Phyllis Porter, Frances Owen, Cherokee County Commissioner Gene Hobgood and Everett Porter.

county to call an election in November 1989 to decide the question. The bill allowed for a part-time commission chairperson elected countywide and four post commissioners who must live in the post they represent and are elected from two districts, each made up of two posts. The bill also set qualifications, salaries, filling of vacancies, bid processes and budget procedures.

The referendum passed the voters that November and in 1990 Cherokee County elected a multi-member commission which included Chairman John Brandenburg, Post One Commissioner Rebecca Ray, Post Two Commissioner J.J. Biello, Post Three Commissioner Russ Flynn and Post Four Commissioner Gil Howard. The five took office in 1991.

William G. Hasty, Sr. served at various times in his career as Cherokee County school superintendent, state representative and state senator. He was a school teacher and principal and later worked in state government. He was a columnist for the *Cherokee Tribune* and published several books about the community.

As the new commission worked the first year to find its feet, the five members set their budget for 1992, which topped $20 million for the first time in the county's history. The commission created a county marshal's department to enforce the county's ordinances and a new county road construction department. The board also set money aside in the upcoming budget to establish new county board of registrars to handle elections, which in the past had been handled by the probate judge's office. Another major change was to fund a full-time county attorney and county engineer, jobs which had been outsourced in the past.

Justice Center Becomes County's New Courthouse

The new multi-member commission next turned its attention to other needs in the county. The county commission's next project would change the face of downtown Canton. It also threatened a landmark building in the city. For years a solution to the need for a new courthouse was sought. Until the

The Cherokee County Justice Center was built in 1993 in downtown Canton and began serving the community in 1994 with eight courtrooms and judicial offices. At the time the Cherokee County Administrative Offices were located in the facility, but they were moved as demands for the courts increased and more space was needed.

1990s, Cherokee County was still served by its white marble courthouse which was completed in 1929. The county's first courts met in a log cabin near Canton, known as Etowah at the time in the early 1830s. A courthouse was then built in Canton, but burned by Sherman in 1865. In 1871 the county built another courthouse, but it fell into disrepair by the 1920s and finally burned. It was replaced with the white marble structure on the square in Canton.

A plan to build a new court facility during Gene Hobgood's time in office and even back to Commissioner Trammel Carmichael failed to ever get public support, and finally in the early 1990s the commission tried once more to come up with a plan that the taxpayers would approve. A study committee appointed by the new commission in 1991 took up the issue and looked at several potential sites outside the downtown area. Sites they were considering included one next to Cherokee High School and another across from the old Canton Textile Mill No. 2. However, the consideration to move the courthouse out of the downtown was not popular. Mayor James Cannon at the time said, "I am the mayor of the city and I want to see it remain downtown. Take the courthouse away and you can put locks on all the businesses."

Business owner Bud Chambers agreed, calling it devastating and saying that downtown businesses would cease to exist without the courthouse. Superior Court Judge Frank Mills called on the county to look at all land available in the downtown area. "We need to look at all possibilities and intangible factors," Judge Mills told the newspaper. While some suggested putting the new courthouse where the white marble structure was, members of the community lobbied against that plan and urged renovation of the old historic building. The new court facility could not be built behind the white courthouse because the land was unsuitable.

Finally voters in 1992 approved a plan to construct the three-story building next to the white courthouse. Officially called the Cherokee County Justice Center, the building was opened in 1994 and housed eight courtrooms and most of the county's judicial offices. For a number of years it also housed the county commission. The county maintained some offices in the old Jones building next door. The marble courthouse received a $3 million renovation during the construction of the new building.

Politics Take a Fast Right as County Goes Republican

The November 6, 1990, election in Cherokee County not only ushered in a new multi-member commission, it also marked a changeover in party politics for the county. For more than 100 years, since the time of Reconstruction, Cherokee County voted a majority Democrat. During Reconstruction Lincoln's party ruled in Georgia, but as the influence of the Carpetbaggers faded, Georgia became a solid Democratic Party state. Likewise in Cherokee, most local and state officials elected were affiliated with the Democratic Party. The tough times of the Depression and the popularity of Franklin D. Roosevelt and many of his programs underscored the commitment to the Democratic party.

In 1986 all but one local and state official elected in Cherokee County was Democrat. The lone office holder elected as a Republican was Justice of the Peace and later Magistrate Judge Frank Gramling. In 1988 the GOP began making serious inroads into the county when Sheriff John Seay was elected as a Republican, as well as District Attorney Garry Moss and state Representative Steve Stancil. That election marked the beginning of the GOP takeover in Cherokee County. In 1990 the changeover was almost complete.

During the election that year Cherokee County voters gave the nod to all five county com-

Woodstock gave President George Bush a Main Street welcome on August 22, 1992, when the Republican kicked off his bid for re-election in what was considered the quintessential small town. More than 40,000 people attended the rally that put Cherokee County on the map in a big way. Four years earlier during the 1988 presidential election United States Senator Dan Quayle brought his vice presidential campaign to south Cherokee County when a rally was held for him at Etowah High School.

missioners, three of the four school board members up for election and also cast the most votes for the GOP gubernatorial candidate. Both state House seats went to Republicans, with popular long-time county politician Democrat Bill Hasty retaining his seat in the Senate, beating Republican challenger Ben Whitaker. Democrat Pierce Neese beat Republican Frank Cipolla by only 38 votes to take the School Board Post 3 seat. Just over half of the county's 31,661 registered voters at the time went to the polls.

Cherokee County Republican Chairwoman Florence Cauble said that the large amount of Republican vote in the south end of the county was what helped send the GOP into power. The south end contained more than 70 percent of the county's registered voters in 1990, and while turnout percentagewise was stronger in the north end, the higher numbers of the voters in the south end helped carry the day for the Republicans. "I have heard people in the south end of the county say they are not being heard in county government as much as they would like," Mrs. Cauble said. "I guess they got their chance." After the 1988 election, state Senator Bill Hasty said that the southern portion of the county would not elect another Democrat, and he proved to be right.

Agriculture Still Growing Strong

Even as Cherokee County evolved into a suburban metro community, agriculture continued to play an important role in the county's economy. Poultry production still provided a solid base of jobs and revenue, beautiful horse farms dotted the landscape of southeast Cherokee County, and the county became a leader in production of materials for landscaping and gardening. As available land began to shrink and as new homes dotted the landscape, many still chose to farm their land. Cherokee County had a working dairy, a commercial egg farm, hog farms, and, of course, plenty of chickens. But as the suburban landscape pushed up against the rural environment, a subtle shift began.

Although the glory days when poultry dominated Cherokee County's economy in the 1950s and 1960s were long over, the Georgia Census of Agriculture in 1987 ranked Cherokee County ninth in broiler production in the state. The county was

Horse farming in Cherokee County became big business with farms such as this one in Ball Ground growing in popularity. In the 1990s horse farming was contributing an annual estimate of as much as $4 million to the economy.

producing more than 28 million chickens per year, including egg breeders, layers, broilers, and pullets. Jobs directly related to the poultry industry in Cherokee County were at 1,200 and there were 149 poultry farms in Cherokee County.

Cherokee also still had a large livestock industry in 1990, with more than 10,000 head of cattle, placing it in the top 50 counties out of Georgia's 159 in beef production. A number of well-known purebred cattle producers were in Cherokee County at that time. The beef production was tied to the cattle production, with poultry litter the primary source of fertilizer used on the pasture land of the county.

Cherokee County continued to have a strong agricultural industry in the 1980s and 1990s, despite residential growth. Cagle's Dairy Farm is one agricultural business that continued to remain successful in the 1980s. As land became more valuable and tax values increased, many of those who owned large tracts of land sold them for development.

Cherokee County also produced large quantities of hay, which required a large investment in fuel and equipment, helping further fuel the economy.

In 1990, Cherokee County was also one of the state's top greenhouse plant production counties, with annual sales of more than $10 million in plants which were sold throughout the Southeast. The county was also home to eight Christmas tree farms, making it one of the top Christmas tree producing counties. The nursery industry, which supplies markets in and around metro Atlanta with everything from container plants to plant materials, was also a big part of the total agriculture industry in the early 1990s. In those years the production of sod grass was a relatively new agricultural endeavor for Cherokee County. At the time, the county had one sod farm but hoped the future would bring more.

Horse farming was also a multi-million dollar industry in Cherokee County in the 1990s, with annual estimates of $3 million to $4 million pumped into the economy by the business of raising horses for fun and for profit. The bucolic nature of horse farming also made the areas where it was prevalent, especially southeast Cherokee where it bordered north Fulton County's horse country, an attractive place for prospective estate owners. Many of the horse farms consisted of a few acres and a few horses, but there were some larger operations for boarding and riding lessons. There was also a horse auction each week in Cherokee County.

Cherokee County had one of only two family-owned dairy farms which processed their own milk in the state in 1990, Cagle's Dairy in the Hickory Flat community. Cagle's Dairy was established in 1952 by Bernese and Albert Cagle and began processing milk in 1959 when the Cagles and four other dairy operations bought the Etowah Maid Dairy processing facility in north Canton. Etowah Maid Dairies was opened as Cherokee Farm Products Creamery in 1927 at the intersection of Waleska Road and Highway 5 in north Canton. The creamery in those days sold its milk and buttermilk under the trademark of Etowah Maid. In 1971 Albert Cagle bought

Bernese and Albert Cagle look out over their farm and dairy in Hickory Flat.

out all the other stockholders in Etowah Maid and moved the processing plant from 9 Waleska Road to his dairy farm in the Hickory Flat community. The dairy operated there as a family enterprise which produced, processed and distributed milk and other products until 2008 when the main facility was moved to Gilmer County. The family continued to operate a smaller version of the dairy farm as a tourist attraction and educational opportunity. In the 1990s, the Cagles sold whole milk, 2 percent milk, buttermilk, chocolate milk and a fruit punch made from a unique recipe. In 1990, Cagle's Dairy delivered to more than 60 locations in Cherokee County, including day care centers, convenience stores and independent grocery stores.

Cherokee County farmers also produced 12,000 head of swine, most of which were raised on Haley Farms. The wholesale market value of swine produced in Cherokee County was more than $1.5 million annually in the 1990s.

Since the earliest settlers, Cherokee County's rich forests provided a major asset to the growth of Cherokee County. According to a 1989 Georgia Forestry Report and a Profile of Agriculture in Cherokee County, the county had almost 191,000 acres of forest. Cherokee County also had four sawmills and two pulpwood yards. J.P. Haynes Lumber Co. was opened in Keithburg in 1947 and continues in 2011 to serve the community with building materials including treated and untreated lumber. As Cherokee County continued to grow as a suburban metro county, the forests would shrink and the demand for lumber and other building materials would increase.

Poet Laureate Pens Odes of Cherokee

In 2000 Cherokee County native David Bottoms was named the Georgia Poet Laureate by then Governor Roy Barnes. Bottoms was born in Canton in 1949, the son of David and Louise Bottoms. He graduated from Cherokee High School in 1967 and previously attended Canton Elementary School. After graduating from the local high school, Bottoms attended Mercer University in Macon, which would become the setting for many of his later poems. His first book, *Shooting Rats at the Bibb County Dump*, won the

Dr. David Bottoms, the state Poet Laureate, hails from Canton. Many of his poems recall his early days growing up in the community. *Photo courtesy of Carina Bernard, Georgia Humanities Council.*

1979 Walt Whitman Award of the Academy of American Poets. He received his PhD in creative writing and poetry in 1982. Bottoms became a professor at Georgia State University teaching creative writing. He was later named associate dean of fine arts at the university.

In his first book of poetry, Bottoms began writing of southern woods and good old boys, often in graphic and violent terms. He searched for meaning in everyday life and wove religion and life and death into his poetry. His next book of poetry published in 1983 was titled *In a U-Haul North of Damascus*. The 31 poems in that collection are called sensitive and spiritual, as he began to explore the relationships between danger and beauty. In 1987 he published *Under the Vulture Tree*, which explored his interests in nature and scenes from childhood and family life. Bottoms also published two novels.

Bottoms was not the only Georgia Poet Laureate to live in Cherokee County. Dr. John Lewis, who practiced medicine with Dr. Grady Coker from 1945 to 1946 and went on to become a well-known surgeon in Atlanta, was appointed Poet Laureate of Georgia in 1974 by then-Governor Jimmy Carter.

Towne Lake Brings Surge in Population

Meteoric growth was already a reality in Cherokee County by the late 1980s, and a new planned development about to take off in the south end of the county was destined to propel population figures even higher. The 4,000-acre Towne Lake project was already under construction in 1989 when the United States Census Bureau released figures that showed Cherokee County as the 16th fastest growing county in the nation. With a population of around 86,000 people calling Cherokee County home in 1988, the county had already experienced growth. But now Towne Lake was expected to bring an additional 30,000 or more people to the county. The development would have around 8,000 homes. At that time in Cherokee County most subdivisions contained around 50 to 100 homes.

Cherokee County Commissioner Gene Hobgood said at the time that while Cherokee's growth in the 1980s was phenomenal, placing it in the top 20 counties in the nation for growth during the decade, the next decade should be even bigger. Speaking of the planned Towne Lake community and a proposed large development near Holly Springs that would eventually be Bridgemill community, Hobgood said, "These developments don't mean a greater impact, just a better planned and organized growth pattern."

Towne Lake was the brainchild of Larry Johnson, a developer out of Texas who began purchasing the 3,700 acres of undeveloped land in the mid-1980s, most of it owned by large timber companies, and known by local residents as the "Thousand Acre Woods." Johnson began putting together a group of Georgia developers to make the project a reality. At the time the land had no water or sewerage and no decent roads. Much of the topography was rocky and hilly. Developers who signed on included Arvida, a home building company, and Means Brothers, an Atlanta development company, as well as several local Cherokee County builders and developers. Many of those considering helping to develop the property thought it might be too far from Atlanta, but its proximity to Interstate 575 was considered a metro growth generator. The development was expected to offer country club living at more attractive prices than neighboring Cobb and other metro communities. Cherokee County had less traffic on the interstate

highway than its southern neighbors, and taxes were lower.

Commissioner Hobgood persuaded the developers to pay for the construction of Towne Lake Parkway to serve the property and to donate land for a new school, library and park, which is now named Hobgood Park. The land donated for schools was used to construct Woodstock High School and Woodstock Middle School. Rose Creek Library was built on the land donated for libraries.

Local banker Hollis Lathem, who later became chairman of the county commission, was chairman of the Cherokee County Water and Sewerage Authority. He came up with a plan to build the needed water and sewer infrastructure and pay for it with fees generated from the homes that would be built, according to an article in the *Atlanta Journal and Constitution*. In the article Lathem praised the plan to build Towne Lake. "I felt it was an opportunity we did not want to miss," Lathem is quoted as saying. "It was going to bring new commercial development. It was going to increase the tax digest tremendously at no cost to the county."

The Towne Lake development continues to makes a massive impact on Cherokee County. This map shows along Eagle Drive.

Community leaders praised the development because it offered one large uniform plan including homes, apartments, shopping and offices. Arvida agreed to develop Eagle Watch, one of the many neighborhoods planned for Towne Lake. Eagle Watch was slated to have around 1,300 homes and include a golf course designed by Arnold Palmer. Other amenities of the new communities included neighborhood swimming pools, clubhouses, playgrounds, tennis facilities and wooded lots, some of which backed up to Allatoona Lake. Other neighborhoods included Parkview, The Arbors, Deer Run, Eagle

View, Rose Creek, Summerchase, Towne Lake Hills, Wellesley and Wyngate. Means Brothers built Deer Run and commercial development along Towne Lake Parkway.

Homes in the new planned community sold rapidly, attracting at least two-thirds of the new homeowners from out of state or from a foreign country. The influx of new residents quickly began to affect local politics and bring new ideas into the county. Shopping centers, restaurants, gas stations and other commercial development also sprang up in the area to serve the new population. For the first time in more than 150 years since the founding of Canton, the county seat was seeing a new power base emerge with a population greater than that of the town in north Cherokee.

Woodstock blends historic preservation with new developments such as Hedgewood in Olde Towne Woodstock which offers in-town living, shops and restaurants in a vibrant setting.

Chapter Nine

Setting Course for the Future

Cherokee County leaders saw the new millennium in at the Cherokee County Emergency Center in downtown Canton as problem 2000 fears for computer rollover, or Y2K, had governments on alert. But despite the fears, the new millennium dawned quietly with little forewarning of what lay ahead in the decade that would bring the 9/11 attacks and the worst financial crisis since the Great Depression. In the years following the attacks on the World Trade Center and the nation's capital on September 11, 2001, Cherokee County saw many people leave to fight in the ensuing wars in Iraq and Afghanistan. The division of the National Guard in Cherokee County was called up and many volunteered to go overseas to participate in the battle for freedom. At home, Homeland Security made itself felt as local leaders prepared to ensure the safety of the community from any threat that might come.

For Cherokee County the start of the 2000s would herald more years of rapid growth and home construction. In the preceding years, as Cherokee County continued to experience phenomenal growth, an emerging political movement to slow development began to make its impact felt. By 2000 a moratorium on new development was put into effect to slow the rapid residential growth many felt was overburdening the county's infrastructure including schools and roads. Lower interest rates, competition between local banks and the influx of population made Cherokee County a community where the housing bubble was present. Then, beginning in 2007, the subsequent rise in interest rates and the collapse of the housing market fueled by subprime mortgages caused a massive number of foreclosures and a severe financial crisis that hit Cherokee County hard. Issue after issue of the *Cherokee Tribune* contained hundreds of foreclosure notices on homes, businesses and land within the county. But by the end of the decade, the county was beginning to see some signs of recovery and had once again weathered the worst of a crisis to emerge intact.

As Cherokee County moved into the new millennium and the start of the next century, the community had seemed poised for a bright future. Especially in the first part of the decade Cherokee County continued to grow, and by the 2010 U.S. Census the population had surged to an impressive 214,346 people. Cherokee County welcomed 72,443 new residents from 2000 to 2010, a 51.1 percent increase, according to the United States Census figures released in early 2011. Minorities were a major percentage of the new population. Cherokee County's African-American population increased by 230 percent from 3,519 in 2000 to 11,633 residing in the county in 2010. The county's Asian population increased 201 percent to 3,484 during the same time. But by far the largest impact was the increasing Hispanic population, many of whom moved to Cherokee County because of the building boom of the late 1990s and early 2000s. In 2010 the county reported 20,566 Hispanic residents, an increase of 67 percent from the year 2000 census when less than 8,000 Hispanics were reported as residing in the county.

Those early settlers in the 1830s who ventured into the north Georgia wilderness to lay claim to the first land lotteries would never have dreamed that in less than 185 years Cherokee County would attract so many people. The very features of the county that drew those first hardy souls, the natural beauty of rivers and mountains, proximity to transportation routes, possibilities of jobs and pleasant surroundings to raise a family, continued to bring new residents each year throughout the history of Cherokee County.

In the early 2000s, Cherokee County emerged as a vibrant part of the metro Atlanta area while still offering small town living, friendly communities, ample churches, solid law enforcement and public safety and a continued emphasis on education for its citizens. But the growth did not please everyone and it came with its own set of problems.

In another round in the continuing battle over development in the county, Woodstock resident and retired media executive Mike Byrd defeated Cherokee Commission Chairperson Emily Lemcke in 2002. Ms. Lemcke was an activist from southeast Cherokee County who had never held political office when she defeated incumbent Commission Chairperson Hollis Lathem in 2002 on a promise of slowing residential growth in the burgeoning county. According to an article in the *Atlanta Journal Constitution*, Ms. Lemcke and other commissioners elected on a platform of slowing growth put a moratorium on new developments for months. She fought against the Northern Arc, a highway planned to bisect the county and Cherokee County commissioners were the first in the state to implement development impact fees.

Byrd served one four-year term before being defeated by another slower growth candidate, L.B. Buzz Ahrens, who moved to Cherokee County and purchased a horse farm after retiring from the corporate world. In 2010 Commission Chairperson Ahrens was the first chair to be reelected to a second term

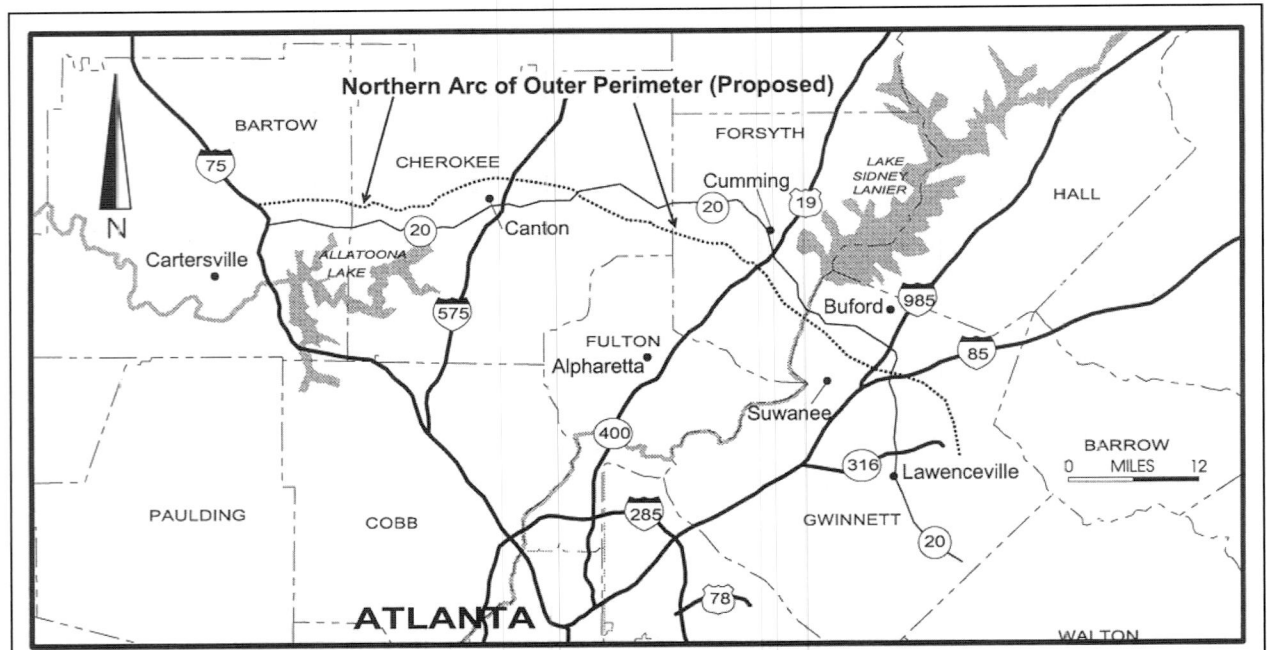

The proposed Northern Arc was never built, but was originally planned to come through Cherokee County. The political battle to stop the highway was a major factor in local politics. The 1990s were a time of political upheaval fueled by the pressures of heavy residential growth and the profits to be made. Many residents were in opposition to the changes the growth would bring.

since the commission became a multi-member board in 1990. Other Cherokee County Commissioners included Post One Commissioner Harry Johnston, Post Two Commissioner Jim Hubbard, Post Three Commissioner Karen Bosch and Post Four Commissioner Jason Nelms.

In 2009 Cherokee County voters approved a $90 million Parks, Recreation and Green Space bond referendum. The monies were to be used for passive parks, walking trails, an aquatics center and new team parks for softball, baseball, soccer, football and other sports, as well as enhancements to existing parks throughout the county. The cities would also benefit from the parks expansion plan, with each city getting new facilities.

Cities Continue to Grow

Much of the decade's growth occurred in the county's cities. In Canton by 2010 the population reached 22,958, almost tripling in size from the 7,709 residents in the county seat in 2000. Ball Ground almost doubled in size, growing from just 730 to 1,433 residents in 2010. In Holly Springs, 5,994 residents moved in over the decade, bringing the city's population to 9,189. Woodstock expanded from 10,050 residents in 2000 to 23,896 in 2010. And even Waleska in north Cherokee County got 28 additional residents in the 2010 population count, growing from 616 to 644 in the college town.

During the decade of growth Canton experienced a number of changes, including several new recreational opportunities for residents. The first half of the decade was under the leadership of Mayor Cecil Pruitt. In 2004 Canton was on a fast track of growth. In May 2004 the city opened the new Heritage Park and constructed an $8 million YMCA community center in

The Hickory Log Dam and Reservoir is an important component of the Bluffs at Technology Park in Canton and is one of the tallest dams in the state not built by the U.S. Army Corps of Engineers or Georgia Power Company. The lake it creates has 15 miles of shoreline.

north Canton next to the new park. The Cecil Pruitt YMCA was built with city funding in partnership with the Atlanta Metro YMCA and has a gymnasium, indoor swimming pool and houses the Cherokee Sports Hall of Fame. Canton also saw the advent of a new shopping area off Interstate 575 at Highway 20 called Canton Marketplace. The new strip shopping area included several national retail stores such as Kohl's and Target as well as restaurants and other commercial operations.

The city also was part of a project to build a reservoir to increase the city's water supply which is from the Etowah River. The Hickory Log Creek dam project was done in partnership with the Cobb County/Marietta Water Authority which owned 75 percent of the new reservoir on the Bluffs Parkway. In 2008 former county Commissioner Gene Hobgood became mayor of Canton.

In Holly Springs, Mayor Tim Downing took office in 2004. In the ensuing years the city experienced phenomenal growth, both in population and size as the city annexed expansive areas of land between the city and the Hickory Flat community to Highway 140. In 2006 the city celebrated its centennial.

The Holly Springs Serpentine Marble Quarry, here in 2006 before being filled in, was drained and filled with rocks and dirt. New residential developments and subdivisions have grown up around Holly Springs and the old quarries.

Many of the city's longtime industries had by then closed their doors, including Able Lumber Company and several poultry operations. The old cotton gin had been demolished and the stone quarry that had once produced green stone was filled with water and in disuse and disrepair. Subdivisions had grown up around the quarries themselves. The city was facing pressures to provide infrastructure for the rapid residential growth and looking for ways to improve and revitalize the downtown core. The historic depot was still a centerpiece of downtown and was used by the city as a community center. The downtown district retained its historic integrity with the depot as well as the former E.M. Barrett Store and the Hardin House anchoring the area. A new city hall was constructed on Holly Springs Parkway.

For Waleska, the smallest town in the county, the new millennium brought change at the school that had defined the northeast city for the past century. Reinhardt College became Reinhardt University under the leadership of President Dr. J. Thomas Isherwood.

The university offered 41 undergraduate programs and master's degrees in business, education and music. The college boasted 18 sports teams supported by scholarship and plans for a football program to kick off in 2013. The Floyd A. and Fay W. Falany Performing Arts Center, named for the former college president and his wife and opened in 2002, provided a nucleus for both student participation and

enrichment concerts and performances such as the Vienna Boys Choir and the Atlanta Symphony. The college campus also had a new visual arts center, student center and other facilities to provide for the growing student population. At Waleska City Hall, Mayor Doris Jones was at the helm after several years of city leadership by Mayor Marguerite Cline, a former county school superintendent and member of one of the city's prominent families for much of its history.

In the first years of the decade in Woodstock, Mayor Bill Dewrell led the community on an agenda of continued growth. A new mixed-use development got under way in the city's historic district bringing additional housing, restaurants and stores to the downtown area. Dewrell

Dr. J. Thomas Isherwood and a group of students celebrate Reinhardt College becoming Reinhardt University with a new banner. The university now offers a number of graduate programs in addition to four-year degrees.

was followed by Mayor Donnie Henriques, who led the city during the last portion of the decade. Despite the economic downturn and the housing crisis, Woodstock continued to be a dynamic community attracting growth and business. Under Mayor Henriques' leadership, and with an active Downtown Development Authority and Convention and Visitors Bureau headed by Director Billy Peppers, the city worked to improve downtown parking and to make a more pedestrian friendly environment. In 2001, the Woodstock Visitors Center opened in Historic Dean's Store, circa 1906. and served as a hub for those coming to the downtown area. The city finally saw construction begin on the Rope Mill Interchange on Interstate 575 to relieve traffic congestion from the Towne Lake area. The Rope Mill Park got under way and the construction of the pedestrian bridge over Little River was completed. While historic homes still lined Main Street as they had for 100 years and many still housed descendants of the original families who built them, the city continued to welcome legions of newcomers. Gift shops, spas and salons, restaurants, a tea room, and other businesses thrived in the downtown area. The city has embraced its motto, "Experience Woodstock, Her Heritage, Her Vision."

For Ball Ground, the new millennium meant a renewed sense of community and spirit of growth. While the city had seen a decline in the 20th century, the beginning of the new century brought a significant rise in population and interests in the historic downtown area. Mayor Rick Roberts, whose family traced its roots back to the 1800s in the community, served in the leadership role as Mayor from 1988 to 1993, and then from 1996 through the first decade of the 2000s. By 2011, the city was home to about 1,500 residents, a number of new subdivisions and industry. Businesses and residents were attracted by the city's proximity to the North Georgia Mountains and easy access to Interstate 575.

The new Ball Ground City Hall, which opened in 2007, celebrates its heritage with a bell tower. The city has experienced tremendous growth in the last 10 years.

Industry and Development Bring Jobs

Cherokee County continued to work to attract jobs and businesses to the community. A new corporate park called Cherokee 75 and located in southwest Cherokee County was attracting interest from companies looking to locate. Throughout Cherokee County industries such as Universal Alloy in Canton, Chart Industries near Ball Ground, and Belnick, Inc., also known as the BizChair.com, were expanding and offering opportunities for jobs in the community.

In July of 2010, Chart Industries, which makes products for the biomedical industry, expanded its Cherokee County presence with a $5 million investment and the addition of at least 50 jobs. Chart was one of the county's top industrial employers. The company had expanded in 2008 by relocating its regional administrative office to Cherokee County where it had been in operation since 1982.

BizChair.com began a 149,000-square-foot expansion in 2010 at its building north of Canton. The company, which sells office chairs, stack chairs, folding chairs and recliners, as well as office, home and medical equipment, made the decision to expand to make room for more inventory. The expansion added 20 jobs to the company. The company was created in 2001 and moved into its first commercial warehouse space in 2004. It moved to Cherokee County in 2007.

The Bluffs Parkway was opened off Riverstone Parkway in 2004, funded in part with $8 million from the state Department of Transportation and expected to help bring new jobs to the area. The city of

Canton in partnership with Cherokee County worked to bring the Bluffs at Technology Park to the north end of the city. The commercial development was expected to bring 15,000 new jobs to the county. However, the recession in 2008 stymied the plan and saw new job creation and development of the technology park grind to a halt. But the county still saw several companies expand within Cherokee County, according to the Cherokee Office of Economic Development, formerly the Cherokee Development Authority. In 2010 more than $16 million was invested in new and existing industries and 135 jobs were created.

The Cherokee County Conference Center at the Bluffs has the county open for business in the new millennium. *Photo courtesy of David Johnson.*

The Bluffs did see the addition of two major enhancements for Cherokee County. In 2008 the Cherokee County Board of Commissioners moved their offices and the county government to a new facility on Bluff Parkway. Voters approved funding the plan at the polls in 2004. The Cherokee County Administrative Building also includes the Northside Hospital Cherokee Conference Center which offers 8,000 square feet of conference space and can accommodate as many as 600 people seated for an event. The conference center is used for meetings, banquets, weddings and other social and business events. The County Administrative Offices house the county's Planning and Zoning, Building, Mapping, Finance, Community Services, Environmental Health and other offices.

As a $34 million expansion of the Cherokee County Airport is completed, the runway was lengthened to 5,000 feet making it possible to welcome corporate jets to the facility. The project was a collaborative effort between federal and local governments and is hoped to spur companies to locate in Cherokee County.

Another major advancement was the location of Chattahoochee Technical College, which opened its 62,500-square-foot Cherokee County campus in the Bluffs in 2011. The Canton campus, which began construction in 2008 is on 25 acres in the technology park. Along with classroom space, the new campus features a library, four computer laboratories, a bookstore, student center and tiered lecture hall. Chattahoochee Tech offers classes in eight counties, including the newest campus in Canton and the Woodstock campus which opened as Appalachian Tech in 2005 in the old Woodstock Elementary School complex.

The Cherokee County Airport has a new corporate passenger airport terminal to better serve those utilizing the airport. A new 65,000-square-foot hangar was also built as part of the airport expansion and more new hangars are planned in the future.

After the rapid expansion of banks in the 1990s and opening decade of the new millennium, the recession of the late 2000s saw a number of financial institutes in Cherokee County fail, among them Bank of Woodstock, a division of United Community Bank of Sparta, and Security Bank in Woodstock. The bank crisis was compared to the Savings and Loan crisis of the late 1980s, which up until that time had been one of the hardest hitting financial troubles since the Great Depression. However, Cherokee County weathered that earlier crisis better because its economy was more diversified among agriculture and industry than in 2008-2009 when much of its economy was dependent on building new homes for the ever- burgeoning population. With the county's dependence on construction and growth for economic stimulus, many industries within that field struggled to survive, and several large developments were put on hold.

Cherokee County did receive a Work Ready Community designation in 2011 from the Governor's office of Workforce Development. Cherokee County Commission Chairman L.B. Buzz Ahrens began the process which partnered the county with the Cherokee County Chamber of Commerce and Chattahoochee Technical College to pursue the designation. As a Work Ready Community, Cherokee County can increase employment opportunities and attract new business and industry to the county. The county had to have a plan to boost high school graduation rates, profile jobs within the community and recognize companies involved in the program. Piolax Corporation in Canton was one such company recognized for its pioneering efforts in implementing the program.

The extensive $34 million airport expansion was funded by federal monies and local dollars. The project included a new 5,000-foot runway open in 2011, allowing corporate jets to land. The runway was widened from 75 feet to 100 feet. There is a new passenger terminal already open. A 65,000-square-foot hangar is adjacent and additional hangars under construction and planned. The airport is located just off Interstate 575 Exit 27 in Ball Ground. The county has created an airport area master plan to expand the surrounding business development, and has acquired property for eventual lengthening of the runway to 6,000 feet.

Art Takes Center Stage

Cherokee County put emphasis on the arts in the early years of the 21st century, with several venues in operation and more on the drawing board. The new Elm Street Cultural Arts Center was on the drawing boards in Woodstock, art offerings at the Cherokee Arts Center and the Canton Theatre were expanding, and in Waleska the Falany Performing Arts Center at Reinhardt University contributed exemplary performances for the community. The Cherokee Arts Center sponsored the Canton Festival of the Arts each spring in May in downtown Canton. The popular festival features fine artists and crafts people, performers and entertainers, concessions and a wine and beer garden. A literary fair held as part of the festival features nationally known authors, as well as local writers, with literary panels and book signings.

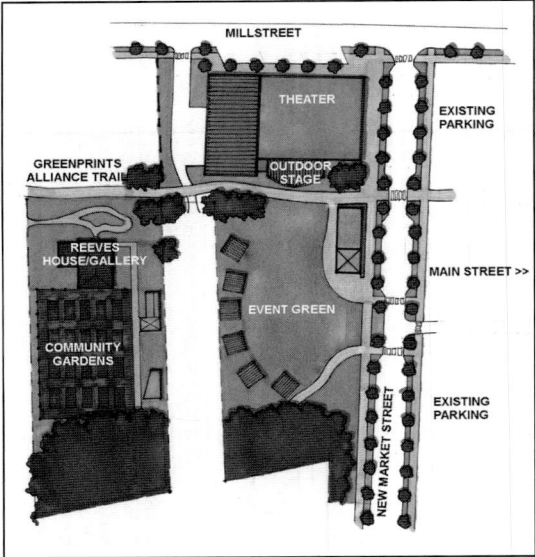

Plans for the new Elm Street Cultural Arts Center in Woodstock are under way. The Towne Lake Arts Center has included a new Theater, renovated historic house and community garden for their new home.

The Cherokee Arts Center also offers performing arts such as Blue Grass performances, visual art exhibits and school art exhibits throughout the year, as well as the popular Camp Imagine for children.

The Towne Lake Arts Center, which for almost a decade had presented audiences with plays and musicals featuring local talent, had a new location in downtown Woodstock in the City Center located in an historic former church. The organization was calling the location at 8534 Main Street home, but planned to move to the Elm Street Cultural Arts Village a few blocks away when that site opens. The organization produces and presents a diverse playbill including popular musicals like "Hello Dolly" and classics such as Thornton Wilder's "Our Town" on stage at the City Center. There is a plan to bring Shakespeare to the boards of the Towne Lake Arts Center.

The Cherokee County History Museum and Visitors Center opened to the public in February 2011 and from the start was making history itself as better than anticipated numbers of visitors came through its doors. Located in the Historic Marble Courthouse in downtown Canton at 100 North Street, the museum is operated by the Cherokee County Historical Society volunteer members and staff. The Museum tagline says that "Cherokee County is Where North Georgia History Begins!" and Historical Society Executive Director Stefanie Joyner said she was pleased with the contribution the new facility is making. "The History Museum gives visitors a chance to connect with local history and learn in a fun, interactive way," Ms. Joyner says. "The museum is a great way for newcomers to learn about our past and engage us in the present. It is a great introduction to our unique history."

The Museum was one of the first in the country to uses iPad computers to help enhance the experience for those who visit. The iPad stations offer presentations about The Trail of Tears, archaeology, slavery, desegregation, gold mining and moonshining. The iPads were donated by local businesses and individuals, and are a great way to quickly get acquainted with the county's extensive history. The topics chosen for the iPad presentations are some of the most dramatic and interesting subjects in the county history.

The Cherokee County History Museum and Visitors Center is opening up the county's past to those who tour the exhibit in the historic white marble courthouse in downtown Canton.

The infamous Trail of Tears had some of its beginnings in Cherokee County, and the county also has dramatic history from the Civil War days. The 1829 Georgia Gold Rush saw many miners coming into the region, and Prohibition brought a different kind of riches to the region, this time in an illegal industry.

Education Key to Success

Public education in Cherokee County experienced what school administrators called a renaissance in the 21st century under the leadership of Dr. Frank Petruzielo, superintendent of schools from 1999 to 2011 and beyond. When Dr. Petruzielo assumed the reins of the local system in 1999, the school district was facing loss of accreditation. By 2011, Cherokee County schools ranked some of the best in the state of Georgia and the nation. Cherokee was one of the first school systems in the United States to earn the designation of "District Accreditation of the Quality School System" through the Southern Association of Colleges and Schools. Test scores and other criteria placed all five Cherokee County high schools in the top 25 in Georgia. Cherokee County public schools had 38,600 students in attendance by 2011.

The Cherokee Arts Center is located in the building that was originally the Canton Methodist church. It has been home for the Arts Center since 1998. The Cherokee Arts Center promotes arts in the community through performances, exhibits, camps and classes.

In 1999 Cherokee County had less than 26,000 students. By 2011, with 38,600 students enrolled, it was the eighth-largest school district in the state and the largest employer in Cherokee County with more than 4,500 full-time employees including teachers, administrators and support staff.

Dr. Petruzielo was named the Superintendent of the Year in 2004 by the Georgia PTA. He became the first superintendent in the state to serve on the Georgia PTA Board of Directors. Active Parent Teacher Associations were providing support in all elementary, middle and high schools in Cherokee County.

However, Dr. Petruzielo, who came to Cherokee County from the same post in Broward County, Florida, one of the largest school systems in the nation, did have his detractors. Dr. Petruzielo had several run-ins with city leaders over the location of schools and state legislators over funding and other issues. Hot topics such as charter schools brought out heavy opposition at school board meetings. He also drew community ire early on in his term when a proposal that the historic Canton High School be torn down and a new facility for county offices be constructed in the downtown Canton area. Graduates of the facility, which closed in the mid 1950s when

The former Canton High School was preserved by the Cherokee County Board of Education and used as a meeting center and offices. The project was awarded the Historic Preservation Award by the Cherokee County Historical Society in 2003.

Cherokee High School opened, led a protest of the proposed demolition. Members of the Cherokee Historical Society and other residents who favored preservation joined the effort. School leaders eventually reconsidered and Historic Canton High School was renovated with funds from a special purpose local option sales tax. The auditorium of the building became the headquarters for Cherokee County School Board meetings and other activities for the school system.

Monies generated from the special purpose local option sales tax in the 2000s also allowed the public school system to construct eight new elementary schools, three new middle schools, two new high schools, and undertook eight major school addition or renovation projects. Other improvements included significant technology enhancements and new support facility projects. The new high schools brought the county to a total of six: Cherokee High, Etowah High, Sequoyah High, Creekview High, Woodstock High and River Ridge High.

The school system still faced a number of challenges, including continuing growth in the student population and overcrowding conditions at a number of schools in the county. With economic woes plaguing governments and causing a reduction in available funding, the Cherokee County School System was forced to implement reductions in a number of areas. Cherokee County was expected to add 500 to 1,000 students per year in the near future, and that figure could increase when the economy revived. State and federal funding for education was shrinking and reports indicated that high school students throughout the United States needed better education to compete in a global market.

A National Landmark of Remembrance

Members of Canton's National Guard Unit, Company B of the 1/108th Calvary of the 48th Infantry Brigade Combat Team, are welcomed home after serving in Afghanistan in 2010.

In every war the United States waged the people of Cherokee County stepped forward with acts of patriotism and sacrifice. So it is perhaps fitting that in 2006 the site of one of only two national cemeteries in the state of Georgia and 123 nationwide was located in Cherokee County. The Georgia National Cemetery occupies an historic site of 775 acres overlooking the Etowah River and near Allatoona Lake and the foothills of the Blue Ridge Mountains. The land for the cemetery was donated by World War II veteran and land developer Scott Hudgens in 2001. Hudgens was instrumental in the development of Riverstone Mall and other major mall and land developments in the metro area.

The cemetery is located off Highway 20 near Knox Bridge on land the early Native Americans first roamed looking for food and the Cherokee later hunted and fished. The property was eventually a hunting camp and used for timber. Only 330 acres of the property will comprise the actual cemetery. The rest will be left natural because of the terrain of the property and its unsuitability for development. Initially, 50 acres are in use for gravesites for veterans. Upon completion the project is to include a total of 33,000 full-casket gravesites, 3,000 in-ground sites for cremation remains and 3,000 columbaria niches for cremation remains. In addition the cemetery will include an entrance area, an information center, administration and maintenance building, public restrooms, flag plaza and shelters for committal services.

The Georgia National Cemetery in Canton provides a fitting final resting place for veterans and their families. The National Cemetery is situated on 775 acres of land near the Etowah River and overlooking Allatoona Lake and the Blue Ridge foothills.

Burial arrangements will be made after death, as with all national cemeteries. The Veterans Administration does not reserve grave space. Veterans or spouses wishing to be buried in national cemeteries need to have the veteran's military separation papers available to establish eligibility, which requires a discharge other than dishonorable. Dependent children of veterans may also be buried at the national cemetery.

The new 775-acre national cemetery in western Cherokee County will serve veterans for the next 50 years. As of fiscal year 2008, there were 2,154 interred on the site. The Georgia National Cemetery attracts immense interest from the public, who are appreciative of the beauty and meaning of cemeteries honoring the veterans. Thousands of families make visits each year to pay respect to those who are buried there. The cemetery is open to the public sunrise to sunset each day.

Forward to the Future

As Cherokee County moves forward into the future, many things have changed since the days of the Cherokees and the earliest settlers, and yet much remains the same. Cherokee County's history traces through generations of committed, dedicated and hard-working residents. From the county's earliest roots to its present days, those who have called it home have enjoyed many opportunities while meeting numerous challenges. The same perseverance and spirit of adventure which marked the first settlers helped propel the community and its people toward a bright future in 2011.

In 1932 when Lloyd G. Marlin wrote *The History of Cherokee County*, the nation was sunk in the darkest days of the Great Depression. Many obstacles were still ahead before economic stability would again be achieved, and yet he was confident that the county would weather the storm and come out on the other side stronger than before. Similarly in 2011 at the time of the writing of this history, Cherokee County and the rest of the country were still trying to escape out of the Great Recession. Despite the difficulties that the economy of Cherokee County was feeling and the toll those concerns took, the future appeared bright.

As a part of the dynamic metro Atlanta region, Cherokee County was still experiencing growth. The conservative leadership by local governments in Cherokee County kept taxes among some of the lowest in the state. Unemployment was less than the national average and businesses in Cherokee were still expanding with new jobs created each year. While the housing and home construction markets were still feeling the effects of the recessionary times, developers and builders were optimistic that the market would soon rebound. As traditional ways of doing business hit economic roadblocks, Cherokee County residents adapted with more entrepreneurial techniques.

The Hickory Log Reservoir Lake provides a beautiful view at dawn and emphasizes the beauty of Cherokee County. Cherokee County has a long history of providing adequate resources such as water for its residents and is looking to a bright future. *Photo courtesy of Gary Mullet.*

Technology was playing a greater role in day-to-day life for local residents. Social media might have replaced the old small-town customs of neighbor visiting neighbor, but the new information streams allowed for communication unheard of just a decade ago. Computers and smart phones enabled residents to know what was going on down the street or across the country. Cherokee County was courting technology industries and white collar jobs.

Transportation and the link it provides for commerce and business still holds the key to economic growth and success. Whether it was through the expanded airport, continued road improvements and expansions, or new modes of transportation yet untapped, the future was on the road to success in Cherokee County.

Planned communities such as Woodmont, Bridgemill, Rivergreen, Towne Lake and Lake Arrowhead offered a new sense of community to those locating here, as well as a wide range of amenities such as golf, tennis and social clubs to make life more pleasant. Vast areas of farm and woodland had changed to neighborhoods of homes so quickly that it seemed to happen almost overnight. But despite the major development that occurred, immense expanses of forest and undisturbed land still remained.

As the population grows, new schools seem to spring up in almost every community. The new educational facilities featured the latest technology, new ways of teaching and new opportunities for learning. The future of education seems limitless. A new generation is being prepared for the future in ways not thought of in past decades.

Marlin said in 1932, and was proven to be right, that Cherokee County would continue to be "a good place to live." He wrote that the generation of that time could not even guess at the changes that would take place in Cherokee County in the coming years. In 2011, the motto of Cherokee County, "Where Metro Meets the Mountains," was evocative of the merging of the old more rural Cherokee County with the progressive urban influences that had begun to take over.

Yet the essence of the community was still reminiscent of the past. People still reached out to help neighbors in need. Churches and civic organizations were going strong in the community. Cherokee County is headed in the right direction and the future may not be clear but it is certain to be bright.

Cherokee County stood ready to welcome the 21st Century, its challenges and its opportunities as the community moved into a new era.

2011 Elected Officials for Cherokee County

Cherokee County
Commission Chairman L.B. Buzz Ahrens
Commissioners: Post 1- Harry Johnston, Post 2 - Jim Hubbard, Post 3 - Karen Bosch, Post 4 - Jason Nelms

Cherokee County Sheriff - Roger Garrison
Cherokee County Tax Commissioner - Sonya Little
Cherokee County Coroner - Earl Darby
Cherokee County Surveyor - Ron Wikle

Ball Ground
Mayor Rick Roberts
City Council Members - John Byrd, Mickey O'Malley, Frank Homiller, Lee Prettyman, Andy Stoner.

Canton
Mayor Gene Hobgood
City Council Members - John Beresford, Bill Bryan, Jack Goodwin, Amelia Rose, Bob Rush, Pat Tanner

Holly Springs
Mayor - Tim Downing
City Council Members - Karen Barnett, Dee Phillips, Jeremy Smith, Kyle Whitaker

Nelson
Mayor David Leister
City Council Members - Paul Feldman, Johnny Hopkins, James Queen, Penny Thacker, Martha Tipton

Waleska
Mayor Doris Jones
City Council Members - Bill Cline, Edna Cook, Paul Ice, Mary Helen Lamb, Floyd Puckett, Dennis Cochran

Woodstock
Mayor Donnie Henriques
City Council Members - Tessa Basford, Randy Brewer, Chris Casdia, Tracy Collins, Bud Leonard, Bob Mueller

Cherokee County Court System

Cherokee County District Attorney - Garry Moss
Cherokee County Clerk of Court - Patty Baker
Cherokee County Probate Judge - Keith Woods
Blue Ridge Circuit - Chief Judge Frank Mills, III,
Judge N. Jackson Harris, Judge Ellen McElyea

State Court - Judge Clyde J. Gober, Jr.,
Judge W. Alan Jordan, Judge Dee Morris
State Court Solicitor - David Cannon, Jr.,
Magistrate Court Judge - James Drane
Juvenile Court - Judge M. Anthony Baker,
Judge John B. Sumner

Cherokee County Board of Education

Post 1 - Robert Wofford
Post 2 - Mike Chapman
Post 3 - Michael Geist
Post 4 - Janet Read

Post 5 - Rick Steiner
Post 6 - Rob Usher
Post 7 - Kim Cochran

State Legislature

Majority Leader Senator Chip Rogers, District 21
Senator Jack Murphy, District 27
Representative Charlice Byrd, District 20

Representative Calvin Hill, District 21
Representative Sean Jerguson, District 22
Representative Mark Hamilton, District 2 3

History in Photographs

Magnolia Thomas was born in Canton in 1890 and later moved to Woodstock where she had a respected career as a school teacher. Miss Thomas, right side, fourth from the right, was a member of the class of 1918 at Spelman College in Atlanta.

Henry G. Gibbs takes a ride on horseback in Ball Ground circa 1912 with the Ball Ground cannery visible in the background. The cannery was never operational and the ruins still exist.

Family members of Newt Adams, who later became sheriff of Cherokee County, gather in 1924 in front of the Bruce/Bice family home, still extant, on Trinity Church Road. Front row, from left, Lois Griffin, Judge Fowler, Jesse Mae Voyles, Margaret Fowler. Newt Adams, Laurence Adams, H.L. Adams, Marie Bailey, Mattie Bruce, Jeanette Bailey, Willie Mae Bruce, Sadie Bruce. Second row, Thelma Bice, Monteria Bice, Johnny Fowler, Pearle Fowler, Homer Adams, Lee Adams, Jesse Bruce, Queen Victoria Bruce, Elizabeth Sidale Griffin, Irene Bailey, E.J. Bailey, John Williams Bailey, John Willie Bailey on lap, Ardella Cook. Third row, Ciscero Bice, Herbert Bruce, Burton Bruce, Mattie Bruce, Jessi Mae Bruce, Ora Bruce, Berdie Bruce, Sarah Bruce, Willie Bruce, Anderson Brannon, Irene Brannon, John Henry Cook. Fourth row, Clinton Bice, Bertha Bice, Verna Mathis Hawkins, Charlie Hawkins, J.L. Griffin, Ethel Fowler, Captain Fowler, Clara Belle Bruce, Amy Cook, Addie Brannon, Ernest Brannon, Eva Agnes Sears, Charlie Sears. Fifth row, Alonzo Mathis, Pearle Mathis, Mary Beck, John Beck.

William (W.E.) Richardson was an overseer at Augustus Coggins' Crescent Farm and served during World War I in the U.S. Army. He is seen here with his son Jack in 1934.

Robert Wilson Hillhouse, center, along with two other workers operate the Hillhouse steam sawmill engine. Bob Hillhouse would travel to different sites to cut lumber and then sell to Stephens Lumber in Holly Springs.

During the Great Depression it was not unusual for neighbors to give the only thing they could afford, a helping hand, to a neighbor in need. Here, in the summer of 1935, many of the residents of the Buffington community came together to work out the cotton crop of Bud Ponder after he was killed in a car accident on July 4, 1935. The field was located on what is today the W.W. Denney property on Highway 20 and many of those who pitched in are still living today.

Stumptown was the traditionally African-American community off East Main Street in Canton. One of the main thoroughfares of the community is Crisler Street, shown here in the 1940s. The community most likely grew up as freed slaves following the Civil War established homes for themselves and their families. The name came because as the trees were cut down, some of the houses were built over the stumps. The community maintained its own commercial identity for decades with a store, funeral home and other businesses, as well as a church.

The Hotel Canton was a centerpiece of downtown Canton for many decades. Shown here in 1949, the local hotel offered a place for those who were drawn to the cooler temperatures of the foothills of the North Georgia Mountains. Many visitors arrived by train and found the hotel a stylish place to stay the night or even longer. The hotel had a dining room and was the site of many parties and meetings in the community.

Diana Lathem and her family do a little boating at Allatoona Lake in the 1950s. The coming of the lake was an economic boon for the county, attracting tourists, fishermen and boaters from neighboring counties. Constructed by the United States Army Corps of Engineers in the 1940s, the lake today draws seven million visitors annually. The lake was constructed on the Etowah River.

Edwin Bell Jr., left, and Georgia Bell take a break in front of their family's store in 1950. The E.M. Bell Store on Highway 20 served the Buffington community for many years. The tight-knit community got its name and grew up in the vicinity of Fort Buffington, the removal fort used in the Cherokee roundup of 1838.

Marvin Bell, left, here with an unknown soldier, served in Korea in 1952. A number of Cherokee County residents fought in the Korean War and are honored at the Thomas M. Brady Post 45 of the American Legion in Canton and the South Cherokee Post 316 in Woodstock.

The Georgia Marble Company, in 1959, prepared to ship the new columns for the United States Capitol before John F. Kennedy's 1960 inauguration. In this photo, Earl Ingram is standing in the railroad car and Garland Cagle is to the far left.

At a baptism at Mt. Pisgah Church in 1956 pastor Jay Bottoms baptizes twins Billy and Evelyn Sewell while family members and friends, including Lottie and Anderson Sewell, Charles Sewell, Lois Sewell, James Bearden, Marcus Bearden, and Willy Bearden look on. Religion has always been an important part of life in Cherokee County.

Pamela Rountree Owen places a call from the Holly Springs Depot, circa 1959. Many Holly Springs residents in 1959 were sad to hear the news that the Louisville & Nashville Railroad Company had decided to close the depot and no longer provide a stop in the city. Holly Springs leaders and residents did not want to see the depot abandoned, so they negotiated a 10-year lease for $36 per year with the option to renew. In 1960 Holly Springs had a City Hall at the depot.

The Burger Chief was a popular spot with local students in the 1960s and 1970s. The restaurant was one of the earliest spots for fast food for the community of Canton and became a popular hangout for young people. Teens loved to "cruise the Chief" after school and after sporting events at Cherokee High School. The Burger Chief was located on Marietta Highway in North Canton next to Northside Pharmacy.

The William Bearden/Amos Cline Home in Waleska, 1949. The home was built circa 1910 and still retains many historic features.

The Brown Farm in Canton was built in 1838 by Dr. John Washington Lewis, whose daughter, Harriet Frances Lewis married Judge James R. Brown, brother of Georgia Civil War Governor Joseph E. Brown. Dr. Lewis helped the Brown brothers get an education. The bricks of the side dependencies were made on site, and the buildings served as Dr. Lewis' office and the laundry. The house has been modified many times, including the addition of the second story in 1892. The upper porch and Victorian details have since been removed.

The City of Canton Fire Department, headquartered in the old post office in downtown Canton, prides itself on providing the highest levels of service through fire prevention, education, suppression and rescue activities and the mitigation of effects from natural and man-made disasters. Here, firefighters Tony Ferguson and Tyrone Gates are on duty in the late 1980s.

Mary Elizabeth Davis receives an award from the Cherokee County Chamber of Commerce at a banquet at the Pine Crest Inn. The Chamber promotes good business practices in the community by regularly recognizing members for their contributions to the county. Mrs. Davis and her husband, former Canton Mayor Walton Davis, have a long history of community service.

The Canton Cotton Mill Office was built in 1929 and later expanded in 1949. The office headquartered the management of the textile mills until they closed in 1981 and then became home to the Cherokee County Board of Education Executive Offices. Here, Jim Wheeler is in front of the building during the 1970s.

Bibliography

Books and Papers:
Anderson, Mike. "The Moonshine King of Georgia." *Georgia Backroads* 9:2, Autumn 2010.
Bernhard, Jayne. "Ball Ground Historic District Nomination." Cherokee County Historical Society, 2007.
Bernhard, Jayne. "Canton Historic District Nomination." Cherokee County Historical Society, 2007.
Cadle, John. "Mayors of Canton" unpublished research.
Canton Cotton Mills, *A Man, A Town, and A Mill.* 1949.
Carver, John. Bivouac of the Dead Confederate Soldiers of Cherokee County, Georgia. 2008.
Cherokee County Chamber of Commerce Minutes and Records- 1944-1951, 1970
Cherokee County Heritage Book Committee. *The Heritage of Cherokee County.* Walsworth Publishing Co., 1998.
Cherokee County Historical Society. *Glimpses of Cherokee County.* Canton, 1981.
Cherokee County Historical Society. The Crescent Chronicle IX: 3 (2008).
Cherokee County School District, "District Progress Annual Report, 2009-2010"
Chupp, David, First Baptist Church of Canton, Georgia 1833-1983.
Davis, Anita Price. *Georgia During the Great Depression.* McFarland, 2008.
Felton, Alice Dean. Interview with J.H. Johnston, 1937.
Free, Mary Howard. *Edward Leslie Stork Cherokee County Folk Potter.* Canton: Cherokee County Historical Society, 1995.
Fox, Jack F. *The 1850 Census of Georgia Slave Owners,* Baltimore: Clearfield Publishing Co., 1999.
Guidry, Jennifer. *Elizabeth Grisham Brown:"A Strong and Sunny Soul".* MA Thesis. Georgia College and State University, 2003.
Hasty, William G. Sr. *I Remember When.* Self published, 1994.
Hickory Log Cemetery. Canton: Advanced Placement Students Sequoyah High School.
Hill, Sarah H. *Cherokee Removal: Forts Along the Georgia Trail of Tears. (The National Park Service and the Georgia Department of Natural Resources/Historic Preservation Division, March 2005, http://www.nps.gov/trte/TRTE/Georgias%20Trail%20of%20Tears%20Report% 20ONLY.pdf).*
Hubbard, Glenn. *Before Allatoona.* Personal papers published in Woodstock, 1990.
Hudson, Charles. *The Southeastern Indians.* Knoxville: University of Tennessee Press, 1994.
Hughes, Juanita, *Set Apart: The Baptist Church at Woodstock.* Published by First Baptist Church of Woodstock, 1987.
Huxford, Judge Folks. *Genealogical Material from Legal Notices in Early Georgia Newspapers.* Easley:Southern Historical Press, 1989
King, Duane. *The Cherokee Trail of Tears.* Graphic Art Books, 2008.
Jackson, Olin, *A North Georgia Journal of History,* Volume II, Legacy Communications, 1991.
Jones, Ben Perry. "Robert Tyre Jones: A Family Perspective" Published privately.
Latty, John W. *Carrying off the Cherokee, History of Buffington's Company Georgia Mounted Militia.* CreateSpace, 2011.
Levin, Rob. A *Foundation of Growth: The Story of the Bank of Canton.* The Bank of Canton, 1992.
Lewis Historical Publishing Company, *Georgia Through Two Centuries, Family and Personal Records,* 1965
Krakow, Kenneth K. *Georgia Place-Names.* 3rd ed. Macon: Winship Press, 1975.
Krueger, Thomas, Canton Copper Mine Thesis, Kennesaw State University
Marlin, Lloyd G. *The History of Cherokee County.* 2nd ed. Cherokee County Historical Society: Wolfe Publishing, 1997.
McFarland, Jimmy," Wreck of the Little Hook"
McLoughlin, William G. *Cherokee Renascence in the New Republic.* Princeton: Princeton University Press, 1986.
Miller, Zell, *They Heard Georgia Singing: Great Georgians - Vol. 2,* Lee Roy Abernathy. Advocate Press, Franklin Springs, GA, 1984
Mooney, James. *History, Myths and Sacred Formulas.* Asheville: Bright Mountain Books, 1992.
Moore, Peggy McClure, Family Papers of Charles Alfred McClure
Parks, Joseph H., *Joseph E. Brown of Georgia.* Baton Rouge: Louisiana State University Press, 1977.
Petruzielo, Frank, Superintendent of Cherokee County School District, "Cherokee's Renaissance in Education, 1999-2011"
Profile of Agriculture in Cherokee County. Canton: Cherokee County Extension Service. October 1991.
Public Education in Cherokee County. Canton: Cherokee County Board of Education, 1982.
Read, Joseph, J.W. and Mary Beth. *Ore, Water, Stone and Wood; Historical and Architectural Investigations of Donaldson's Iron Furnace, Cherokee County, Georgia.* Atlanta: Garrow and Associates, Inc. 1987. Report prepared for The U.S. Army Corps of Engineers, Mobile District. Contract No. DACW01-87-C-0007.
Reflections of a Century: Holly Springs, Georgia 1906-2006. Holly Springs Centennial Committee, 2006.
Roberts Marble Company, Company Literature
Saxon, Randy, Family Papers of Elias Earle Field
Sawyer, Gordon. *Northeast Georgia A History.* Charleston: Arcadia Publishing, 2001.
Scaife, William R. and Bragg, William Harris. *Joe Brown's Pets: The Georgia Militia, 1861-1865.* 2004, Mercer Univ. Press Macon, GA
Shadburn, Don L. *Cherokee Planters in Georgia 1832-1838.* Roswell: WH Wolfe Associates, 1990
Silliman, Garrett W. and Thompson, Lori C. "Life Along the Etowah: An Archaeological Study and Historic Perspective" 2010
State of Georgia, Land Lotteries, Available at the Georgia Archives.
State of Georgia, Department of Banking, "A Statement of Condition for Etowah Bank, March 27, 1931"
State of Georgia Department of Industry and Trade, Economic Profile of Canton, Georgia, 1970-1971
Tuck, Stephen G.N. *Beyond Atlanta: The Struggle for Racial Equality in Georgia, 1940-1980.* Athens : The Univ. of Georgia Press, 2001.
U.S. Archive, Georgia Land Lot Distribution, 1831 (Gold Lotteries), Acts of the General Assembly of Georgia, Vol. 1, Page 64,
U.S. Supreme Court, *Cherokee Nation vs. Georgia 30.* Chief Justice C.J. Marshall
U.S. Bureau of the Census, 1900-2010
Utley, F.L. and Humphrey, Marion, *Place Names of Georgia, Essays of John H. Goff.* Athens, Georgia. Univ. of Georgia Press, 1975.
Walker, Charles O. *Cherokee Footprints...* Vol. 1. Canton: Industrial Printing Service, Inc, 1988.
Warren, Mary B. and Weeks, Eve B. Whites Among the Cherokees, Georgia 1828-1838. Athens Georgia, Heritage Papers, 1987.
Webb, Patrick, "Hands of God at Work: The Life and Contributions of Mr. and Mrs. Alfred Webb Roberts" Kennesaw State University
Whitmore, Felicia S. *Georgia's Woodstock: A Centennial Tribute 1897-1997.* Fernandina Beach: Wolfe, 1997.
Wright, G. Richard and Kenneth H. Wheeler. "New Men in the Old South: Joseph E. Brown and his Associates in Georgia's Etowah Valley." *The Georgia Historical Quarterly* XCIII.4 (2009): 363 – 387.

News Articles, Chronological

"Extracts from Cherokee-Mountaineer." The Cherokee Advance. 1861.

Cherokee Advance. April 14, 1880

"Contract Let for New School Building" The Cherokee Advance. April 1913.

"Reinhardt Opens to Large Attendance." The Cherokee Advance. January 9, 1913

"Cherokee County," "Judge James R. Brown," "Sheriff Joshua Spears," "The Success of Gus Coggins," "Georgia Marble Finishing Works," "E.A. McCanless," "Jones Mercantile Co." The Cherokee Advance, 24-Page Trade Edition. July 3, 1913

"From a Confederate Soldier," The Cherokee Advance. November 28, 1913

"Another Letter Written When War Clouds Were Hovering the South." The Cherokee Advance. December 5, 1913

"Hon. R.T. Jones on the School Question." The Cherokee Advance. June 12, 1914.

"Issue Passed to Build New School Building." The Cherokee Advance. June 19, 1914

"McCanless Elected Mayor for 1915." The Cherokee Advance. December 18, 1914

"German U-53 Gets 6 Boats." The Cherokee Advance. October 12, 1916

North Georgia Tribune. August 2, 1918.

"Mr. D. J. Haney Found Dead In Bed." The Cherokee Advance. February 21, 1930.

"Reinhardt College Has Fine Rating With Senior Colleges." The Cherokee Advance. March 14, 1930.

"Reinhardt College." The Cherokee Advance. April 18, 1930.

Parham, Mrs. J. B. Social and Personal Mention. The Cherokee Advance. May 23, 1930.

Reid, Albert T. "Election Trail Which Way." Cartoon Caption. The Cherokee Advance. May 9, 1930.

"Cherokee Superior Court Will Convene Monday Morning with Judge Maddox of Rome Presiding." The Cherokee Advance. 8 August 1930.

"Banking and Agriculture Discussed at Well Attended Meet in Canton." The Cherokee Advance. October, 1930.

"Christmas Gifts Of High School Go To Charity." The Cherokee Advance. December 28, 1930.

"Wm. Galt Improving In Atlanta Hospital." The Cherokee Advance. 1930s.

Durden, Henry W. "God Farm Practices Reduce Weevil Loss." The Cherokee Advance.

"Canton Playground Wins $50.00 Prize." The Cherokee Advance.

"We View With Alarm." The Cherokee Advance. 1931.

"Auction Sale of 22 Residence Lots in Sunnyside Saturday, Nov. 14 At 1P.M." The Cherokee Advance. 1931.

"Ex-Sheriff Josh P. Spears Passed Suddenly Tuesday at Ripe Age." The Cherokee Advance. January 23, 1931

"Robert Strickland, Prominent Banker and Civic Leader, To Address Chamber Commerce." The Cherokee Advance. Feb. 24, 1931.

"Chamber Commerce Banquet Friday Night Most Successful in History of This Cherokee Co. Organization." The Cherokee Advance. March 6, 1931.

" ' Help Yourself' to be Presented Tues., 17." The Cherokee Advance. March 13, 1931.

Parham, J. B. "Space Fillers." The Cherokee Advance. April 3, 1931.

"Chamber Commerce Directors Discuss Educational Needs at Regular Monthly Meeting." The Cherokee Advance. 1931.

"Canton Meeting Reveals Much Food Produced By The Farmers." The Cherokee Advance. September, 1931.

"Chamber of Commerce to Protest Against Reduction of Passenger Train Service on L. and N. Railroad. The Cherokee Advance. October 24, 1931.

"Do Your Christmas Giving Early." The Cherokee Advance. October 28, 1931.

"Here Goes Old Man Depression." Crisler's Department Store Add. The Cherokee Advance. November 1931.

"Bank Canton Directors in Meeting Wednes, Usual Dividend Declared." The Cherokee Advance. December 12, 1931.

"A Future Paradise For Fishermen and Pleasure Seekers." North Georgia Tribune. 1949.

"New Poultry Dressing Plant to Begin Operating in October." North Georgia Tribune. 1949.

"Allatoona Dam Sluice Gates Closed Tuesday." North Georgia Tribune. December 30, 1949.

"City, County To Vote Separately on Local School Merger Question." North Georgia Tribune. September 30, 1954.

"Cherokee Water Authority Legislation to Be Introduced." North Georgia Tribune January 27, 1955.

"Fire Aftermath Finds Canton Business Houses In Plans For Reconstruction." North Georgia Tribune. June 1955.

"Ground Broken Wednesday For New Co. High School." North Georgia Tribune. 1955.

$1 ½ Million Fire Razes Canton; 1 Man Dead In Worst Disaster In City's History. North Georgia Tribune. June 30, 1955.

"State Awards Contract for Cherokee School Buildings." North Georgia Tribune July 21, 1955.

"Ground Broken for Woodstock Medical Center." North Georgia Tribune. 1960.

"Abernathy Plays In Piano Contest at Gospel Sing." North Georgia Tribune. July 28, 1960.

"Burtz Takes Judgeship Oath Thursday, Pope Makes Move for Solicitor's Post." North Georgia Tribune. August 4, 1960.

"Contract Signed, Hospital Start Expected Monday." North Georgia Tribune. August 11, 1960.

"New Hospital Gets Formal Send Off As Authority Observes Ground Breaking." North Georgia Tribune. August 25, 1960.

" Sen. Kennedy Carries Cherokee for President; Stringer, Hannah Win Other County Contests." North Georgia Tribune. November 10, 1960.

"Cherokee Citizen Nominated for "Farmer of the Year"." North Georgia Tribune. November 17, 1960.

"Cherokee's Dean Rusk Named Secretary of State by Kennedy." North Georgia Tribune. December 15, 1960.

"Barnett Named Administrator of New Hospital." North Georgia Tribune. January 12, 1961.

"New Hospital Now Ready for Memorializing." North Georgia Tribune. June 8, 1961.

"Equipment For New Hospital to be Displayed." North Georgia Tribune. July 13, 1961.

"Canton, Ball Ground Winners Here Wednesday." North Georgia Tribune. October 12, 1961.

"Ball Ground Moves Ahead Adding City Improvements." North Georgia Tribune. July 6, 1961.

"M.G. Hendrix, Ball Ground Physician, Dies." North Georgia Tribune. September 28, 1961.

"3 Major Road Projects On State Plan for Cherokee." North Georgia Tribune. February 9, 1961.

"Curtain Drops On 14th Convention Of Poultrymen." North Georgia Tribune. February 2, 1961.

"Leaders Named For S.E., Poultry and Egg Convention." North Georgia Tribune. March 9, 1961.

"Officers Raid, Destroy Still; One Arrested." North Georgia Tribune. April 6, 1961.

Two Make Bond Following Sheriff's Raids Sunday." North Georgia Tribune. March 30, 1961.

"Esteemed Doctor Paid Tribute By Rotary, Lions, Kiwanis Clubs." North Georgia Tribune. May 11, 1961.

"County Commissioner Speaks to Kiwanis Of Roads, Taxes." North Georgia Tribune. May 25, 1961.

"Dean Rusk Day at Reinhardt To Draw 2,000." North Georgia Tribune. April 20, 1961.

"Freedom and Tolerance Declared Action Guides By Rusk at Homecoming Day Fete." North Georgia Tribune. Apr. 27, 1961.

"Secretary of State Dean Rusk to Visit Waleska." North Georgia Tribune. April 13, 1961.

"4th Celebration in Canton Next Tuesday." North Georgia Tribune. June 29, 1961.

"Early Signs Point to Big Road Building Year for Cherokee County." North Georgia Tribune. March 23, 1961.

"Grading of Lake Road Fits Into Govt. Park Plans." North Georgia Tribune. May 31, 1962.
"Routes Announced for Canton Highway By-Pass." North Georgia Tribune. July 13, 1963.
"Commission for Cherokee Airport Study Named." North Georgia Tribune. July 25, 1963.
" Cherokee County A Robust Market, Survey Shows." North Georgia Tribune. August 1, 1963.
"Commission is Formed to Study County Airport." North Georgia Tribune. August 8, 1963.
"Thomason Leaves Banking Service After 52 Years." North Georgia Tribune. October 10, 1963.
"Cotton Mill Workers Out On Strike; Outlook Dim for Early Contract Settlement." North Georgia Tribune. October 31, 1963.
"Cotton Mill Employees Vote To Strike Sunday Night." North Georgia Tribune. October 24, 1963.
"Canton Mills Closed 'Indefinitely.' " North Georgia Tribune. November 7, 1963.
"World Mourns, Pays Tribute to Assassinated President." North Georgia Tribune. November, 1963.
"Mill Operation Agreement Said To Hinge On Rehiring Workers." North Georgia Tribune. December 5, 1963.
"Canton Mill- Union Strike Settled." North Georgia Tribune. 1963.
"Mill Contempt Hearing Begun, Interrupted by Snow." North Georgia Tribune. January, 1964.
"Legislation To Be Introduced To Expand City Services." North Georgia Tribune. January 9. 1964.
"Mills Offer to Reemploy Persons Working at Strike Outset; Rejected." North Georgia Tribune. January 23, 1964.
Mr. L.L. Jones, Sr. Chairman of the Board, Canton Cotton Mills."To All Employees Of Canton Cotton Mills." North Georgia
    Tribune. September 26, 1963.
"House Resolution Calls For Four-Lane Highway to Canton." North Georgia Tribune. February 20, 1964.
"Canton Telephone Co. Sold To General Tel & Electronics Corp.." North Georgia Tribune. February 27, 1964.
"Capacity Filled Allatoona Adds Threat To High Water Damage In Canton Area." North Georgia Tribune.   April 9, 1964.
"13 Candidates Qualify For County Primary Set May 27." North Georgia Tribune. April 16, 1964.
"LBJ to Visit North Georgia Friday, To Make Talk at Gainesville." North Georgia Tribune. May 7, 1964.
"10 Entrants Qualify for County Democratic Primary Set May 27." North Georgia Tribune. 1964.
"County Primary Vote Returns All Incumbents But Coroner." North Georgia Tribune. May 28, 1964.
"Talmadge Featured Speaker in 4th Celebration." North Georgia Tribune. July 2, 1964.
"Voters to Make Choice at Polls Wednesday In State Primary; Run-Over Election Possible." North Georgia Tribune.
    September 3, 1964.
"WCHK to Start FM Broadcasts This Friday." North Georgia Tribune. September 3, 1964.
"Cherokee Allotted $61,000 for Airport." North Georgia Tribune. October 22, 1964.
"Goldwater- Miller Wins Six States; Georgia Voters Break Tradition." North Georgia Tribune. November 5, 1964.
Cherokee County Young Democrats. "What About The Civil Rights Bill !!" North Georgia Tribune. 1964.
"Eastern Route for I-75 Sought By Large North Georgia Group." North Georgia Tribune. February 25, 1965.
"Health Center for County To Be Constructed Soon." North Georgia Tribune. March 25, 1965.
" Highway Department Calls Hearing For Rt. 5 Location and By-Pass." North Georgia Tribune. August 19, 1965.
"Air Show to Accompany Port's Dedication Saturday." North Georgia Tribune. September 29, 1966.
"Cherokee Industries Expect 'Good Year'." The Cherokee Tribune. February 14, 1974.
"Major Headlines from 1975." The Cherokee Tribune. 1975.
The Cherokee Tribune November 13, 1975.
 "Voting Districts for Multi-County Commission." Cherokee Tribune. 1975.
"Major Headlines for 1975." Cherokee Tribune. January 8, 1976.
Cagle, Mike. "Atomedic Hospital Now Operating At Full Capacity." Cherokee Tribune.
Barnes, Jean. "Dean House Over a 100 Years Old." Cherokee Tribune.
Cherokee Tribune. April 25, 1979.
Samples, Cheryl L. "Sewerage, Water, Head List." Cherokee Tribune . February 14, 1980.
Budd, James. "Ballard Assumes Job As Top Cop." Cherokee Tribune. January 7, 1980.
Budd, James. "County to Begin Steps to 'Fix Up' County Jail." Cherokee Tribune. Fall 1980.
Budd, James. "Old Stone Structure Was Pig Iron Smelter." Cherokee Tribune. 1980.
Duff, Karl. "Boddy's Nursing Facility Took 12 Years, $1 Million." North Georgia Tribune. 1980.
Budd, James. "Escapees 22, 23 Leave Cherokee County Jail." Cherokee Tribune. November 18, 1980.
Fiddelke, Michele. "Commissioner Discusses Revenue Sharing Funds." Cherokee Tribune. November 24, 1980.
Fiddelke, Michele. "Commissioner Adopts Budget." Cherokee Tribune. December 17, 1980.
Fiddelke, Michele. "Holly Springs Residents Question City's Proposed Treatment Plant." Cherokee Tribune Dec. 22, 1980.
Budd, James. "Mills Named New Superior Judge." Cherokee Tribune. 1980.
Hefner, Bobby. "Former Lawmen Turn to Crime". Cherokee Tribune. January 28, 1981.
Cagle, Mike. "Canton Textiles, Local Institution." Cherokee Tribune. February 4, 1981.
Waitman, Bruce. "I-575 Work Continues in North Canton Area." Cherokee Tribune. 1980s.
Fiddelke, Michele. "Demos Meet, Get Home for Debate." Cherokee Tribune.
Waitman, Bruce. "Group Formed to Aid Mill." Cherokee Tribune. April 1, 1981.
Hefner, Bobby. "Canton Textiles to Close Doors." Cherokee Tribune. March 18, 1981.
Budd, James. "New $1.7 Million Jail Recommended." Cherokee Tribune. March 4, 1981.
"Coker Nursing Home, A Cherokee Landmark." The Cherokee Tribune. February 4, 1981.
Budd, James. "Rapid Growth May Help County Get Federal $$$." Cherokee Tribune. 1981.
Cherokee Tribune. August 31, 1983.
Woody, Laura and Chuck Blake. "Parolee Arrested in Double Murder." The Cherokee Tribune January 16, 1985.
Fouts, Jeff. "Lickskillet / Old, New Exist Side by Side." Cherokee Tribune. 1985.
Woody, Laura. "Mid-School Bids to Be Retaken." Cherokee Tribune. 20 January 1985.
Anderson, Larry and Sally Charles. "County Voters Reject Three-Man Commission." Cherokee Tribune. May 11, 1986.
Feeney, Joe. "Historical Society to Save Rock Barn." Cherokee Tribune. 1989.
Feeney, Joe. "Work on Rock Barn Nearing Completion." Cherokee Tribune. 1989.
Johnston, Rebecca. "County ranked 16th." Cherokee Tribune September 13, 1989.
Johnston, Rebecca. "County Swings Hard Right." Cherokee Tribune.
Howell, Candace. "Georgia's Poet Laureate Once Lived in Canton." Cherokee Tribune.
Bennett, D.L. "County swings to GOP." Cherokee Tribune. 1990.
Bennett, D.L. "Outer perimeter draws local views." The Cherokee Tribune November 18, 1990.
Bennett, D.L. "GOP sweeps commission." Cherokee Tribune. November 7, 1990.
Bennett, D.L. "Seay allies try to stifle recall." Cherokee Tribune. October 31, 1990.

Johnston, Rebecca. "Sheriff Seay off the hook." Cherokee Tribune. October 17. 1990.
Harper, Craig. "Some Voters Seay 'We've Had Enough'." The Cherokee Tribune October 21, 1990.
Bennett, D.L. "Sheriff Seay: I Didn't Lie." Cherokee Tribune. October 24, 1990.
Bennett, D.L. "Scaled-Down Courthouse Controversial." Cherokee Tribune. August 5, 1990.
Bennett, D.L. "Sheriff's 'Hit List' Sends Grand Jury Into Session." Cherokee Tribune. October 28, 1990.
Groves, Kim. "Library Checks Out." Cherokee Tribune. April 14, 1991.
Bennett, D.L. "GBI Launches Probe of Sheriff's Office." Cherokee Tribune. April 17, 1991.
Cherokee Citizen, "Cagle's Dairy: Homegrown Success in Hickory Flat" July 3, 1991
Cherokee Citizen "Canton Woman's Club" Unknown Date
Johnston, Rebecca. "Hobgood led Cherokee through booming growth." Cherokee Tribune. 1991.
Bennett, D.L. "Panel Culls Possible Sites for Courthouse." Cherokee Tribune. 1991.
Bennett, D.L. "County's finances on verge of disaster." Cherokee Tribune. April 4, 1993.
Graham, Doug, "McClure's Altruism' Atlanta Journal Constitution
Cherokee Ledger News, "Veterans Share WWII Stories", September 26, 2007

Websites

Encyclopedia of North Carolina, "Cherokee Indians" http://uncpress.unc.edu/rc_encyclopedia/cherokee.html
Galileo, "Cherokee County Historical Population Profile" "County Maps", georg_ainfo.galileo.usg.edu/countypop/ Cherokeepop.htm.
J.H. Johnston Family History, www.jhjohnston.org
New Georgia Encyclopedia, Mississippian Period Overview, Georgia History Overview. www.newgeorgiaencyclopedia.org.
North Georgia Gold Rush and Cherokee Removal Forts, ngeorgia.com/history
Railroad History, www.railga.com
U.S. Army Corps of Engineers, History of Lake Allatoona http://www.sam.usace.army.mil/allatoona/
U.S. Bureau of the Census, Cherokee County Quick Facts, quickfacts.census.gov

Interviews

Pam Carnes; Dave Caughman; Cynthia Durham; Roger Garrison; Billy Hayes; Juanita Hughes; Nell Magruder; Edward McMickens; Priscilla Strickland Moody; Peggy McClure Moore; Samuel Pitts; Judson Roberts; Randy Saxon

Index

FAIR PLAY 1028

SIXES 1274

BELLS 817

WOODST 896

21

T.A.GARREN
PHELOS BRIDGE
DARY
FIELD BROS
M.M.SESSIONS PROP
A.B.COGGINS
B.F.PERR
GOLD MINE
G.W.ALEXANDER
McCURLEYS MILL
P.S.BEDELL
STEELS BRIDGE
SIXES MINE
LAUGHING GAL
SWEETWAT
SWEETWATER CH.
N.J.WHEELER
E.L.LOVINGOOD
CHEROKEE MILLS
O.W.PUTNAM
O.W.PUTNAM
PUTNAMS FORD
RIVER
LOVINGOODS BRIDGE
J.T.ROBERTSON
GOLD
R.B.HANCOCK
GALTS FERRY
O.W.PUTNAM
CREEK
O.W.PUTNAM
H.C.BRYANT
McCOLLUM
E.L.MARR
M.A.LOVINGOOD
MORGIANA MINE
A.J.WILLBURN
J.H.McCLURE
R.H.TRIPPE
Q.McMINIMEN
A.T.HUEY
C.E.BAKER
J.E.TYSON
W.M.ROBINSON
J.Q.H.TYSON
J.J.BROOKE
W.C.ATTAWAY